DATE DUE

MAR 25 1981		
DEC 14 1981		
DEC 6 1982		
6-29-89 Page		
JUN 09 1992		
11-02-92		
8-8-97 JL		

DEMCO NO. 38-298

Analyzing Real Estate Opportunities

Director of Publishing—Llani O'Connor
Book Editor—Peg Keilholz
Project Editor—Helene Berlin
Production Manager—Meg Givhan

Analyzing Real Estate Opportunities

Market and Feasibility Studies

Stephen D. Messner
Byrl N. Boyce
Harold G. Trimble
Robert L. Ward

NATIONAL ASSOCIATION OF REALTORS®
developed in cooperation with its affiliate, the
REALTORS NATIONAL MARKETING INSTITUTE®
of the NATIONAL ASSOCIATION OF REALTORS®
Chicago, Illinois

International Standard Book Number: 0-913652-11-3
Library of Congress Catalog Card Number: 77-21264
REALTORS NATIONAL MARKETING INSTITUTE®
Catalog Number: BK123

Printed in the United States of America
First printing, 1977, 9944
Second printing, 1979, 5000

Analyzing real estate opportunities.

Bibliography: 30 pages
Includes index.
1. Real estate investment—United States.
2. Real estate investment—United States—Case studies. I. Messner, Stephen D.
II. Realtors National Marketing Institute.
HD255.A64   332.6'324   77-21264

Foreword

REALTORS NATIONAL MARKETING INSTITUTE® of the NATIONAL ASSOCIATION OF REALTORS® devotes much of its effort to produce educational courses, periodicals, audio-visuals and other training aids for brokers and their salespeople. Some of the most competent real estate brokers and salespeople in the country credit the Marketing Institute's high quality teaching and educational materials for contributing to their success. Marketing Institute books are also widely used in colleges and universities and in fields ancillary to real estate, such as finance, government and law.

About the Authors

Dr. Stephen D. Messner heads the Finance Department of the University of Connecticut and is Professor of Finance and Real Estate. He holds an M.B.A. in Finance and a D.B.A. in Applied Urban Economics from Indiana University. Messner co-authored the Marketing Institute's book, *Marketing Investment Real Estate*, in 1975. He is also a co-author of *Effective Business Relocation, Industrial Real Estate* and *Management of an Appraisal Firm*. In addition he has written numerous articles and research monographs in the field of real estate.

Dr. Byrl N. Boyce is Professor of Finance and Real Estate, School of Business Administration, University of Connecticut. He holds an M.B.A. in General Business from Indiana University and a Ph.D. in Transportation and Finance from Pennsylvania State University. Boyce authored the 1975 award winning *Real Estate Appraisal Terminology* as well as a number of articles and monographs on real estate-related topics. He is Executive Vice President and Treasurer of The Real Estate Counseling Group of Connecticut, Inc. and holds offices in several regional and national urban economics associations.

REALTOR® Harold G. Trimble, Jr., C.R.E., C.C.I.M., heads his own firm in San Francisco, which provides appraisals, market analysis and feasibility studies for clients specializing in development projects; he also consults on property management problems in the residential income field. He is president of Toddy Investment Company in Oakland, California, a firm involved in development of apartment houses and commercial real estate projects for major national industrial clients. Trimble serves the Marketing Institute as a member of its Governing Council, Education and Publications Committees and is a senior instructor in the Institute's Commercial-Investment Courses. He holds a Class "A" membership in the International Council of Shopping Centers.

REALTOR® Robert L. Ward, C.C.I.M., is president of his own firm in Orlando, Florida, which specializes in investment counseling, syndication, taxation, commercial acquisitions and dispositions and exchanging. Past President of the Orlando-Winter Park Board of REALTORS®, Ward has been active in central Florida real estate for more than eight years. He serves the Marketing Institute as Vice Chairman of the Commercial-Investment Council and is a member of the Educational Courses Committee and the Board of Governors.

Acknowledgements

The preparation of this book involved the substantial and substantive input of a variety of individuals who collectively supplied case materials, typed successive drafts, provided guidance, criticism and suggestions, did editorial work and performed various other important tasks. The authors would like to recognize in these few paragraphs the significant contributions of several individuals.

Brenda C. Pace (Oakland, California) provided materials for the development of one of the case studies. Daniel R. Crow (Englewood, Colorado) provided the entire case study completed by the Real Estate Research Corporation that appears as the Appendix to Chapter 8. In addition, he spent several hours providing the background data and raw materials that were used in the case study illustration in Chapter 8. Finally, William A. Strickfaden (Denver, Colorado) was primarily responsible for the initial development of the loan package materials contained in Chapter 9.

Nancy Easton and Sandra Mazzola typed much of the preliminary draft material and did their typically excellent job. Judy Paesani was involved in editing certain portions of the manuscript and was also primarily responsible for compiling the annotated bibliography.

Two students who deserve special recognition are Mark Goldman for his yeoman efforts in checking computations and in aiding in the development of the financial analysis contained in Chapter 8, and David Scribner, Jr. for his efforts in gathering basic data and in preparing a portion of the preliminary draft of Chapter 1.

Llani O'Connor of the Marketing Institute performed the important task of directing and coordinating the entire publishing effort, while Peg Keilholz and Helene Berlin of her staff provided editorial support.

The review group for this book included REALTORS® James F. Bell, Jr., C.C.I.M.; Albert J. Mayer III, C.R.B., R.M.; Victor L. Lyon, C.C.I.M., C.R.B., C.R.E., M.A.I.; and Jerome S. Metzger, C.C.I.M.

Contents

Introduction

As brokers and market analysts become more conscious of the many variables and problems encountered in even routine analysis of local real estate, they seek ways to improve decision-making processes and increase their effectiveness in advising both investor and user clients.

This book is designed to fill a variety of needs.

First, it can be used as a guide to conducting market and feasibility studies. The framework of analysis provided here may be applied to a variety of locations and land uses if proper account is taken of the variables involved. It is unlikely that most brokers will undertake major market and feasibility studies in any formalized way. The more important use of such studies is in the related marketing and investment functions the broker performs.

This book is also designed to aid in understanding, interpreting and even updating studies conducted by competent analysts for use in marketing properties. In addition, enough detail is provided in several areas so the broker has some basis for evaluating the quality and applicability of market and feasibility studies for use in solving these problems.

A growing role of the broker/counselor is to serve as the advisor to investors who wish to explore the feasibility of undertaking development ventures or to test the advisability of purchasing an existing property. In this role the broker is placed in the position of obtaining market analyses, feasibility studies and appraisals that will aid in reaching a decision. A further use of this book may be as a guide to the broker in interpreting his or his client's data and analysis requirements to the consultants who will conduct the market or feasibility study.

This text may also be used as a training tool for salespersons in commercial-investment brokerages who are not yet familiar with these studies and who want an overview of the market process. There are few sources of information that explain and interpret these studies for the person new to the field.

Finally, it is the goal of this book to formalize and improve the process of market analysis which is conducted regularly by brokers and other market analysts.

Section I

Use and Relevance of Studies

Chapter 1

Market Analysis as a Tool for Brokers

1

Succeeding chapters will be introduced with a list of key terms and their definitions. Since Chapter 1 basically consists of introductory terms, we have not included such a glossary here.

This is a book about the real estate market, the urban environment in which it operates, and methods that may be used to analyze the economic potential of proposed (or existing) real estate developments. Since a primary focus of this book is the identification, collection, analysis and forecasting of market data relating to real estate, it is a logical, and intentional counterpart to the earlier text entitled: *Marketing Investment Real Estate*.[1] The purpose of this present volume is to illustrate *how* market information is obtained for use in analyzing the relative performance of real estate investments, as well as a wide variety of other brokerage applications discussed below.

Nature of Market Studies

Often a market and/or feasibility study is thought of as a "necessary evil" in obtaining mortgage financing for a project that the developer/investor was already committed to even before a careful analysis was undertaken to determine if it was financially feasible over the long-run or forecast economic life of the investment. It was certainly not uncommon to observe this type of environment throughout the early 1970s and consequently to see the effect of undertaking real estate investment projects on the basis of whim and unsubstantiated judgments about the market.

It is the basic tenet of this book that a market and/or feasibility study is a first step in the development/investment process and often in the design of marketing strategies and plans for existing properties. A logically con-

---

1 Stephen D. Messner, Irving Schreiber and Victor L. Lyon, *Marketing Investment Real Estate* (Chicago: REALTORS NATIONAL MARKETING INSTITUTE®, 1975).

structed and well documented feasibility study offers a wealth of data and information to the real estate broker who is concerned with marketing the property or even designing an investment strategy once the local market has been delineated and the future demand for real estate forecast.

Scale of Investment and/or Land Use

In recent years a large number of real estate development failures have been highly publicized with one common feature to all—they were large-scale investment projects which had a widespread and significant impact on the local market area. What has not been so clearly documented and as widely publicized is the even larger volume of small individual properties that also fail. The important point to note is not that a larger number of smaller properties fail and go virtually unnoticed on the national scene, but that they fail for many of the same reasons as do the widely publicized projects—*lack of proper market analysis that might have identified the nature of market demand or other factors that caused the project to fail.*

Smaller scale developments do not have the economic or market impact, nor do they have the visibility (publicity) of the large-scale developments; yet they still represent the same investment problem (the balancing of the risk of loss of venture capital and the problem of liquidity in the early stages of development). They require the same general framework of market and feasibility analysis. The responsibility of the real estate analyst/consultant is the same with the smaller scale investments as it is with the larger scale investments even though the degree of sophistication applied and the extent and nature of data gathered may be considerably less for the smaller properties. The market analyst must be aware of the *general framework* which is to be applied no matter what the size of the investment.

At this juncture of the text, however, it is well to ask, "Who is this real estate market analyst?" The answer is *anyone* who attempts to forecast the future net income stream or amenities from a proposed or existing land use of any size.

A broker or developer may become aware of a market opportunity because of his own personal needs and requirements. For example, in a small urban area, the lack of a fast food operation may appear obvious to the casual observer when there simply are no such land uses in the area. It does not follow, however, that there is sufficient market demand to support such an investment even though there is presently no supplier meeting the apparent demand and there is no competition. A variety of factors may be brought into a formal analysis which could lead to the conclusion that the development of such a land use is presently infeasible. This conclusion would be based upon the typical investors' return and risk criteria coupled with a wealth of experience in this particular field which suggests certain minimum requirements based upon number of households, income levels, traffic volume past a particular location, etc.

Whatever decision is made in this case, the outcome will hardly be earth-shattering, nor will the local economy suffer or be significantly enhanced if the real estate associated with the fast food operation is developed. However, the point here is that the process of analysis is just as important to the prospective developer/investor as it is to the promoters and developers of major regional shopping centers. The actual analysis may be much less costly and perhaps even less sophisticated. Consumer surveys relating to the shopping habits and tastes of the most likely consumers of the fast food products may be unnecessary for such a small market area, for example. The major components of supply and demand, however, are the same as in major undertakings and the elements which spell success or failure are also similar.

Existing vs. Proposed Developments

There is often confusion over the type of analysis undertaken for an existing property as opposed to a proposed property. There is no question in the minds of most brokers and prospective investors that a feasibility study is needed in the case of a new development since it is one of the prime requisites of the lender when negotiations are undertaken to acquire debt financing for the project.

Such is not the case for an existing property since it represents "sunk cost," and a commitment has already been made to the particular site, especially in the case of a relatively new improvement. However, many serious errors in judgment occur for just the reason that the apparent commitment fixes the use and thus the potential market for the existing property. All too often significant market opportunities are overlooked because the broker and owner cannot see beyond the property as it exists today. They often neglect the alternatives of conversion of use or even complete demolition because they are wedded to the existing structure and the use that it implies. Take for example the many gasoline stations that remain vacant because of a failure to consider and promote alternative uses.

Even if there is no question that the existing use is most appropriate, it is important to reassess the market if a marketing plan is being devised to dispose of the property at the highest possible price within a reasonable period of time.

Focus on the Future

The primary time horizon of real estate market analysis and feasibility analysis is the future, whether dealing with an existing improved site or a proposed use on an undeveloped site—whether dealing with an investor who is seeking specific risk and return characteristics in an investment, or the user who has specific physical and locational requirements in mind for his business operation. In spite of the fact that the bulk of information

5

collected is historic data relating to the near present, the use of this information is for the purpose of making a forecast. Obviously, the investor is buying the right to enjoy future, not historic, income.

The entire focus of investment analysis is on the prospects for the future of a particular property and its future potential in generating cash flows. This posture is well established in the pertinent literature and in the minds of investors and investment analysts. However, the time dimension is often forgotten or overlooked when the bulk of the analyst's efforts are taken up with collecting information on the market as it exists today or as it has functioned in the recent past.

All of this information is useful only to the extent that it provides an indication of the market conditions which will prevail during the relevant period of the investment—THE FUTURE. It is all too simple to carefully examine the present situation and then cavalierly extrapolate the present into the future without careful consideration of those variables which are most likely to change and thus affect any forecast of the "status quo." The whole point of examining the past and present is to provide insights as to the most likely future; it is not to assume that the future will be a duplication of the present or recent past.

Some brokers and market analysts fall into the trap of exclaiming that they are willing to forecast only very short-term futures in an attempt to underscore their desire for honesty and conservatism, as well as to emphasize the problems associated with longer term forecasts. Unfortunately, life is not that simple nor is the process of real estate investment analysis and counseling. If the investor intends to hold the property for ten years or more, it is hardly sufficient to make a one-year forecast for the future of the property and then advise the client as to the relative desirability of a purchase based upon this forecast. The only logical and defensible basis for this advice would be if the investor intended to hold the property for one year only. Otherwise, it must be assumed that the one year "stabilized" forecast of net operating income is *implicitly* forecast over the actual or intended holding period of the investment.

Few real estate investments are held for only one year or for periods of relatively short duration. The reasons are obvious: the long economic as well as physical life of improvements, and the current framework of federal income tax laws. Even the selling costs associated with the transfer would provide basis alone for longer-term holding periods. In any case, real estate investments are typically held for periods in excess of seven years, and the trend of current tax legislation is pushing this time horizon even further into the future as the tax benefits of accelerated depreciation are being lost for various classes of investment properties. Thus, it is hardly a service to the prospective investor when the broker/analyst claims conservatism by forecasting the cash flows of the property for one or two-year periods into the future when the intention of the investor is to hold it for a much longer period. Such a so-called conservative approach to forecasting is or may be a misrepresentation of the most probable future for the property.

The user is also concerned with the future since the use of the property will occur over the future and not at the present or recent past. The real concern of the user is how the property, including the location, will meet his needs both as he perceives them today and over the future time period that he intends to use the property. For example, if a user finds a property improvement that is ideally suited to his needs, he may find that the property itself diminishes in utility as the environment around the improvement changes.

In summary, existing as well as proposed real estate developments require a market analysis and perhaps even a feasibility study when disposition is being considered. The primary orientation of such analyses is the future. Existing improvements are in reality a constraint on the use of the site; a market analysis is necessary to determine if the present use should be continued, altered or completely converted by demolition and replacement. A well constructed market analysis is the key to real estate investment decisions whether they involve existing properties or new development proposals.

Importance of Conducting Market Studies

Successful real estate development depends upon the symbiotic relationship of three elements: (1) the physical entity (the property in its market environment); (2) the financial structure; (3) and the people involved in development and management. It is only in the successful combination of these three that real estate developments can succeed. An analysis of the debacles of the recent past indicates that all the people involved had good track records, and while money was generally available, some restraint was indicated. "The REITs shovelled out money without stopping to analyze local real estate markets."[2]

The weakest area, however, was the property in its market environment. In examining the office building market in New York, *Fortune* magazine concluded that the market had not been properly studied:

> Because of an extraordinary boom in white-collar employment from 1965 to 1969, both interim and permanent lenders thought the demand for new space was a sure thing, even without tenants on the dotted line. They began competing furiously for the right to finance new building. . . . Banks for their part became eager to lend without

2 "How the Bankers Got Trapped in the REIT Disaster" *Fortune*, March 1975, Wyndham Robertson, p. 168.

7

the backup of permanent 'take-out' commitments. In that rich rental market of the late 1960s, moreover, most calculations assumed virtually 100 percent occupancy, top rental rates and minimum expenses for alterations or concessions.[3]

Even if the office demand had kept growing at the accelerated pace of the late 1960s, the growth in office space would have far outpaced it. In fact, office employment peaked in 1969 and declined just as the building boom began in earnest. A proper market study might have indicated that the growth in white collar jobs during the late 1960s was abnormally high, but the optimism that tends to surround real estate tends also to treat anything negative as temporary and everything positive as both permanent and indicative of the future. A cursory examination would have shown that overbuilding was occurring. While lenders and developers were operating on the assumption of prolonged growth, any analysis of economic feasibility based upon such optimistic projections would have led to disastrous consequences.

Improper Market Analysis

Similar assumptions were being made in real estate throughout the nation; the old wives tale that real estate is a good hedge against inflation helped fuel the debacle further when inflation started to run rampant in the mid 1970s. The point is clear—to determine the economic feasibility of any real estate development, the market needs to be identified and, most importantly, verified. To assume without basis for assumption (particularly for large scale projects) leads to dire consequences for all parties to the project as well as the market area in which the project is located.

Problems in the real estate market stem from a variety of causes but central to these problems is unquestionably poor market research or perhaps no real research at all. Hopefully, it is clear by now that before proceeding with the development of additional spatial units within a particular market, that market must be analyzed in some fashion. All too often, development takes place only on the basis of hunch, intuition, availability of money from lending sources and a whole host of less than scientific means of judging the demand for (in relation to existing supply of) space.

In the case of poor quality market research, perhaps the most significant problem is overly optimistic projections that evolve from boom periods in real estate development. Even though the boom may be experienced in another part of the country and in a spatial use different from that being considered in the market being analyzed, there has historically been a tendency to transfer the euphoria of success rather indiscriminately. The traditional emphasis placed upon the "bandwagon effect" has to be re-

---

8   3 *Fortune*, op. cit., February 1975, p. 162.

jected and markets assessed on the basis of relevant statistical data compiled from both primary and secondary sources within that market.

A second problem giving rise to poor quality market research is definitional in nature. Often it is not clear what type or form of study or analysis is needed. For example, institutional lenders often ask for an appraisal report for a construction loan when, in fact, a feasibility study would be more suitable to their purpose. Clients have difficulty in precisely articulating their objectives and consultants therefore have trouble in identifying precisely the purpose of the study or analysis. As a result, there has been substantial imprecision built into terminology. It is not uncommon to see or hear the terms market, marketability and feasibility used interchangeably. One prime function of this book is to indicate that these terms are *not* interchangeable; that they have very precise requirements; and that they provide information at critical decision points within the framework of the development process.

Along with these problem areas, inflexibility in the projected results may lead to a rigidity in a development plan that remains inflexible even in the face of changing market conditions. The precision of the mathematical processes by which data are manipulated often leads the analyst to the unwarranted conclusion that his/her projected results are just as precise. Even if the analyst is not unduly influenced by mathematical processes, certainly a client reading the analyst's report is often so influenced. The narrowness of the data used to make projections leads to rather sterile (and perhaps even dangerous) projections.

The success or failure of many, if not most, projects is based upon the extrapolation of first operating period revenues coupled with questionable projections of sell-off price at a stated future point in time. Perhaps the optimism of such forecast revenues and reversions were reflected in the successes projected by reports, studies and analyses for projects acquired by the real estate investment trust industry in 1973 and 1974.

Peculiarities of the Commodity and the Market

Real estate is a unique economic good for several reasons. It is the only major economic good that is immobile and therefore is subject to geographically oriented forces outside itself. Real property comes in relatively large economic units usually acquired with the nominal owner (or owner of record) supplying less than half the money needed to purchase the property and a lender supplying the remainder. Because of its immobility, each parcel of real estate is unique. This is the dominant characteristic of the real estate market within which marketability and feasibility are considered.

The real estate market in which the commodity is traded is far from a model of pure or perfect competition; in fact, it is very imperfect. As previously indicated, the property is immobile; therefore, the market must come to it rather than it going to the market. That is, the market must pre-exist, grow or change if the property is to serve it at its location. The "spatial units" are heterogeneous; no two are the same. Furthermore, the market is stratified or segmented by property type, location and price level. At any one point in time there are relatively few spatial units in any segment available and relatively few buyers seeking that particular type of unit. The quantity of money required is relatively large; the accompanying transactional process is complex, costly and time consuming. The time required to complete transactions restricts effective communications among owners, tenants, buyers and other market players. In such an imperfect market, then, price is indeterminate. It is imperative, however, that the real estate analyst consider all of these factors when examining a specific problem.

Spatial Activities and Spatial Units

In and of itself, space has no value. Space, however, in a proper location and in combination with some use or activity that has been determined feasible, may have considerable utility. In urban areas (which is the focus of spatial activity and use in this book), space has value by accommodating activities of people within that area (however defined or delineated). Activities of people are quite diverse between and among urban areas and thus require units of space which are different in aggregate amount for the area under consideration and in the size of individual units being absorbed.

Spatial activity, then, identifies the use to which the property (actual or proposed) is being put in much more specific terms than that of zoning or other forms of use classification, although the term itself is generic. For example, zoning regulations may indicate an industrial use, but the term spatial activity, which incorporates industrial use, calls for that specific form of activity taking place within that space, such as manufacturing (by type), warehousing (of what), commercial (retail or wholesale), etc.

Spatial units refer to the manner in which space is being used or absorbed in the market. Once the activity has been clearly identified, then how it is perceived (bought, sold or leased) in the market as an economic good can be expressed in spatial units. For example, rather than reflect potential residential demand by number of households requiring space (over and above existing supply) it would be more beneficial to the analyst to break that demand down by specific spatial units—single family residential, apartments (by type), condominiums, etc.

For analytical purposes, it is imperative that the specifics of activity and units be identified. Without these, the latter stages of market analysis and the whole of marketability studies and feasibility analysis cannot be accomplished.

Use of Market and Feasibility Studies by Real Estate Brokers

The presumption throughout the present discussion is that market and feasibility studies are conducted within the framework of sound methodology and careful, professional data collection and analysis. Within this context, then, it is important to note the various specific ways that a real estate broker may use such analyses. The following is a partial listing of such applications with no attempt to provide an exhaustive list—only the fertile imaginations of the many brokers throughout the United States can complete this task.

Identifying Opportunity

A market analysis may measure effective demand in the relevant market area and compare this with supply. The result is the need or "market gap" in order to identify both current and future investment and user opportunities. To the enterprising broker and/or developer, this particular application is especially important during economic slumps when opportunities seem few and clients appear scarce. Identifying market shortages in the entire market area or locational deficiencies in specific sectors of the market area are particularly useful applications of market and feasibility studies.

Designing Marketing Strategies and Plans

Market and feasibility studies can provide useful estimates of magnitudes of potential consumers by location, which can serve in pinpointing the most effective advertising strategies and in designing specific marketing plans for an existing or proposed development. For example, the more a broker knows about existing industrial users, their past and present use of warehouse space, the better able he will be to direct his specific promotional campaign to that segment of the market which could most effectively use the existing or proposed warehouse development.

Formulating Development Proposals and Plans

A well-conceived market study can serve as an invaluable aid in designing development proposals for new properties or even improved properties where conversion or rehabilitation is being considered. A market study can serve as an invaluable guide in determining what land use is appropriate at a particular site, what building configuration is most marketable and profitable, and over what time period the construction should begin and end where staged construction is possible. Although pin-point accuracy is obviously not possible when so many imponderables are present, the process of new development design is carried out more effectively when sound market and feasibility studies are used in the decision-making process.

Establishment of Rent Levels

Market studies are also an invaluable aid in setting rents that are competitive in the marketplace and yet attractive enough to achieve the use ratios that are necessary to achieve investor objectives. Once a rental structure is completed, there is little that can be done to change the inherent profitability of the development except through sound property management which includes the use of market information to determine the rent schedules which will provide a level of occupancy that will best achieve the return objectives of the owner.

In the case of most real estate investments, the major operating expenses are fixed expenses and the primary return on investment is related to the large capital outlay in the improvement and the land. It is a rare instance when the most logical investment strategy is to allow an improvement to remain vacant rather than to rent it at prevailing market rates. Thus, the real question is to determine prevailing market rates so as to achieve the highest possible rent while still maintaining acceptable levels of occupancy. This determination can only be made by a careful study of the existing market as well as a forecast of demand for the future when longer-term leases are involved.

Economic Justification for Debt Financing

One of the most frequent uses of a feasibility study is to provide the market justification for advancing funds to finance a development project, whether it is a new development proposal or a market value appraisal for an existing property.

Cash Flow Forecasts

The most fundamental use of a market and feasibility study is to aid the analyst in forecasting cash flows associated with a specific property or for a group of properties. Indeed, nearly all other applications are subordinate to this application. The investment analyst is most concerned with the use of market studies specifically to assess the degree of risk associated with his cash flow forecast. He is concerned with the likelihood of a particular rent level being sustained over the forecast holding period of the investment. A sound market study can provide the basis for estimating the lowest rent level that could occur, however unlikely, as well as the most optimistic possibility. The analyst can then "bracket" his forecast within these limits even though his final analysis will likely rest on specific dollar amounts per year rather than brackets or ranges of amounts.

Marketing "Problem" Properties

Marketing studies can provide invaluable assistance in the marketing of "problem" properties by identifying a broader range of uses than might otherwise be considered by a casual analysis of the market. Such studies can also help in the marketing of problem properties by establishing "absorption" rates for existing and alternative uses. Finally, problem properties can be marketed more effectively if more specific target markets are segmented through market analysis.

Framework of Analysis

This book will cover a variety of tools and techniques used in conducting "market studies." It should be noted that within the context of this book, the terms "study" and "analysis" are often used interchangeably to refer to the end product or set of final conclusions that result from a process of investigation. Each set of investigations that produce some form of study do so with a specific goal in mind. Typically this goal relates to the determination of a specific real estate investment decision. Indeed, the entire array of studies may be viewed as hierarchy, as shown on page 14.

Forms of Analysis

The primary concerns of this book are *market and feasibility analyses* (*studies*). In a broad and comprehensive framework of real estate investment evaluation, many additional forms of analysis are needed. Each of these has a phase in the general framework and will be discussed in greater detail below.

In general, *market analysis* represents the broader aspects of analysis that might identify a variety of potential uses. *Feasibility analysis* provides the basis for determining which of a variety of alternative uses meets the investment requirements of a specific investor. Highest and best use studies and investment analysis specify the most probable and profitable use from among the alternatives remaining after determining feasibility.

Given a specific site, a preliminary *highest and best use study* might be conducted in which the physical, legal, and locational characteristics of the site are considered in eliminating land uses which blatantly violate the constraints placed on the site. From that point, a market analysis would be conducted, the purpose of which would be to determine the potential or opportunities for proposed development, rehabilitation or conversion by establishing the range of spatial activities and the time of development indicated as most appropriate by market conditions. The market potential or opportunities identified helps establish the need for expansion of appropriate land uses and the rate at which development can take place. Additionally, they set the basis for income forecasts and provide the framework for timing the development and financial analysis.

A *marketability study* provides the basis for determining whether forecast market forces (as determined by market analysis) will support develop-

Market Study
A study of the market variables which influence the supply of and demand for real estate. (This is the broadest possible form of analysis and it encompasses all other types of demand-oriented real estate studies.)

Marketability Study
A narrowly defined study to determine the conditions under which a specific property can be sold. The key conclusions relate to both price and time required to sell.

A Feasibility Study
A study to determine the probability that a specific real estate proposal will meet the objectives of the developer and/or investor.

Highest and Best Use Study
A study to determine that use among other possible and legal alternatives uses which results in the higher land value for a specific site.

ment of each potential use and the rate at which such developmen
take place. Marketability identifies precisely each use type or
income projections, and density or land requirements and ab
rates for each use. Analysis of marketability is conducted within
work of the broader market analysis of past, current and potential futu..
patterns of metropolitan area development. Development patterns and
trends in the project market area (and the competitive strengths of the
site, if known) with regard to other competitive offerings are evaluated to
determine the specific use potentials and development timing.[4]

A *feasibility study* involves the determination of "go" or "no go" decisions from among a variety of potential uses with a given specific location. As a result of feasibility analysis, it might be concluded that all,
none, or some of the uses may be feasible in light of the various constraints
imposed. Among the various potential uses to be considered, the general
question to be asked in feasibility analysis is, "Will it work?"

While no decision need be made in feasibility analysis regarding which use
is most appropriate (since they might all be feasible), there is the requirement that if the answer to the question posed above is *no* or perhaps
marginal, then it is incumbent upon the analyst to consider those changes
in constraints, resources, and/or proposed actions that would be necessary
(and at the same time reasonable) to make the project work.

The final analysis of *highest and best use* identifies the most probable use
from among a variety of uses identified as feasible. Specifically, highest and
best use is that use which contributes to community environment or development goals as well as maximizing the wealth of the individual property
owner. In more practical terms, the concept of highest and best use
analysis involves the selection of those land uses with favorable economic
potential for site development.

Finally, *investment analysis* involves the determination of scale of development, the selection of the most beneficial financial package and/or
determination of the most favorable leasing terms, and a precise after-tax
analysis of overall financial performance—all in a mix that best achieves
the client's objectives.

General Overview of Feasibility Studies

Graaskamp, in his *Guide to Feasibility Analysis*[5], identifies three situations under which a feasibility study would be conducted. They are: (1)

4 Michael D. Wilburn and Robert M. Gladstone. *Optimizing Development Profits in Large
Scale Development Projects*. ULI Technical Bulletin 67, (Washington: Urban Land Institute,
1972), p. 12.

5 James A. Graaskamp, *A Guide to Feasibility Analysis*, (Chicago: Society of Real Estate
Appraisers, 1970).

a site or building in search of a user; (2) a user in search of a site and certain improvements; (3) an investor looking for a means of involvement in (1) or (2).[6] In essence, our view of a feasibility analysis matches that of Graaskamp, although we have incorporated the third situation into the first two.

It is our judgment that an investor/user would be involved in either of the first two circumstances and although (as will be noted later) the format would be slightly altered, the concern for investor/user objectives would be handled in pretty much the same manner regardless of circumstance. We are also taking very explicit recognition of the fact that a feasibility study can only be conducted after the market has been fully investigated and analyzed and some indication of the marketability of the space or activity over some representative and realistic time frame has been determined.

The market analysis/feasibility process described in this book is fairly elaborate. It is, however, similar to the intuitive feasibility study that commercial/investment brokers face daily. Those brokers are generally familiar with the area in which they operate and from their own knowledge of consumption patterns for a variety of activities, recognize or are sensitive to, investment/brokerage opportunities. For example, commercial/investment brokers are aware (if only unwittingly) of a variety of statistics or trends in the general area in which they operate. Generally, the broker will attach a subjective judgment or analysis of the relative importance of these general statistics or trends regarding the opportunity observed. In other words, they are utilizing experience and intuition in a relatively informal way of analyzing a perceived opportunity within the market.

The less sophisticated broker will simply look at general conditions of the area in which he works and recognize that it is either a growth area, a transition area, or a declining area and utilize a form of shot-gun approach to the variety of opportunities that might be pursued within these different classifications of market area. The more sophisticated broker would look behind the reasons for growth, transition or decline and ask a number of questions regarding the vitality of the area and the reasons for transition or for decline. It may be noted, for example, that in growth areas marginal operations succeed in spite of themselves. That is, growth absolves or at least mitigates a large number of mistakes or bad decisions.

All of this points up the need for some formalized process to analyze markets and marketability of space. The need for such a formalized process is much more apparent than ever with the recognition of the levels of sophistication among those within the brokerage field in conjunction with rather substantial changes in the economy that we have seen in the past several years. One thing is quite clear; that is that the broker

---

6 Ibid., p. 13.

does not create the need or demand for space—the market does. The broker, however, is in a position to anticipate or recognize this need/demand.

The procedure or format for the situations under which a feasibility study would be conducted, considered above, differs depending on what information is known at the outset. The difference is not only in the order in which the various parts of the study are carried out, but also in the determination of highest and best use. Highest and best use is not a requirement where the use is known or given. In such a case, the use is either feasible or not and the question of highest and best use is of little or no consequence to the analysis.

The Process of Analysis

The following represents schematics (flow charts) of the process of analysis under each of the situations discussed above.

Use Known/Site To Be Determined

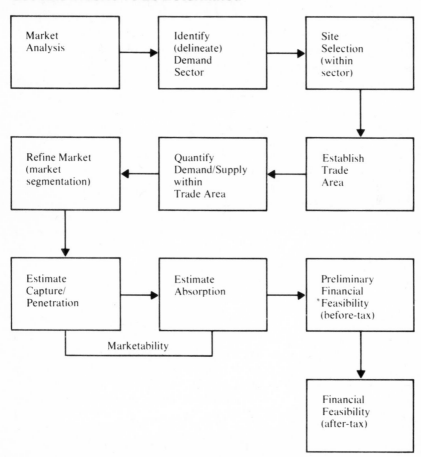

Site Known/Use To Be Determined

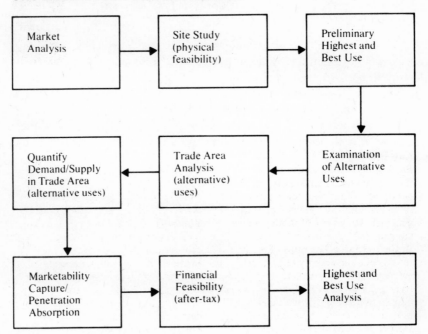

Chapter 2

Urban Growth Process

2

Key Terms

Basic Activities Land use activities (i.e., manufacturing), which produce goods and/or services for export out of an economically defined area *or* generate the import of money and/or consumers.

Basic Multiplier The ratio of an area's total economic activity (e.g., total employment) to basic activities (e.g., basic employment).

City A political entity with clearly delineated political boundaries.

Decentralization A shift in population growth and ancillary land use activities associated with population growth away from central cities.

Economic Base The employment and income-generating activities in an economically defined area.

Location Quotient A ratio of a specific local activity (i.e., employment) compared to national norms for that activity.

Non-Basic Activities Those economic activities (service activities) which support basic activities and thus have their entire market within the economically defined area.

Spatial Patterns The manner in which land use activities develop within urban areas. An observed phenomenon that provides insight to future development patterns.

SMSA Standard Metropolitan Statistical Area: an urbanized area with economic boundaries, as opposed to political or locational boundaries.

Urban Places Densely populated, non-rural areas.

Urbanized Area A population center of at least 50,000 persons.

Market and feasibility studies are most often conducted within the context of urban areas, since the nature of urbanization is one of agglomerations of people and activities that represent potential markets. The primary causes of such geographic concentrations are economic in nature. Thus, an understanding of and appreciation for the forces that influence the location and extent of economic activity, and in turn the resulting spatial patterns of land use, are fundamentally important in estimating the extent and nature of selected urban markets, and in assessing the financial feasibility of a specific land use.

The locational attributes of a specific site are typically viewed in terms of the existing urban environment—that is, in a static context. Data, after all, are a picture of what has happened in the past and are generally available on an "as of" date. However, as any investor well knows, it is the future, not the past nor the present, that is truly relevant in determining the financial feasibility of a particular land use for a site.

Likewise, the measure of market variables—consumers' tastes, family income levels, age distribution and other demographic variables—begins with an analysis at a single point in time. In both cases, the more critical consideration is the future, and how each of the key variables have and will change over time. How many families will reside in the relevant or specified market area; what will be their income levels and/or disposable income; what will be the age distribution, education, employment, etc. of the projected population, and how will each of these population characteristics bear on their consumption of a wide variety of goods and services? These are the types of questions, along with many others, that must be answered with approximations and forecasts. Generally speaking, they can be answered best by viewing the city or urban area as a large single *labor market* area.[1]

This portion of the text, then, is devoted to the city and to an analysis of where, how and why it grew in the United States. With an understanding of this growth and development process, we can then turn to a discussion of how to analyze the markets and the economic potential of individual sites which are located in or which fall within the sphere of influence of such cities.

Extent and Cause of Urbanization

Urbanization can be defined as the concentration of both people and economic activities in political units called cities, the fringe areas of cities, and large urban agglomerations. The United States is an urban country and the trend is clearly toward increasing urbanization. When our first census was taken in 1790, less than 6 percent of the nation's population resided in urban places of 2,500 people or more; by 1970 nearly three-fourths of our total population lived in such urban places.[2] In fact, over 40 percent of the 1970 U.S. population were recorded as living in the larger cities or urbanized areas of 500,000 population and over.

The most simple and persuasive explanation for this dramatic trend toward concentrated urban living was the technological advances in agriculture which steadily reduced the need for manpower to feed our growing population. As farm productivity increased, farm workers were drawn to the urban areas where jobs in manufacturing and services were

---

1 Wilbur R. Thompson, *A Preface to Urban Economics* (Baltimore: The Johns Hopkins Press, 1965), p. 67.

2 It should be noted that some discrepancy in comparison exists between the definition of "urban" before and after the 1950 census. Prior to 1950, the definition of urban included only cities *of 2,500 population or more.*

plentiful. This migration from rural to urban areas has continued since the turn of the century:

Our rapidly growing per capita income—the reflection of a generally advancing technology—has not, however, increased the demand for foods and fibers at anywhere near the same rate; food consumption is increasing only about half as fast as over-all productivity and per capita income, and not much more than half as fast as the productivity growth rate in agriculture itself.[3]

The resulting long-term growth trends both in the number of large cities and the relative share of the nation's population living in such population concentrations is clear, as shown in the table below:

Table 1   Growth in U.S. Urbanization 1850–1970

Year	Number of Urban Areas 500,000 Population & Over	Total Population in Such Urban Areas (in millions)	Percentage of U.S. Population
1850	1	0.7	3
1860	2	1.6	5
1880	3	3.6	7
1900	7	11.0	15
1920	15	23.9	23
1940	19	36.6	28
1960*	37	65.9	37
1970*	42	85.0	42

* Includes Alaska and Hawaii

Source: David W. Rasinussen, *Urban Economics* (New York: Harper & Row, 1973), p. 2. Taken from Jerome P. Pickard, Office of the Under-secretary, U.S. Department of Housing and Urban Development, "Growth of Urbanized Population in the United States: Past, Present and Future," (Presented at Conference on the National Archives and Urban Research, Washington, D.C., June 18, 1970.)

The trend is unmistakably toward an ever-increasing proportion of our population residing in cities—the creation of a nation of cities—as the migration from rural areas to cities continues and as the 90 million people who will be added to our population between 1970 and 2000 choose cities over rural areas as their residences. By the year 2000, it is possible that two-thirds of our population will live in the *large* urban areas of 500,000 population and over and that well over 80 percent of our total population will live in urban areas.

There is little disagreement among urban economists as to the cause of urban growth in the United States through the 1970s. Up to now, the farm-to-factory (or service establishment) is the widely accepted explanation. However, the future changes or shifts in population are likely to be

---

3 Thompson, *op. cit.*, p. 11.

more complex in nature. In the 1950s, the rural population declined not only in relative terms but also in absolute numbers. The change in definition of "urban" contributed in part to this phenomenon, but nonetheless, actual depopulation did occur in many areas. Wilbur Thompson sees great significance in this for the future:

> ... the nation's rural areas are rapidly emptying out; the great farm to city migration has about run its course and will soon belong to economic history. Today, the most challenging urban growth problems arise out of inter-urban competition for growth and the development of the national system of cities.[4]

The analysis of urban markets and the feasibility of developing (or redeveloping) urban land uses is thus becoming an increasingly complex process. No longer can we assume that the general trends in rural-urban migration plus population increases will guarantee the continued growth of any single city, even though we have concluded that the national trend in urbanization will continue. Cities and geographic regions are in competition with one another, and this competition will produce major shifts in population over the next several decades, both within and among cities. Today, more than ever before, it is important that the analyst understand how and why cities grow and change with respect to land use, population number and mix, and the many other related characteristics of urban areas that combine to determine market potential.

Before turning to a discussion of economic factors that are the primary determinants of city growth and change, it is helpful to trace some other important population changes and shifts that have taken place within the urban areas of the United States. Profound changes which have been taking place in the ever-growing urban population during the twentieth century suggest future patterns of growth and continued change. Since 1950, there has been extensive and systematic collection of metropolitan area statistics by the U.S. Bureau of the Census and other federal agencies.

For earlier periods, back to 1900, Donald Bogue converted census data to conform to modern definitions of metropolitan areas to allow the analysis and intertemporal comparison of urban versus metropolitan growth. It will be helpful to define some terms that are used throughout this discussion and text.[5]

Definitions
City

While widely used to describe many varieties of large and/or dense population settlements, a city is most precisely defined as a political entity which

---

4 Thompson, *op. cit.*, p. 12.

5 Most definitions are taken from the U.S. Bureau of the Census, *1970 Census of Population*, Vol. 1, *Characteristics of the Population* (Washington, D.C.,: Government Printing Office, 1972).

has clearly delineated boundaries. Generally, it takes the form of a municipality with a charter of incorporation.

The use of political rather than economic boundaries has the advantage that the area being considered as the "city" is unique at a single point in time, whereby a variety of different "economic" areas might be defined, depending upon *who* was delineating the area, and *what* the purpose is of the delineation. Comparison over time, however, has the disadvantage that political boundaries may change significantly from one reporting period to another. Heilbrun cites the case of Indianapolis, Indiana, which changed from 71.2 square miles in 1960 to 379.4 square miles in 1970—an increase of relative area of more than 433 percent. Population, which increased by 56 percent over the same period, actually declined significantly within the 1960 boundary area.[6] Obviously, care must be taken in making comparisons of city growth over time as long as annexation makes changes in city size possible.

Urbanized Area

This is an area which contains a central city of 50,000 population or more (or contiguous twin cities that have a combined population of 50,000, with the smaller of the two cities containing a population of at least 15,000 persons), the surrounding closely settled area which includes incorporated places of 2,500 or more, incorporated places of less than 2,500 if they contain 100 housing units in an area of five square miles, and unincorporated territory containing more than 1,000 inhabitants per square mile.

This census-defined area is available for the census years 1950, 1960 and 1970 only, and thus provides only a very recent historical record. In addition, comparison over time is difficult because, as in the city, physical boundaries may change over time.

SMSA

Since city boundaries may significantly distort the larger economic and social "area" which surrounds the city and forms the large metropolitan area, the "Standard Metropolitan Area" (SMA) was defined for use in the 1950 census. This geostatistical unit was modified slightly for the 1960 census and renamed the "Standard Metropolitan Statistical Area" (SMSA).

The SMSA is basically an economic unit which has the boundaries of counties or groups of contiguous counties (except for the New England states) that contain at least one city of 50,000 population or contiguous

---

6 James Heilbrun, Urban Economics and Public Policy (New York: St. Martin's Press, 1974), p. 20.

twin cities that have a combined population of 50,000 (with the smaller of the two cities containing a population of at least 15,000 persons). In addition to the county containing the large city or cities, contiguous counties are included in the SMSA if 15 percent of the workers living in them work in the central county of the area, or 25 percent of those working in the contiguous county live in the central country.

In 1970, the Bureau of the Census identified 243 SMSAs in the United States, and collected extensive data on each such area. In New England, towns and cities represent the relevant boundary unit rather than counties, but for all SMSAs, the primary advantage lies in the stability of the area unit plus the fact that data collected for SMSAs are directly comparable with the large amounts of economic, demographic and local government data collected on a county basis by several private and government agencies.

From an economic standpoint, one of the primary criteria in delineating the SMSA is that the area approximate the urban labor force of the central city. This is reinforced by the requirement that at least 75 percent of the resident labor force of the county must be nonagricultural. Further, the SMSA is divided into "central city," "central business district," and "outside central city (suburban ring)," and much of the data collected are available for these subdivisions.[7]

The SMSA then is one of the most important areal units for which data are collected. Since all cities of 50,000 population and above, plus most urbanized areas, are defined as SMSAs, they represent one of the most meaningful units of comparison and analysis for most market and feasibility studies.

Urban Places

Since the primary focus of this text is on the analysis of urban markets and the process of determining the feasibility of real estate investments in urban areas, it is important to draw some clearer distinction between "urban" and "rural." As Heilbrun points out, even SMSAs frequently contain parts that ". . . are thinly settled and essentially rural rather than urban."[8]

Although there are many forms of definitions of "urban," the most useful in terms of the analysis emphasized in this text is that adopted by the Bureau of the Census in 1950 and used to this day. These population size and density criteria include the following places:

1. All incorporated municipalities having a population of 2,500 or more

---

7 Although most of the terms used herein have precise Census Bureau definitions, the "central business district," however, is not so defined except that it refers to the commercial center of the central city and it thus is subject to periodic change.

8 Heilbrun, *op. cit.*, p. 22.

of 1970 would have gained only .1 percent instead of 6 percent in population over the ten-year period.[10]

Changing Functions of the Central City

The decline of growth in the central city raises serious concern over the continued viability of the traditional high-density central city and its focal point, the central business district. It is not simply the fact that population growth in central cities has not kept pace with suburban areas, but rather that the reduced growth rate has been accompanied by loss of jobs, decline in the levels of retail sales and other measures of economic activity, congestion and environmental deterioration.

Industry was one of the first key inhabitants of the city center to leave. The earliest industries in the United States located in or near the city center to take advantage of the transportation routes and facilities, the nearby market for final products, and the available labor force to work in their production lines. As the cities grew around them, however, industrial location became more complex. Manufacturing plants were adopting a larger scale of operation at a time when they were being engulfed by the city. In addition, polluting industries faced social ostracism:

> Early in the industrial revolution in this country, some manufacturing firms encountered social opposition because of the noise, air, or water pollution they created. Their least expensive solution in many cases was to move to areas less intensively developed: the outlying suburbs.[11]

Causes and Catalysts of Growth

As emphasized throughout this chapter, American cities and urban areas have become increasingly important as places of work and residence. Declining manpower demands of agriculture, higher levels of education, greater personal mobility, and increased information about economic opportunities have all enhanced the appeal of urban areas and have increased the extent to which population shifts from one urban area (labor market) to another. Greater production economics of scale, and an improving transportation system are additional factors which fostered urban growth and stimulated inter-urban population shifts.

It is obvious that urban growth occurs. It is more difficult to specify in precise terms the causes and general trends of urban growth. Development of urban areas may be studied through two different approaches.

First, the city can be regarded as one unit in an entire system or complex

10 Heilbrun, *op. cit.*, pp. 30–31.

11 Wilbur R. Thompson, William N. Kinnard, Jr. and Stephen D. Messner, *Employment and Industrial Development Opportunities in the Inner City* (Storrs, Connecticut: Center for Real Estate and Urban Economic Studies, University of Connecticut, 1974), pp. 41–42.

of cities, all interacting with one another. This approach is important in national policy-making and planning, but for purposes of this discussion, the emphasis will be on the role of the city as an autonomous economic entity.

The purpose of this discussion is to investigate the economic growth of a single (though not specific) urban area and to analyze the changes which occur within an urban area over time. To accomplish this investigation, the urban area will first be defined. Next, the basic component parts of the area will be identified, within the context of an economic evaluation. Finally, the probable influence, and interrelationships of these economic, social and political factors will be discussed, as they relate to future urban development.

An urban area may be thought of as any area which encompasses some major economic, social or political focal point. It includes not only its densely utilized center, but also the immediately adjacent areas which are dependent upon the central place. The essence of the urban area is concentration of economic and social activity. *Cities exist because there are economic and social benefits which result from proximate location.* The interdependencies of many activities, the need for concentrated consumer markets for effective and efficient distribution of consumer goods, and economies of scale in production all tend to enhance the development of cities.

Urban areas are dynamic, not static entities. Social, political, and especially economic factors can result in significant and broad changes in the urban area that should be anticipated in most market and feasibility studies. Although specific cities can be quite unique, especially during their early development stages, they must all adapt to a constantly changing environment. For our purposes here, we must understand the basic factors which can cause cities to change; further, the most probable and general development trends must be determined. We are concerned with two major facets of city growth. First, will a particular city grow? And if so, to what extent? Second, with a certain degree of proposed change in absolute size, what will be the character of change with respect to land use, area economics, and social and political structure of the urban area?

A developed urban area, then, is most essentially an economic entity. It owes its existence, both historically and as a vital going concern, to the fact that certain major economic activities can only be efficiently conducted in a concentrated environment. Stated differently, some activities (such as retail shopping, industry and professional services) presuppose the existence of large groups of resources, including people, for their successful conduct. Given a specific city, our purpose is to determine, or predict, what changes will take place in its structure. The first task is to estimate the future size of the subject city. Economic base analysis is one method of accomplishing this.

Economic Base Theory

When we examine the urban community as a functioning economic unit, our primary focus will be on the employment and income-generating activities that are often referred to as the "urban economic base." These activities are the economic "heart" of the community and are thus responsible for its economic health.

Basic and Non-Basic Activities

The economic base concept separates the economic activities of an area into two major categories: basic and non-basic. Basic activities (alternately termed primary, or exporting activities) are those land use activities which produce goods or services for export out of the specified limits of the relevant area. Non-basic activities are those which perform merely a supportive function; those which supposedly exist because they are demanded by the factors of production which are associated with basic activities.

Basic activites can encompass both the production of goods and the provision of services; both an automobile factory and a regional hospital are basic institutions because of the consumers they serve. It is the relationship between the production of the goods or services and the consumption of that good or service within the area which is critical in determining whether an activity is basic or non-basic, not the specific activity which the production encompasses.

Location Quotients

Location quotients, which compare the production and consumption of a good or service in a specific area, as opposed to national norms, provide one method of determining which economic activities are basic to an area. Location quotients seek to identify basic industries by comparing employment (or value added or sales or income) in a given industry within the area with total national employment in that same industry. This ratio is called the "location quotient." The location quotient (employment, in this example) is calculated as follows:

$$\frac{\text{Local Employment in Industry}}{\text{Total Local Employment}} \div \frac{\text{National Employment in Industry}}{\text{Total National Employment}}$$

If the location quotient is greater than 1.0, the industry is an "export" or basic industry. For example, suppose a university employs 2,100 people in a city with total employment of 31,500. The national percentage of college and university employees is 0.8 percent. The location quotient is then:

$$\frac{2,100}{31,500} \div .008 = .067 \div .008 = 8.333$$

29

Clearly, the university is in large part a basic ("export") industry in this city.

More specifically, the extent to which the basic industry is an export industry is measured by the difference between the location quotient and 1.0, divided by the location quotient. This is because a location quotient of 1.0 means that the industry has exactly the same proportion in the local economy as it has nationally. In this instance, $7.333/8.333 = .88$; which means that 88 percent of the product (as measured by employment) of the industry is exported, while 12 percent is consumed locally.

A location quotient of less than 1.0 means that the industry is non-basic for the area. In essence, such an industry serves the local community by selling its goods and services to residents. To the extent that the location quotient is significant is less than 1.0, it is an indicator that the non-basic industry in question cannot meet all of the local demand for the particular goods or services.

To be truly effective, the identification of basic industry should use detailed data (four-digit Standard Industrial Classification categories rather than two-digit) and measure not only employment, but also income, value-added and sales data ratios. Limitations of time and money frequently dictate a simpler approach; however, properly applied, the heart of the economic base provides both a valid concept of urban growth and change and a potentially useful tool to analysts.

The importance of basic activities lies in the belief that it is these activities which bring money into the city. Thus, the urban area is seen as an exporter. When sufficient exporting services exist, ancillary services (non-basic) will be demanded. Proponents of the economic base theory assign critical importance to basic industries. Non-basic services are seen as relying upon the profitability of basic export activities.

The Economic Base Multiplier

Once the importance of the area's economic base is accepted, the method of predicting future economic growth is relatively straightforward. The methodology encompasses two separate but related topics: the identification of basic activities of the area and prediction of the future level of these activities, and the development of a basic multiplier.

Major basic industry sectors can be identified through the use of location quotients. Future prospects for these industries are evaluated on the basis of consideration of national trends in the industry, the general ability of the area to provide necessary inputs to the activity, and the specific prospects of the area's ability to get products to the final consumer. Using this information, the level of future activity (measured by employment, or dollar sales) for each basic industry is estimated. All of these employment predictions are summed, to develop a gross factor for future growth. This factor indicates the relationship between expected and current basic activity.

Concurrently, an economic base multiplier is developed. This indicator depicts the relationship between the total economic activity of the area and the basic activities of that area. The economic multiplier is obtained by dividing the total level of economic activity of an area (as measured by an indicator such as number of people employed) by those activities which comprise the area's economic base.

The total future economic activity of the area is obtained by multiplying the expected basic activity by the already developed economic base multiplier. The result yields a gross indication of the absolute amount of economic growth which will occur in the urban area over the prediction period.

Limitation of Use

Problems with the data required for analysis and theoretical difficulties limit the effectiveness and validity of the economic base concept. Differentiation between basic and non-basic activities is not always easy. Although some activities, like the example supplied above, are relatively obvious, there are considerable areas which present difficulty.

For example, a regional bakery would combine both basic and non-basic activities; products consumed within the urban area would be non-basic, while baked goods exported to the surrounding area would be basic. In theory, the resources employed in the bakery's activities would have to be broken down into basic and non-basic components for economic base predictions to be valuable.

Also, location quotients rely upon national or regional norms for the determination of what percentage of a good should be consumed within an area. To the extent that an area engages in non-normal consumption, the economic base model will fail to depict the actual situation. Non-normal consumption could be expected in many types of activity, due to differences in knowledge of and access to the products, plus simple differences in geography, climate, income, facts, etc.

Perhaps the most damaging criticism of economic base analysis comes from critics who maintain that export is not the crucial component of an urban area economy. These critics state that supply factors such as a skilled labor pool and good location with respect to output markets are of utmost importance. Given a certain level of depth and maturity, a consumer market area will be sufficient by itself to attract new activities.

Critics also claim that it is impossible for all urban areas to be simultaneous net exporters, although in the aggregate urban areas in the United States have grown dramatically over the past several decades. Another shortcoming of the multiplier is the assumption of constancy in the ratio of basic to non-basic activity.

Other Economic Factors

Once it is established that a particular area will grow, there remains the task of determining how the change will affect the urban area's component parts: land allocation, transportation, and social and political factors.

Allocation of Land

Land allocation essentially is based upon market forces operating within the constraints of social and political considerations such as zoning and the desire of people to live in homogeneous neighborhoods. Market forces allocate land as follows: The demand for land is derived from land use activities which require land. Since any single site potentially could be used to support a variety of activities, there is the need to determine which activity will most probably occur at a specific site. The amount that any activity can pay for the land is a function of the wealth-producing power of that use, at that specific site. The economic desirability of a site depends on input (resources) and output (consumer markets) considerations. Within a specific industry or activity category external economies of agglomeration or disassociation may have profound influence upon the spatial location of individual units. Through a market bidding process, the land use which is most suited to a specific site is rationally self-selected to occupy it. The land use which utilizes the site most profitably, the "highest and best use," will generate the most rental which can be applied to the land.

It is obvious that the best use of a particular site will not always occupy that site; personal motives, inertia, and incomplete understanding of urban economics will occasionally result in less than optimal land use. However, subject to the constraints mentioned above, land will generally be allocated according to its highest and best use.

Importance of Change. Growth, age, changing personal tastes, and a changing state of technology all result in different market demands for specific goods and services. As demand for land is derived from the demand for other resources, each resource, as its relative importance and value changes, will yield a changing residual which is available to pay for land. It is this constantly shifting residual to land (especially in relative terms to other uses) which results in changing patterns of land use.

General Trends. Through time, American cities have tended to develop both vertically and horizontally. Vertical (intensive) growth—the construction of multi-story buildings—is a direct result of growth of market demand for specific services, which result in greatly increased land values. Given a certain level of land prices, a single-story building represents a less than adequate intensity of use of a site. If the activity is such that a central location is considered essential, then vertical development will occur. Horizontal (extensive) development is the lateral growth of the city. The spreading of the concentrated area beyond the prior city boundaries is the most significant and obvious cause of the relocation of land use activities. There are several reasons for this. First, most land use activities depend on neighboring uses of land. As the demand for office space and other high intensity uses increases, the price of land rises. Other, less intense users of land, who cannot afford the new occupation costs, are forced to relocate out from the center of the city. The eventual relocation site of these displaced activities depends on their specific locational needs.

Subcenters. When a city undergoes significant development, in terms of absolute numbers, subcenters are likely to develop, distinct from the central portion of the original city. These subcenters encompass activities which require access to a concentrated market, yet are not oriented specifically to competing for the expensive land found in the central core. Eventually, these subcenters may attain considerable size. Functions such as retail sales and professional services are often represented here. These units may include branches of the main downtown store or office. The development of subcenters tends to reduce the total travel time needed to access activities, and promotes non-radial travel.

Residential Neighborhoods. Land use activities depend to a great extent upon the surrounding uses of land. This is especially true of retail, residential and industrial uses. Use tends to be homogeneous within immediate neighborhoods, yet some diversity must be available within a limited area, because of the diverse activities in which people engage.

Residential patterns are especially pronounced. People tend to live near other people of similar socio-economic status. Most people prefer quiet, clean and relatively new neighborhoods.

Economic considerations affect the location of residential clusters. Access to employment and to shopping facilities are perhaps the most important of these concerns. New housing tends to be built along existing roads of access to central place activities. The severely limited nature of mass transit in this country makes good road access especially important to residential areas.

Change. In combination, economic and aesthetic factors have resulted in tremendous suburbanization of residential populations. As high intensity uses occupy larger segments of the inner city, the large homes of the relatively well-to-do are abandoned. Some are converted into multi-family residences or small professional offices. Displaced families relocate according to the social and economic factors mentioned above. With people living outside the central city, light industry, and especially retail sales, tend to follow, creating subcenters. This general trend of suburbanization is a mixed blessing. It reduces congestion in the central city, which is good; but it also tends to deprive the urban area of tax revenues, and may lead to a general decline of central city areas.

Transportation

Transportation is a major component of the urban situation. As activities require land on which to be conducted, so a physical site is dependent upon access to give it value. Two aspects of transportation have an effect on urban growth. First, an urban area must have adequate transportation to market its economic output effectively. Second, the urban area's local transportation system must be constructed so as to facilitate the human mobility which is essential to both the production of goods for export and the ultimate consumption of finished goods.

Output Considerations. Transportation has become relatively cheaper and faster over time. Existing air, rail and especially truck transport has resulted in an efficient system of transportation. Since roads are used by automobiles, as well as trucks, the general public has, in effect, subsidized the cost of goods transportation. The output transportation function is largely dependent upon the interconnections between individual cities. With the existing highway system, these demands seem to be met. However, if a city lacks adequate access to outside markets, it would be very difficult to remedy this situation as a result of the city's own efforts. Thus, it is doubtful that significant future growth would occur.

Input Considerations. Human inputs into the manufacturing process and individual consumers of finished products require a great amount of effort, time and expense to transport, especially when opportunity costs are considered. Thus, workers and consumers tend to be located close to employment and shopping centers, along established routes of transportation.

Transportation and Urban Growth. An urban area's existing and proposed local transportation system will significantly influence the area's growth. If the system is adequate, or especially fine, and able to meet the needs of most potential users, further economic development and orderly growth will be enhanced. A good transportation network makes an area relatively more attractive than another area which is similar in all other respects.

More obvious than the benefits associated with a good transportation system are the detrimental effects which result from systems inadequate to handle existing or proposed needs. With an insufficient transportation system, the basic function of an urban area—to promote human interface—will not be accomplished. Older, more fully-developed cities are especially vulnerable to this danger, as narrow streets and the location of existing buildings may not allow significant improvements in the network. If the existing or proposed system is overloaded, congestion and the associated problems of time loss, inefficiency, pollution and general frustration will keep people from the city. At first, marginal travelers, and later more basic users of transport facilities, will seek alternate opportunities. Because trip attractions and assignments are usually based on perceived costs, measured in travel time, an inefficient transportation system will encourage the development of subcenters away from the central place. These subcenters will tend to reduce the perceived cost of transportation. However, if the city's transportation system is exceedingly poor, it may tend to hinder the development of transportation in the surrounding areas.

Mass Transit. Mass transit seems to offer an opportunity to avoid detrimental congestion in the central city. Its efficient use helps to maintain the efficiency of the urban area. However, three basic difficulties limit the usefulness of mass transit systems at this time: (1) transit systems are very expensive; (2) they offer only limited flexibility to users; (3) people seem reluctant to forego the use of their automobiles.

Social and Political Considerations

Our discussion has emphasized economic and transportation factors. This is partially due to the tangible, and to some degree, measurable aspects of these factors. However, in addition to these items, political and social considerations are also important.

As an organized body, society through its officials controls urban growth with devices such as property and income taxes, building codes, and zoning policies. These and similar entities create the social-political environment within which the market forces detailed above must operate.

Thus, decision-makers with power over these tools have considerable influence on the future of the urban area. Used knowledgeably, these tools may be utilized to fine-tune development. For example, taxation may be used to speed or slow increased industrial development within a specific area. Tax incentives (temporary tax forgiveness) are useful to attract industries. Conversely, heavy taxation can result in an exodus of industry, as experienced by New York City during the late 1960s and early 1970s.

Section II

Methods of Market and Feasibility Analysis

Chapter 3

Framework of Market Analysis

3

Key Terms

Marketability The ability of a market to absorb space with a specific use.
Market Analysis A dynamic process involving the projection and analysis of the components of demand (e.g., income, population, employment, retail sales, etc.).
Market Study The comparison of market analysis projections with supply of space for a specified activity (both existing and potential) in an effort to identify market opportunities.
Spatial Use A specific activity that occupies space (i.e., medical office space).

When advising a client on either the acquisition, development, sale and/or lease of a property type or use, advice based upon hunch or intuition can be and often is as speculative as the investment itself. Decisions based upon hunch or intuition incorporate implicit assumptions that must be recognized by both the consultant and the client. Those implicit assumptions include: (1) that demand for a specific use exceeds existing supply in the magnitude necessary to assure success; (2) that alternative uses have been deemed less desirable (insufficient demand, less profitable, provides lesser tax shelter, insufficient leverage advantages and the like) than that use which has been selected; and (3) that client objectives have been precisely articulated and are understood by both the consultant and client and, further, that they have a high probability of being achieved.

This is not meant to suggest that hunch and intuition are to be discarded altogether. Knowledge and experience (in the form of hunch and intuition) in specific markets provide considerable insight in selecting appropriate uses, but do not provide substantive measures without some formalized type of framework in which these decisions are made. The numerous difficulties and high costs associated with the proper researching of local markets for whatever use often result in decisions being made in precisely the manner outlined above rather than by more rigorous analysis.

Without the more rigorous forms of analysis, upswings in local market activity can bring about various forms of destructive competition. Often

39

lesser quality real estate investment opportunities emerge during these turns and become intermingled with quality opportunities in the market at that time, and generally command prices that will doom even the most conservative investment criteria of the client. In addition, developers tend to over-build markets (and lenders over-lend markets) and cause investors to experience high vacancies and the resulting negative cash flows.

In more recent years, a new level of sophistication has been achieved in all levels of real estate analysis, and exclusive reliance on hunch and intuition is neither necessary nor very prudent in judging the merits of alternative real estate investment opportunities. All too often, traditional market analysis has involved the collection of a large mass of data, placing it in tabular form, and then ignoring that data and stating conclusions that were arrived at before the data were even collected. While there was never justification for this form of approach, the application of more sophisticated tools of analysis provides us with the opportunity to obtain some very meaningful insights from data collected but heretofore not properly analyzed or perhaps even ignored completely.

Nature of Market Analysis

In general, market analysis involves the projection and analysis of the determinants of demand; i.e., it is demand-oriented. It is the initial structured form of analysis utilized in projecting or forecasting those variables (income, population, employment, retail sales, etc.) which determine the demand for various forms of space or spatial activities. In effect, then, market analysis is concerned with the existing economic health of a specified market area (region, city, community, neighborhood, etc.), its future and the potential for new, rehabilitated or converted spatial units (uses) within that area. It is important to note at the outset that although market analysis is demand-oriented, it would be meaningless to project demand determinants without making some provision to match these projections with supply of spatial activity or activities within the area under consideration. Supply is not simply an enumeration of existing spatial activity but also takes into consideration changes (current or potential) to the stock.

Gathering Data

Market analysis is an ongoing process and, in most general terms, is an analysis of the components of demand without any necessary regard to specific use at the outset (although specific use may determine at some subsequent point in the analysis the form in which variables are projected or forecast). Those general market forces that make up the demand for space include population, employment, income, market interest rates, housing starts, land absorption analysis, retail sales, etc.

For each of the determinants our concern is with the estimation of change over time. The requirements for market analysis at this stage were provided in aggregate form from a variety of private and governmental sources. Census data, for example, provide a particularly good source and a starting point for population, business and housing projections. *Sales Management* magazine (as an example of a private source) utilizes census data and updates those data annually for a number of market areas. The Federal Reserve System publishes in its monthly bulletin a broad range of financial information, and Reserve Banks within the system publish economic data pertinent to their respective districts. Individual firms (consulting firms, in particular) maintain in-house libraries containing data from the foregoing sources, as well as refinements of that data resulting from past consulting assignments.

Whatever the source of the data to be utilized in market analysis, it should be emphasized that the data are not to be uncritically accepted, i.e., without consideration of how and for what reason the data were collected or the manner in which the data are presented or have been processed (manipulated). It would be an unusual circumstance, indeed, where data can be utilized directly in a market study from either secondary or primary sources without some refinement.

Aggregate data, regardless of source, often requires breakdown or "reduction" to more useable units to measure the effects of change within the broader category. For example, aggregate figures on population projections, while important, reflect only a starting point from which that data is broken down into such categories as age distribution, sex, race, marital status, birth and death rates, density and number of households among others. Aggregate employment projections might be further refined by type, as basic or non-basic, by relating historical levels of employment and area projections to national averages and trends or to reflect projected levels of unemployment. Income in the aggregate or in the form of wage rates might be refined or converted to personal or disposable income and then further to effective buying income in the aggregate or per household or per capita.

Demand and Supply

Once the components of demand have been projected (forecast) and refined according to the analyst's needs and that of the market study being conducted, the next step in the process is to compare these projections to existing supply, also considering anticipated additions to supply. Determination of supply is essentially an enumeration (inventory) process typically done by someone else, e.g., renewal agencies, local assessors, consultants, etc. Supply analysis (as an input into market analysis) is also an ongoing process requiring constant updating for new additions to and deletions from stock or recognizing those additions about to come on line. **41**

The extent to which demand exceeds supply can provide insight into the opportunities for development, rehabilitation or conversion in terms of type, size and appropriate timing. The latter represents analysis of marketability (discussed below) which should be investigated even though initial projections of demand may not be thought to be sufficiently in excess of supply to warrant further investigation. For most spatial uses, there is generally an excess of demand over supply in most market areas. This is due in large part to overlaps in market areas, some of which are worldwide with respect to certain classes of goods and services.

In any event, in addition to the importing of goods and/or services from outside a relevant market area, the existence of poorer quality (but competitive) space within the market area and the packaging of a potentially more marketable spatial activity or good or service warrant investigation of marketability. Even if projected market forces appear to be inadequate to support new activity, marketability should be studied carefully.

Market vs. Marketability Studies

The marketability of spatial activity (typically identified in unit forms such as square feet, apartments, number of beds, number of motel rooms and the like) implies the ability of the market to accept the transference, salability, or exchange of some or all of the rights in that spatial activity. The marketability study usually considers a specific use or uses of spatial activity. This activity may or may not represent the highest and best use since the marketability study does not necessarily consider optimal use, but rather marketable use. A marketability study has been defined as:

> A study to determine to what extent a particular piece of property can be marketed or sold under current or anticipated market conditions. It is inclusive of a market study (analysis) of the general class of property being considered.[1]

As noted above, the marketability study incorporates data pertinent to a market study of the general class of property under consideration. In effect, this suggests that once the determinants of demand have been identified and contrasted with supply, marketability carries the analysis one step further by identifying the number of units that can most probably be absorbed within that market and over that time period.

As indicated previously, studies are often mistitled. This is particularly true of the marketability study which is frequently confused with the feasibility study. The marketability study ". . . seeks to establish the relative rentability or salability of a project by estimating the rate at

---

1 Byrl N. Boyce, Editor, *Real Estate Appraisal Terminology* (Cambridge, Massachusetts: Ballinger Publishing Company, 1975), p. 137.

which the space will be absorbed by the market over a time period at certain rent or sales levels. The marketability study does not involve consideration of the development costs or profitability."[2]

A marketability study is, in effect, sandwiched in between the market study on the one hand and a feasibility study on the other (see Chapter 1). The complexity of analysis increases as one progresses from one form of analysis or study to the other in the hierarchy of studies. To emphasize the point that a project may be marketable but not feasible consider low income housing. Low income housing is not feasible without some subsidy, although demand for it is high and many cities are experiencing waiting lines. Another marketable item would be new three-bedroom houses for $20,000, but this is not feasible in most markets in today's economy.

The usual conclusions of a marketability study are three: (1) quality, which in economic terms means the price or rent levels at which the market might accept the spatial unit; (2) quantity or absorption scheduled by time periods; and (3) specific conditions, such as terms of financing, sales techniques, amenities, that will enhance the acceptance of the property or encourage its acceptance by the market.[3]

One of the principal uses of a marketability study is to test a proposed project for absorption. For example, a marketability study can be used to answer the question: "What is the size of the market that is available and at what rate will the market develop?" Additional questions would include "What are other plans for similar projects in the area and what effect will this have on the marketability of the proposed project?" Further, "What are the income and price levels in the market and what effect does this have on the decisions of consumers of spatial activity regarding renting vs. buying?" In the location of commercial uses, questions relevant to the site characteristics, accessibility, transportation mode, etc. are quite relevant to the acceptance and absorption of commercial space.

2 John R. White, "Nonfeasence with Feasibility = Failure: Improving the Quality of Feasibility Studies," *Urban Land*, October 1976, p. 5.

3 Anthony Downs, "Characteristics of Various Economic Studies," *The Appraisal Journal*, July 1966, p. 336.

Chapter 4

Projection and Forecasting

4

Key Terms

Coefficient A multiplier. In regression analysis, a statistic computed from the data which indicates the per unit change in the dependent (predicted) variable brought by the per unit change in the independent (predictor) variable.

Confidence Interval A range within which an estimate will be reliable with a quantified probability of accuracy (i.e., a 95 percent probability of being correct).

Degrees of Freedom The difference between the size of a sample and the number of statistics (computed from the data) used up in arriving at an unbiased estimate or equation.

Extrapolation A projection that assumes all influencing factors will remain constant.

Intercept In regression analysis, the point at which the regression line crosses the Y-axis.

Multiple Linear Regression A statistical method used to project a dependent variable with the use of more than one independent variable and with the assumption of linear relationships.

Simple Linear Regression A statistical procedure used to forecast a dependent variable by fitting past experience with one independent variable into the algebraic equation of a straight line.

Slope In simple linear regression, the graphic illustration of the rate of change in the dependent variable brought about by a change in the independent variable. Mathematically:

$$\frac{\Delta Y}{\Delta X}$$

t-table Summary of values that shows the number of standard deviations away from the mean represented by different levels of significance and degrees of freedom.

Trend Analysis The simple examination of past experience (i.e., with unemployment) used to make projections. Typically utilizes time as the independent variable.

Z-table The area under a normal curve measured in number of standard deviations between the mean and observed values (normal standard deviate).

As indicated in Chapter 1 of this book, the primary time horizon of real estate market analysis is the future. Thus, it is not surprising that a major part of most market and feasibility studies is a projection or forecast of selected market information over a time period during which the proposed or existing development will produce an income or amenity stream.[1]

---

1 For further discussion of statistical analysis, see Howard M. Benedict, George D. Herman, and William N. Kinnard, Jr., *Calculator Techniques for Real Estate* (Chicago: REALTORS NATIONAL MARKETING INSTITUTE,® 1977).

Methods of Projection and Forecasting

Forecasting is, at best, an inexact science. Most often, we are dealing with the extension of historic trends or assuming that the past will persist in the future—that observed relationships will extend beyond the range of data inputs. Projections are extremely useful, but in looking at the results of any projection one must be reminded constantly that although the trend now may be a fact, extrapolations represent no more than an educated guess. The presumption is that all factors influencing that which is being projected will continue to act upon the projection in the same way and in the same magnitude.

There are, however, methods of forecasting that allow us the opportunity also to identify measures of reliability associated with the forecast. Thus, more sophisticated techniques of projection render us capable of making more reliable forecasts, i.e., to identify the error associated with the forecast.

In the previous section, economic base analysis was identified as one means by which employment, population, and general land uses might be forecast. A number of limitations were noted regarding the application of this form of analysis and the projections derived from it. Among the limitations were constancy of the multiplier and the stability presumed in the basic/non-basic ratio over time as well as stability in other relationships between total employment and basic employment and population and total employment. To test the reasonableness of forecasts desired from economic base analysis and at the same time to make forecasts independently and with some measured degree of accuracy, a variety of techniques, primarily statistical, are available to us. A number of these techniques are discussed below.

It should be noted that no attempt is made here to provide complete coverage of the topic and tools of statistics as they relate to market analysis. The applications illustrated here utilize standard and conventional statistical techniques which are more fully developed and explained in any basic statistics text.[2]

Trend Analysis (Linear)[3]

Measures of change over time (employment/unemployment, population, household income) are relatively meaningless in and of themselves. To be meaningful for purposes of analysis there must be comparison to measures in other markets for the same time period or with previous levels in the

2 In particular see, William A. Spurr and Charles P. Bonini, *Statistical Analysis for Business Decisions* (Homewood, Ill.; Richard D. Irwin, Inc., 1973).

3 Ibid., pp. 577–605 for a further and more complete discussion of this tool.

same market. Growth or change can be measured in a variety of ways; its direction reflects the influence on spatial resources and their allocation.

As an illustration of the various ways in which growth may be analyzed, the following data will be utilized as a continuing example:

Year	Employment	Unemployment	Unemployment Rate
1966	22,873	1,235	5.4%
1967	23,146	1,250	5.4%
1968	23,653	1,159	4.9%
1969	23,481	1,362	5.8%
1970	23,770	1,260	5.3%
1971	23,965	1,366	5.7%
1972	24,206	1,356	5.6%
1973	24,172	1,281	5.3%
1974	24,367	1,340	5.5%
1975	24,539	1,350	5.5%

Initially, change in employment might be reflected simplistically in absolute numbers, percentages or average rates as follows:

Years	Absolute Change	Percentage Change	Average Rate of Change*
1966–67	+273	+1.19%	+1.19%
1967–68	+507	+2.19%	+1.70%
1968–69	−172	−0.73%	+0.89%
1969–70	+289	+1.23%	+0 98%
1970–71	+195	+0.82%	+0.95%
1971–72	+241	+1.01%	+0.97%
1972–73	−34	−0.14%	+0.81%
1973–74	+195	+0.81%	+0.82%
1974–75	+172	+0.70%	+0.81%
*From 1966			
1966–75	+1,666	+7.28%	+0.81%

The average absolute change in employment per year was 185.11 (1,666 ÷ 9), and the average rate of change 0.81 percent. If we made projections based upon these averages to 1980, the base for each formulation would be 1966 employment. The change over the 14-year projection period would be represented, on the one hand, by the average absolute change of 185.11 times the projection period, and in the case of the average rate of change 0.81 percent times the projection period times the base year employment. Essentially, the projections would be the same (with allowance for errors of rounding) since the average rate of change is simply the average absolute change divided by the base year. Mathematically, the projection formulas might be represented as follows:

$$E_c = a + b(N)$$

for average absolute change *and*

$$E_c = a + r(N)(a)$$

for the average rate of change.

Where:

$$E_c = \text{Projected (Forecast) Employment}$$
$$a = \text{Base Year Employment}$$
$$b = \text{Average Absolute Change}$$
$$r = \text{Average Rate of Change}$$
$$N = \text{Projection Period in Years}$$

Projections for 1980, utilizing the foregoing data and formulas, would be:

$$E_c = 22{,}873 + 185.11(14) = 25{,}465$$

or

$$E_c = 22{,}873 + .0081(14)(22{,}873) = 25{,}467$$

As noted above, the slight difference in the projections result from rounding in the average rate of change. While we have developed a means of projecting employment utilizing these averages, there are some serious limitations to its use in a practical application. The initial difficulty with this means of projection is the implicit assumption that the average absolute change per year (or the average rate of change) will continue in the future. Further, if we also project unemployment, then we are implicitly assuming that the relationship between employment and unemployment remains unchanged over time. Moreover, while we have developed a model for projection purposes, we have no measures of reliability associated with either the model or the projection. Although it cannot resolve all of these limitations (because we are still dealing with averages), regression analysis certainly provides us with a means of testing the reliability of both the model and projections made from it.

Simple Linear Regression Analysis

Regression analysis is used primarily for forecasting or predicting the value of a dependent variable, given the values of one or more independent values.[4] The reliability of the forecast and the extent to which variation in the dependent variable is "explained" by variations in the independent value(s) can be tested and measured.

Regression and correlation analysis can never "prove" anything. They merely demonstrate association between or among the variables, the closeness of that association, and the reliability of the forecasts based upon the analysis.

---

4 Ibid., pp. 448–87.

One simple method of presenting and analyzing data is to plot the data on a scatter diagram and fit a curve to it. In a situation where we are dealing with just two sets of data the independent variable is plotted on the X axis (abcsissa) and the dependent variable is plotted on the Y axis (ordinate). This means that it is assumed that changes in the X axis variable bring about changes in the Y axis variable, not vice versa.

If the curve fitted to the data were a straight line, it would be possible to express its formula as $Y_c = b_0 + b_1 X$; where: $b_0 = Y$ intercept, or value of Y where the line crosses the Y axis; $b_1 =$ slope of line, or $\Delta Y / \Delta X$ or the change in Y for a given unit change in X; and $Y_c =$ computed value of Y at a given level of X. Any number of lines or curves could be fitted by eye to a given scatter diagram. A practical method exists to determine a unique line for a given set of data with certain desirable statistical properties.

In the simple linear regression, the first thing we asked ourselves is what is it we are trying to do? We have two sets of data; we think there may be some relationship between the two sets and would like to know just what that relationship is. The first thing we do is plot the data. If it looks to be linear, we would like to identify the line that best fits the data. Once we have determined that the relationship is linear, there are basically five general steps to take:

1. Determine the line.

2. Measure dispersion about the line.

3. Determine the degree of relationship about that line.

4. Determine the variation in the dependent variable explained by the equation.

5. Make some estimates.

Steps in Linear Regression

More specifically (and in words) the following procedure is followed in simple linear regression.

The first step is to plot the data on a scatter diagram. This shows visually whether there appears to be any association between Y and X. Assuming there appears to be an association, the next step is to calculate the regression equation.

The regression equation, in general form, is: $Y_c = b_0 + b_1 X$. This describes a straight line.

$Y_c =$ the calculated value of Y (the "predicted value" given the value of X). In this case it is calculated employment.
$b_0 =$ the constant. This is the value of Y_c when $X = 0$.
$b_1 =$ the coefficient of X, the "b" coefficient. This is the amount of

48

change in the value of Y per one-unit change in the value of X. The *sign* of the b-coefficient indicates the direction of the change.

Calculating the values of b_0 and b_1 is a slightly complicated process and is accomplished by the method of least squares, which minimizes the sum of the squares of the differences between the observed values of Y and the calculated values of Y_c. Squared differences are called "variances." Minimum squared differences are encountered around a mean. Thus, the regression equation is in effect a moving mean of Y-values, given the values of X.

Since the regression equation has the characteristics of a mean, it has a standard deviation associated with it. This is called the standard error of the estimate, and has the symbol s_{yx}. The standard error of the estimate is used to measure the representativeness of the regression equation in the same way that s is a test of the reliability of $\bar{X}$ in a sample.

Also, since the regression coefficient (b_1) is calculated with the characteristics of a mean, it too has an associated standard deviation. This is the standard error of the regression coefficient, which has the symbol s_b. The standard error of the regression coefficient is used to test whether b_1 is statistically significant. That is, could this association between X and Y have occurred by chance?

To test whether b_1 is statistically significant, the t-value is calculated. This measures how many standard errors the value of b_1 is away from zero. If there is *no* association in movement between X and Y, then $b=0$.

One degree of freedom is lost for every statistic calculated from the raw data. Here both b_0 and b_1 are statistics, so 2 degrees of freedom are lost.

The general formula for degrees of freedom is: $df = n - m$.

      n = number of observations
      m = number of coefficients calculated from statistical data

If $n=25$ in a simple linear regression, then $df = 25 - 2 = 23$. If there were 7 X-variables, there would be 1 b_0-constant and 7 b-coefficients for a total of 8 degrees of freedom lost. Then *m* would equal 8 and $df = 25 - 8 = 17$.

When sample statistics have less than 30 degrees of freedom, the t-table must be used. This is because the reliability of sample statistics (especially averages) decreases markedly as sample size and number of degrees of freedom decreases.

For each number of degrees of freedom (shown in the column headed "df"), the t-table shows the number of standard deviations away from the mean represented by different levels of significance. The level of significance is the complement of the level of confidence. The most common levels of significance used in statistical analysis are .01, .05 and .10. These correspond to the 99 percent, 95 percent and 90 percent levels of confidence. The **49** t values shown in the .005 column are for the 1 percent level of significance (99 percent level of confidence) using the two-tail test. The .025 column is for the 5 percent level of significance (95 percent level of confidence) and the .05 column is for the 10 percent level of significance (90 percent level of confidence) both using the two-tail test to derive a "confidence interval." For the one-tail test, the .01, .05 and .10 columns are for the 1 percent, 5 percent and 10 percent levels of significance, respectively.

The confidence interval around the regression line is given by the standard error of the estimate times the Z or t-value determined by the desired level of confidence and the number of degrees of freedom. Thus, the *95 percent* confidence interval for 30 or more degrees of freedom is $Y_c \pm 1.96s$. The Z value is 1.96 when the probability is .4750; $2 \times .4750 = .9500$. Similarly, the *99 percent* confidence interval for 15 degrees of freedom is $Y_c \pm 2.947s$. The .005 column in the t-table for 15 degrees of freedom is 2.947.

In summary, the uses and limitations of regression and correlation analysis are as follows:

1. Regression analysis can show whether there is association in movement between Y (the dependent variable) and X (one or more independent variables). It describes this relationship through the regression equation.

2. Regression analysis can show whether the relationship in movement between X and Y could have happened by chance.

3. Regression analysis can be used to estimate or predict the value of Y, given a value of X (one or more independent variables). It also can test how reliable that estimate or prediction is.

4. Correlation analysis measures how much of the total variance of Y from its mean is explained or accounted for by the regression equation. It therefore measures how close the relationship is in value changes of X and Y.

5. Regression and correlation analysis are reliable only for relatively large samples.

6. Causation is neither identified nor implied.

7. Relatively sophisticated calculating equipment is required.

8. Regression and correlation are mechanical, mathematical processes. They are not substitutes for judgment and qualitative analysis or evaluations.

9. The results can be no better than the data gathered and used.

Application of the Simple Linear Regression Model

Using the set of data on employment presented at the beginning of the chapter, with employment the dependent variable and time the independent variable, the following regression equation along with various measures of reliability were computed:

$$Y_c = 22{,}867 + 172.76(X)$$

$$r = .97 \text{ or } 97 \text{ percent}$$
$$r^2 = .94 \text{ or } 94 \text{ percent}$$
$$s_{yx} = 134.17$$
$$s_b = 14.77$$
$$t_b = 11.7$$
$$df = 8$$

Before making projections from the model above, it would be well to point out the meaning of some of the measures of reliability that have been calculated from the data. First, an r (the correlation coefficient) of 97 percent suggests an extremely high correlation between time and employment. Secondly, an r^2 of 94 percent indicates that 94 percent of the variability in employment is explained by time. The intercept (b_0) of 22,867 represents the level of employment in the base year (1966) and the coefficient (b_1) of 172.76 represents the average change in employment per year. The standard error of the coefficient (s_b) is a measure of variability in the b coefficient and the calculated value of t (t_b) tells us that the b coefficient is significant at the 1 percent level, i.e., the chances are extremely small that there is no relationship between the two sets of data ($b_1 \neq 0$). Finally, with the degrees of freedom known (8) and the standard error of the estimate (s_{yx}) we have the capability of establishing a confidence interval for our projection.

The employment projection for 1980 using the regression model would then be:

$$Y_c = 22{,}867 + 172.66(14) = 25{,}284$$

We can further state with 95 percent confidence that the actual projection will fall within the range $25{,}284 \pm 2.306 \, (134.17)$ or between 24,975 and 25,593. With 99 percent confidence, the range would be $25{,}284 \pm 3.355$ (134.17) or between 24,834 and 25,734.

Curvilinear Relationships

Had we noted a curvilinear relationship in the above data when we plotted it, there are a variety of ways in which the data may be treated to reflect that relationship in a model for forecasting purposes. One of the more familiar and simplest techniques for expressing a curvilinear relationship is in the application of the basic compound interest formula $[s^n = (1 + i)^n]$. In the case of a trend forecast, the base year is multiplied by the future worth factor as determined by the historic compound rate of growth (i) and the time period (n) over which the forecast is being made. The general form of the forecasting model is the exponential curve $Y_c = a^x$, where

$$a = (1 + i)$$

$$x = n$$

Care must be taken in the utilization of this model for forecasting that the historic compound rate of growth has been computed properly and that the projection is made on the same per-period basis as that represented by the historic data or by the manner in which that data has been processed. Other, more complicated, curvilinear relationsips exist, but are beyond the scope of this book.

Multiple Linear Regression Analysis (MRA)

Any forecast or projection is usually a function of two or more independent variables; a single independent variable often does not serve as an adequate basis for forecasting or predicting. In such cases, multiple regression analysis is frequently more effective. The general equation is:

$$Y_c = b_0 + b_1X_1 + b_2X_2 \cdots + b_nX_n.$$

Multiple regression analysis is a process of separating the dependent variable into its several components or influencing factors and assigning a value or quantity to each. Conceptually, multiple regression is no more complex than simple regression. It does, however, require many more steps in the solution of several simultaneous equations. It is more complicated and time-consuming and really dictates the availability of either a computer or a programmable calculator with adequate storage capacity for its effective use.

Multiple regression still indicates only *association* between the value of the dependent variable and those of the independent variables. Causation is not indicated or implied; it is only inferred from the analyst's substantive knowledge or judgments about the relationships between the variables.

The coefficients derived in a given multiple regression equation are valid *only* for the data, variables and limits (or range) of data that go into the makeup of that specific equation. It is possible to include a variety of characteristics or predictor variables specifically in the multiple regression equation as measurable influences on the dependent variable. Individual adjustment factors (coefficients) for specific characteristics or predictors (independent variables) can be identified and quantified. Moreover, the extent to which a given independent variable is significant as an influence on value (and therefore whether it should be included in the analysis or not) can be tested by comparing R^2, S_{yx} and A.D. in multiple regression equations with and without the specific variable included.

Within a given multiple regression equation, the coefficients may not be what the analyst's judgment or experience would appear to dictate. This underscores the fact noted above that the coefficients are valid and applicable only within a given regression equation with a given set of data. Oftentimes, however, these "inconsistencies" with judgment or experience can be explained by the analyst within the context of the given set of data.

Increasing the number of independent variables often tends to provide a better fit and greater reliability and precision. However, multiple regression analysis contains the potential hazards of *colinearity* resulting from the effect of correlations between independent variables themselves, and *interaction* from one independent variable being a function of the other. These phenomena can cause negative coefficients for what judgment and experience indicate should be positive influences or vice versa. Colinearity can be identified and possibly eliminated by constructing a matrix of the simple correlation coefficients of the variables.

While the *average* error in multiple regression may be quite low, especially as additional independent variables are employed, the *range* of error (or maximum probable error) may be undesirably high. The only correction for this phenomenon is judicious selection of variables—successive testing to identify those which are the "best" predictors. Computer programs are available precisely for this purpose, and those computer techniques involve significantly greater objectivity in the selection process than could be effected by the analyst on the basis of his/her judgment and experience.

For small data sets (sample, number of observations), special attention must be paid to the degrees of freedom lost. This is given by $n - m$, where n is the number of observations, and m is the number of coefficients computed from statistical data in the regression equation.

MRA Application

As an example of a practical application of multiple regression analysis for projection purposes, the analysis of and projection model for rent structure for a six-town area in Eastern Connecticut is discussed below. The study included the total population of 62 apartment complexes in a six-town area. Subsidized housing was eliminated from the sample since the objective of the study was to determine the level of market rentals for a proposed new development anticipated for the area and to be competitive with existing private rental housing.

Initially, the model was constructed with 23 independent variables which were subsequently reduced to nine through factor analysis and stepwise multiple regression analysis. The nine independent variables were "loaded" into four categories through factor analysis as follows:

Category 1—Physical Characteristics
X_2—Square feet per unit
X_5—Number of bedrooms per unit

X_8—Number of bathrooms per unit

Category 2—Financial
X_1—Dollar taxes paid per unit per year

Category 3—Utilities
X_3—Utilities included/not included
X_9—Type of heat (oil or electric)

Category 4—Amenities or Extras included
X_4—Carpeting
X_6—Pool
X_7—Dishwasher

Dummy variables were used for included/not included (1, 0) items and for electric/oil (0, 1) heat. Taxes per unit were determined simply by taking total taxes paid on the complex and apportioning the tax bill to individual units by type, e.g., efficiency, 1 bedroom, 2 bedroom, etc., and on the basis of square footage per unit.

The model developed provides a means for projecting monthly rental by type of unit as a function of the nine variables identified above. The coefficient of multiple correlation (R) was 89 percent, indicating a relatively high correlation between the dependent variable and the nine independent variables. The coefficient of multiple determination (R^2) of .79888 indicates that approximately 80 percent of the variation in monthly rental is explained by the nine independent variables. The standard error of the estimate was $13.04. All the coefficients derived, except that associated with the type of heat, were positive. The coefficient for per-unit taxes (.09) in effect converts an annual allocation of taxes per unit to a monthly amount.

The negative coefficient for type of heat (-10.80) reflects an adjustment for oil vs. electric heat which is representative of that experienced in the market, particularly where utilities are included, i.e., those units with oil heat rent for less than those with electric heat. One additional item of information that was gleaned from the data was that second floor apartment units rent for approximately $8 more per month than those on the first floor. Two-story apartment buildings represent, by far, the modal form of development in this market.

Using the model below, the following projections were established for the proposed new development.

$$Y_c = 46.45 + .09(X_1) + .04(X_2) + 29.50(X_3) + 8.8(X_4) + 11.63(X_5)$$
$$+ 22.31(X_6) + 17.88(X_7) + 38.24(X_8) - 10.80(X_9)$$

Type Unit	Proposed Square Footage	Number Baths	Annual Taxes/Unit*	Projected Rental**
Efficiency	450	1	$ 486	191.81
1 Bedroom	600	1	648	224.02
2 Bedroom	850	1.5	918	289.07
3 Bedroom	1,050	1.5	1,134	328.14

* Assumes construction costs of $30 per square foot with a 60 percent assessment ratio and a tax rate of 60 mils.
** Assumes oil heat, utilities included and all amenities except pool.

Excluding utilities would reduce rentals for each type unit by $29.50. This would provide rent levels of approximately $160.00, $195.00, $260.00 and $300 per month, respectively. These rent levels are slightly higher than those currently prevailing in the market; however, the locational advantage of the proposed development site would warrant the higher rates.

Further analysis might be conducted to establish confidence intervals for each type unit. For example, a 95 percent confidence interval for rent levels by type of unit and assuming all amenities except pool, utilities not included and oil heat, would result in the following ranges:

Type Unit	Projected Rental 95% Confidence Interval
Efficiency	$135–185
1 Bedroom	170–220
2 Bedroom	235–285
3 Bedroom	275–325

In light of the locational advantages of the site, the ranges established above would be extremely competitive at the lower end and moderately so at the upper end. In fact, because of a very low vacancy rate in the market, even the upper end of the range in each category is perhaps more than moderately competitive. More importantly, however, such a range allows the analyst some flexibility in subsequent feasibility analysis of the project where the attempt is made to test the likelihood of meeting a variety of acceptability standards or criteria as determined by the explicit objectives of the parties at interest.

Chapter 5

Data Collection Through Questionnaires

5

Key Terms

Attitudinal Questionnaire A questionnaire designed to generate responses to aid in determining the attitude(s) of the respondents (e.g., toward a type of retail store).

Bias Prejudiced opinion. To be avoided *or* recognized and explained in primary data collection.

Capture (Penetration) Rates The percentage of population in a delineated market area that can be expected to participate in an activity (e.g., buy goods at a particular store). Market share.

Primary Data Information collected as a result of primary research on a specific problem through mail questionnaires or personal interviews.

Secondary Data Information that is available and published through normal sources (e.g., Census of Business, Census of Population).

Structured Questionnaire An organized set of questions about a specific subject that can be objectively summarized.

Unstructured Questionnaire A questionnaire with inquiries in a random order, possibly involving a great range of subject material.

Primary Data Collection

The foundation of most market and feasibility studies is formed through the careful and systematic use of "secondary data," that is, data which is published and available through normal sources. The U.S. Census is an excellent example of a widely used secondary source. Quite often, however, such data are not sufficient in depth or coverage to meet the specific and special requirements of the study. In such cases, "primary data" must be collected; that is, the needed information must be especially generated by the efforts of a researcher through any one of a number of methods. Among the most widely used methods of collecting primary data for market studies is the questionnaire.

Questionnaires can be, in many ways, the crux of any market research operation; however, they are fraught with a series of problems from development of the questionnaire on the one end to the interpretation of responses and presentation of results on the other. In general, there are three major aspects to questionnaires: their form (structured or unstructured), question sequence, and question wording.

Questionnaire Development

In the case of the form of the questionnaire, it will most often be determined by the type of data being sought and the data-collection method to be used. The researcher obviously has a greater degree of flexibility and the opportunity to obtain a wider range of data with the unstructured questionnaire, but runs greater risks of interpretation and bias than with the structured questionnaire. Unstructured questionnaires may be utilized in pilot interviews or in pretests, and the results used to develop a more structured questionnaire.

Wording

Question sequence and question wording can influence both reader and interviewee response. Part of the sequence problem is the necessity for an effective introduction to the questions asked. The respondent's role as either reader or interviewee is somewhat difficult. Either role takes some time and thought on the part of the respondent to answer questions —the purpose of which may not be too clear or the subject matter not of particular interest.

Questions related to personal matters (income/wealth, character, sex, age, education, etc.) have the potential of "turning off" the respondent and require not only proper placement within the questionnaire (typically toward the end), but also proper wording in order to preclude as much as possible imparting bias to the respondent or eliciting bias from him/her. Questions need to be clear (easily understood) to the least literate or least intelligent of those to be surveyed. Complicated terms and phraseology should be avoided. Further, questions should be simple, conveying only one thought, or elicit a single response as much as possible. Finally, questions should be stated concretely and conform as much as possible to the respondent's thought process; i.e., they should be worded such that the situation they portray or the response elicited can be focused more sharply by the respondent.

Responses

Responses sought should be accurate and reflect as closely as possible reality (fact) or the respondent's real feelings (opinion) on the matter. Responses also should be comparable with each other. Questions should be answerable in the same terms or in the same unit of measurement. Overlap in answers is undesirable as it complicates the problems of interpretation. Answers or responses should provide unequivocal reply to a question, and the frame of reference should be as similar as possible for different respondents.

Once the problems of questionnaire development have been resolved and the questionnaire developed, there is the problem of interpreting responses. There is always the problem of translation in the attempt to convert verbal or written response to numerical form for purposes of analysis.

Finally, there is the problem of presentation of results. The problem may lie more in the filtering process where a number of individuals are involved in collecting data (either orally or in writing), yet another group in analyzing the data collected and still another in summarizing results. Beyond all this fragmentation, there remains the problem of the client absorbing all of this in summarized form and applying his/her own interpretation as to what is being said.

Often, the personal interview questionnaire is directed specifically toward delineating a trade area. Most typically several interviews would be stationed at varying locations and times over two to three (or more) shopping days. Results of the interviews are then plotted on maps indicating an existing shopping pattern and trade area delineation. As can be noted from perusal of the questionnaire, other questions relate to the competitiveness of the area in which the interviews are being conducted. This provides some insight into the identification of the potential either for new facilities or expansion of existing facilities within the area.

Without presenting all the tabulations, the following represents information extracted from a mail questionnaire. The researchers are able to determine not only some reasonable estimates of trade area delineation but also information and insights regarding capture (penetration) rates, retail mix, market strategy, shopping preferences, etc. In addition, since the questionnaire was attitudinal in design there were some rather significant findings regarding the image of the shopping area being investigated.

Interpretation and Analysis of Responses to a Mail Questionnaire

This questionnaire was used in a marketability study and was designed to acquire three basic types of information. Initially, the questionnaire sought to develop a socio-economic profile of consumers in the market area. Secondly, it sought to develop an indication of existing shopping patterns for selected items by consumers in the market area as well as preferences of consumers for shopping facilities by type, location (both within and outside the delineated market area), and qualitative aspects of the facility (quality and variety of goods, prices, customer services, and the like). Finally, the questionnaire sought to identify an "image" of the pre-renewal *downtown* shopping facilities in Willimantic, Connecticut.

The Willimantic telephone exchange was utilized as the basic source for sample selection. It was decided by the researchers that this source (with some adjustment) would provide the most complete and up-to-date information on the market area household population. Names of individuals were selected systematically and randomly from each of the areas within the exchange. Eliminated from the sample were businesses, professional offices, and all telephone numbers cross-referenced in areas other than their primary exchange (denoted by capitalized letters over the number indicating the primary exchange). This latter adjustment was necessary to avoid duplication in the selection of the sample.

Students with dormitory addresses at the University of Connecticut in Storrs also were eliminated from sample selection. While it might have been appropriate to include some representation from this group, it was decided that the additional (and considerable) effort to do so would not have been justified. This decision was based upon two assumptions: (1) student representation (from those students most likely to shop in the Willimantic market area) would be obtained from those living off-campus and (2) dormitory students were considered less mobile and thus, to some great extent, captives of the Storrs market.

Of the 776 questionnaires sent out, 30 were undeliverable (for any one of several reasons—occupant moved leaving no forwarding address, occupant deceased, improper address, etc.), thus reducing the net sample size to 746. Overall response to the questionnaire was 41 percent (a range of 30 percent to 53 percent for individual market segments). There was no follow-up to the initial mailing.

The analysis of responses below is preceded by the questions as they appeared on the questionnaire, but not in the same sequence. The grouping of questions (where grouping appears) is in accordance with the information to be analyzed and is identified by topic heading.

Respondent Profile

1. How long have you lived in this area? _____
   (years)

11. What is the sex of the respondent?   a. [   ] Male   b. [   ] Female

10. Who does *most* of the shopping for your household, for items other than food? (Please check one.)

   a. [   ] entire household   d. [   ] spouse

   b. [   ] head of household   e. [   ] spouse and children

   c. [   ] head of household and spouse

8. How many years of formal education has the head of household completed? (Do not include kindergarten.) a. _____
Spouse (if applicable) b. _____

5. How many persons reside in your household? (Insert numbers in appropriate boxes.)

   a. [   ] under 16 years   b. [   ] 16 years and older   **59**

There was a wide range of responses to the question regarding length of residence in the market area (1 to 75 years). The mean response, however, was 18 years, and the modal response was two and four years (bimodal). Of some importance in the cross tabulations of responses was the fact that there was no significant relationship between length of residence and response to whether the individual would shop in the proposed shopping center development. This would seem to indicate (in light of this observation and subsequent observations regarding capture rates) that, regardless of length of residence, consumers would generally view the proposed development positively in terms of their use of it.

Slightly more than 60 percent of the respondents to the questionnaire were female. Correlating this response with that of Question 10 indicates that the bulk of the shopping for the household is done by women. This is not too surprising in light of national statistics which show that the woman spends the bulk of the family retail dollars.

Educationally, consumers in this market have attained relatively high levels of achievement. The mean number of years of formal education for respondents was slightly more than 14.5 years for both the head of household and spouse. The response in this category was again bimodal, with 12 and 16 years representing the greatest number of responses. Certainly the location of a state university and a state college in two of the largest market segments influences these statistics.

The size of household as tabulated from Question 5 was slightly larger than the same statistic determined from secondary sources (3.34 persons per household versus 3.2). The range for persons in the household under 16 years of age was zero to six, with the mean slightly under one. For persons in the household over 16, the range was one to seven, with the mean at 2.35.

Socio-economic Classification

6. What is the occupation of the:

   a. Head of household _____

   b. Spouse (if any) _____

7. Please check appropriate answer. Do you– – –

   a. [ ] rent an apartment   b. [ ] rent a house

   c. [ ] own your own home

8. How many years of formal education has the head of household completed? (Do not include kindergarten.) a. ___ Spouse (if applicable) b. ___

9. How many cars are used by members of your household? _____

From Questions 6 through 9 in the questionnaire, an attempt was made to stratify the sample respondents according to income and status. There are two primary reasons for the decision to acquire information on socio-economic levels in this manner. First, it avoids any tendency for the respondent to over- or underestimate his level via direct response to a specific question. Secondly, it is less personal and prying than directly seeking income level which, on the basis of experience with other studies seeking this same information, would have severely reduced the response rate.

The procedure followed in classifying respondents according to socio-economic level included first noting the occupation of the head of household and spouse, in conjunction with their level of education. Further evidence of the class level was evidenced by home-ownership versus renting and the number of cars per household. On the basis of this information, respondents were classified (albeit somewaht arbitrarily) into the following five classifications: student; lower (unskilled); lower-middle (skilled blue collar); middle to upper middle (white collar); and upper (professional).

The vast bulk of respondents (80 percent) fell into the "middle" socio-economic class. This grouping, coupled with the breakdown of market segments, provides some insight into the composition (or mix) of outlets to be located in the proposed shopping center and the marketing strategy to be followed by those outlets in attracting customers.

Shopping Patterns and Preferences

2. Where do you *most often* purchase the following items? (Please check one box for each item *or* specify location.)

Item	Willimantic Downtown	Willimantic Outlying Areas	Manchester Area	Hartford Area	Mansfield/ Storrs Area	Other e.g., Vernon, etc.
a. Books	[ ]	[ ]	[ ]	[ ]	[ ]	_____
b. Drugs & cosmetics	[ ]	[ ]	[ ]	[ ]	[ ]	_____
c. Sporting goods	[ ]	[ ]	[ ]	[ ]	[ ]	_____
d. Jewelry, watches	[ ]	[ ]	[ ]	[ ]	[ ]	_____
e. Appliances, radio-TV	[ ]	[ ]	[ ]	[ ]	[ ]	_____

Item	Willimantic Downtown	Willimantic Outlying Areas	Manchester Area	Hartford Area	Mansfield/ Storrs Area	Other e.g., Vernon, etc.
f. Furniture, rugs	[ ]	[ ]	[ ]	[ ]	[ ]	_____
g. Hardware & garden supplies	[ ]	[ ]	[ ]	[ ]	[ ]	_____
h. Men's apparel	[ ]	[ ]	[ ]	[ ]	[ ]	_____
i. Women's apparel	[ ]	[ ]	[ ]	[ ]	[ ]	_____
j. Children's apparel	[ ]	[ ]	[ ]	[ ]	[ ]	_____
k. Shoes	[ ]	[ ]	[ ]	[ ]	[ ]	_____
l. Specialty items & gifts	[ ]	[ ]	[ ]	[ ]	[ ]	_____

3. In what type of facility do you do *most* of your shopping for items other than food? (Please check one.)

a. [   ] Large shopping malls (e.g., Enfield Mall, Meriden Square, Corbin's Corners, etc.)

b. [   ] Large department stores (e.g., G. Fox, Macy's, etc.)

c. [   ] Medium shopping plazas (e.g., Manchester Parkade, Vernon Tri-City Plaza, etc.)

d. [   ] Small shopping plazas (e.g., Mansfield Plaza, Holiday Mall, Willimantic Plaza, etc.)

e. [   ] Small local stores and shops

4. When do you shop *most* often for items other than food? (Please check time and day.)

a. [   ] morning b. [   ] afternoon c. [   ] evening d. [   ] lunch hour

e. [   ] Mon.   f. [   ] Tues.   g. [   ] Wed.   h. [   ] Thurs.

i. [   ] Fri.   j. [   ] Sat.   k. [   ] Sun.

12. Indicate the importance of the following items to you when choosing a shopping area. (Check appropriate box.)

Item		Very Important	Moderately Important	Unimportant
a. Quality of goods	_____	[ ]	[ ]	[ ]
b. Variety of goods	_____	[ ]	[ ]	[ ]
c. Price	_____	[ ]	[ ]	[ ]
d. Parking & customer services	_____	[ ]	[ ]	[ ]
e. Atmosphere	_____	[ ]	[ ]	[ ]
f. Convenient location	_____	[ ]	[ ]	[ ]
g. Arrangement of stores	_____	[ ]	[ ]	[ ]
h. Accessibility	_____	[ ]	[ ]	[ ]
i. Restaurants	_____	[ ]	[ ]	[ ]
j. Cinemas	_____	[ ]	[ ]	[ ]

Question 2 provided an indication of existing shopping patterns for selected retail items, for market segments and in the aggregate. For the category "books," the majority of consumers in Willimantic and Lebanon purchase in Willimantic. Significantly fewer consumers in the other three market segments purchase this item in Willimantic. It should be noted that a large number of respondents reported that their purchases of books were through book clubs.

For the category "drugs and cosmetics," the consumers in the market segments Willimantic, Columbia, and Lebanon buy the bulk of items in this category in Willimantic. For the other two market segments (Mansfield and Coventry), there are evidently a number of intervening opportunities both within these specific areas or in market centers competitive to the Willimantic market, e.g., Manchester, Vernon, Rockville, etc.

For the categories "sporting goods" and "jewelry and watches," existing shopping patterns indicate that consumers in Willimantic and Lebanon shop predominately in Willimantic for these items. For Mansfield/Storrs and Columbia, the consumers are almost evenly split between Willimantic and outside shopping areas. Evidently, the Coventry market for these items is, for the most part, lost to outside shopping areas, i.e., the proximity of Coventry (which is on the periphery of the Willimantic market area as delineated in this study) to Manchester significantly offsets any attraction to the Willimantic market. In fact, this is the case for all the remaining items in the Coventry segment, i.e., the preponderance of purchases for all remaining items are outside the Willimantic area.

These remaining items for which Willimantic retains some dominance over outside shopping areas for those segments other than Coventry are "appliances" and "shoes." In the other categories, "furniture," "hardware," "men's apparel," "children's apparel" and "gifts," the Willimantic market segment shops primarily in Willimantic. For "hardware," so does the Columbia market segment. And for "gifts," the Lebanon market segment shops primarily in Willimantic. For all other categories, the bulk of the shopping for the selected items listed is outside the Willimantic area. Of no small significance is the fact that shoppers for "women's apparel" from the Willimantic market segment do most of their shopping for this item outside the Willimantic area, as do the other market segments.

The aggregates of existing shopping patterns for selected retail items within the Willimantic market also were gleaned from the foregoing information. Those items for which existing shopping patterns of the total market appeared particularly low included "books," "furniture," and "apparel" shops (men's, women's, and children's).

Preferences expressed for shopping facilities (by type) appeared relatively consistent throughout the market area. Responses to Question 3 indicate a strong preference for small to medium shopping plazas by respondents to the questionnaire. Additionally, in response to Question 4 on the questionnaire, it was observed that 76 percent of the total market shops between Thursday morning and Saturday evening, with a full 44 percent of the total market shopping on Saturday. There was no significant difference in this shopping pattern between the different market segments.

Summarizing responses to Question 12 indicated the relative importance of a number of variables affecting the preference of consumers for shopping areas. A rank order of the aggregate responses for the more significant items considered very important is as follows:

1. Quality of goods

2. Price

3. Variety of goods

4. Parking and customer service

5. Convenient location

6. Accessibility

Interestingly, there is very little difference in the ratings of these variables when the two classifications "very important" and "moderately important" are combined. Also, the responses regarding the importance of the variables are fairly consistent throughout the market area.

"Image" of the Downtown Willimantic Shopping Area

12. Indicate the importance of the following items to you when choosing a shopping area. (Check appropriate box.) NOTE: Blank spaces following each item are provided for answering Question #13 below.

Item		Very Important	Moderately Important	Unimportant
a. Quality of goods	_____	[ ]	[ ]	[ ]
b. Variety of goods	_____	[ ]	[ ]	[ ]
c. Price	_____	[ ]	[ ]	[ ]
d. Parking & customer services	_____	[ ]	[ ]	[ ]
e. Atmosphere	_____	[ ]	[ ]	[ ]
f. Convenient location	_____	[ ]	[ ]	[ ]
g. Arrangement of stores	_____	[ ]	[ ]	[ ]
h. Accessibility	_____	[ ]	[ ]	[ ]
i. Restaurants	_____	[ ]	[ ]	[ ]
j. Cinemas	_____	[ ]	[ ]	[ ]

13. In the space following the items listed in Question 12 above, rate the *downtown* Willimantic shopping facilities *on each item* according to the following scale:

P=Poor   F=Fair   G=Good   E=Excellent

A large proportion of consumers rate the downtown Willimantic shopping area as poor to fair. Although the ratings were generally consistent throughout the market area, it is interesting to note that Willimantic residents (residents of that market segment relative to the other four) tended to rate the downtown shopping area much lower overall for the items "quality" and "price of goods" than did the rest of the market. This may be, in part, due to the possibility that Willimantic residents tend to shop more exclusively in the downtown Willimantic area rather than other areas. As such, their response may imply some dissatisfaction with the area without making direct comparisons to other areas.

If such is the case, it might logically follow that this dissatisfaction may eventually cause them to alter shopping patterns and seek out other shopping areas. In other words, even though Willimantic has historically had one of the highest retail sales per capita for cities of its size in Connecticut, this could very well change unless something is done to improve the "image" of the downtown shopping area even among what has traditionally been assumed to be its most stalwart supporters.

Potential Capture (Penetration) Rates

14. If a new shopping center were constructed in the downtown area of Willimantic providing ample free parking and an attractive setting for 20–25 merchants, would you shop there?

a. [   ] Yes   b. [   ] No   c. [   ] Maybe

If yes, what type of stores would you like to see in the shopping facility? (If no or maybe, please explain your reasoning.)

_____

_____

_____

_____

Tabulation of Question 14 would seem to provide considerable basis for the proposed development to achieve the necessary capture rates (see Chapter 6). Aggregate figures indicate approximately a 70 percent capture rate as compared to the 66 percent required rate to assure marketability of the project. This observation is not, however, without certain conditions which include both type and mix of retail outlets in the center.

Beyond this, it should be noted that negative responses to the "would shop" question were extremely low throughout the market area, which provides further assurances of the marketability of the project. Upper income (professional) people throughout the area, Mansfield/Storrs students, and low-middle, upper-middle income groups in the Coventry market segment seemed to constitute the groups most reluctant to use the new shopping facility. This observation has obvious implications in the strategy followed in promoting the development and the retail outlets within the development.

Chapter 6

Market Delineation and Penetration

6

Key Terms

Capture (Penetration) Rates The percentage of population in a delineated market area that can be expected to participate in an activity (e.g., buy goods at a particular store). Market share.

EBI Effective Buying Income— Personal income less tax payment and required non-tax payments (i.e., fines, fees, contributions for social insurance).

GAF A general classification for retail activities which includes general merchandise, apparel, and furnishings.

Gravity Models Models, typically of retail activity, which attempt to explain the reasons (time, distance, size, price, accessibility, etc.) and extent to which consumers prefer one market area over another or others.

Market Delineation The process that identifies a location for a use or uses and the area that use will serve.

> **Geographic** Market delineation by defining an area in terms of physical boundaries.
>
> **Political** A market defined by political jurisdictions or boundaries.
>
> **Time/Distance** Market definition by travel cost measured in time and/or distance.

Retail Gravitation The pull or drawing power a retail center has on a market area.

Spatial Activity The general use (i.e., a restaurant) that occupies space.

Spheres of Dominance Defined market areas around a location that draws consumers with various "gravitational" pulls.

Methods of Market Delineation

Up to this point in market analysis, we have concentrated on projecting change in the various components of demand without any necessary consideration of specific location within that market. Feasibility analysis (illustrated in Part IV) requires, however, the determination of a specific site as a condition of proceeding with the analysis. To the extent, then, that there is a gap to be filled in an existing market (as determined by market analysis) and in the absence of a predetermined location, the location of spatial activity is critical to the analysis of feasibility. Market delineation implies either a known location as a starting point or provides the means by which to determine the most effective location in light of existing or proposed competition.

Even if location is a given (site in search of a use), it can be tested for effectiveness in comparison to alternative locations. Although we are dealing primarily with either a site in search of a use or a use in search of a site, it does not necessarily follow that we confine ourselves to a single method of market delineation. Rather, in instances where site is unknown, market delineation is at least a two-step process which first identifies location and then the market for that location and the proposed use or uses. In those circumstances where site is given, in addition to testing for effectiveness, the nature of practical methodology strongly suggests the use of more than a single approach.

Geographic Delineation of Market Areas

Market area delineation can be expressed in geographic terms (physical areas or distances) or in competitive terms. Although the former is perhaps more familiar, the existence of competing firms will impose obvious economic constraints on geographical boundaries. In a geographic sense, market areas may also be defined in political terms. For example, a housing market may be defined in terms of political boundaries of a given community or group of communities, while a retail trade area may be defined by a census tract. School districts also may form a housing market area or at least a segment of a housing market.

Physical or geographic market area delineation also may be expressed in terms of linear, or effective, distance from a given location. The prime market area for a shopping center, for example, may be circular with a radius of a specified distance from the center, or it may be irregular because of limited accessibility which, of course, influences travel time to the center. A housing market may be defined in terms of commutation time to a major employment center. Since real estate markets are stratified, the acceptable commutation time can and usually does vary directly with income, house price and rent level. In physical-geographic market delineation, mapping is widely used, often together with some sort of gravity model.

Competitive delineation of a "market" may best be achieved through some form of regression analysis (see Chapter 4). A basic question to be asked for this form of modeling: Are existing and similar spatial activities likely to be effective competitors or alternatives in the minds of informed buyers or user/occupants of that spatial activity? If they are, then they are in the same market regardless of their geographic location. For example, two homes may be in the same market or submarket whether they are adjacent to each other, down the block or in completely different suburban towns. The competitive markets for a wholesale food distribution center in one city may require the identification of competitive facilities in other centers contiguous to the city under consideration and not within the city under investigation itself. A good fit least-squares regression line, with its accompanying measures of reliability, can suggest the possibilities of whether a specified spatial activity is in the same market (by testing the hypothesis that it does come from the same statistical universe) as the spatial activities that make up the sample from which the regression equation was derived.

Political boundaries are typically given as unchangeable external political constraints. Lines are simply drawn on a map, with the data from external sources, to define the "market area." This method is simple, easy, quick and often used. Such delineation is severely limited by the hazard that social and economic forces often ignore (extend beyond) local political boundaries. In any event, this type of delineation would provide at least a start in terms of a first approximation of trade area, however crude.

Time-Distance Boundaries

Traveling time to a spatial activity is quite important. The cost of travel (commutation) is usually measured in time, which is what the commuter must give up in order to get to work, shop, or attend civic, cultural or social events.

Time "cost" is usually calculated as distance times average rate of speed. Time-distance boundaries can be drawn as circles from the center of employment, or shopping, or other activity, but this simplified approach overlooks the fixed locations of transportation corridors over which travel may be possible at different speeds. The preferred approach would be to locate the major transportation corridors on a map, and then survey average speeds to and from major centers of employment or other activities along these corridors. Distances representing the prescribed travel time are then plotted, and the points connected. The result is a map of the specified market area.

A very popular method of identifying time-distance boundaries is one of simply driving major arterial routes from the subject site and recording distances traveled at specified intervals (typically five minute intervals). These distances are then plotted on a map and the points are connected, so as to provide an indication of the boundaries of the market area. These boundaries indicate specific travel times from the subject site and can be combined with knowledge of other types of constraints (political, economic, social and the like) in order to further delimit the market area. Further refinement would identify boundaries within the market area in terms of primary, secondary and perhaps tertiary trading areas.

Combined with statistical information and projections made in the market analysis, the physical or geographic limits to the market area provide the analyst with a basis for making some judgment regarding the "drawing power" of the spatial activity. In addition to existing competition and accessibility which were considered above in delineating the market area, **69** the image projected by the proposed spatial activity (in the form of merchandising, pricing, services offered, and condition of physical facilities) has substantial impact on the drawing power of the facility and is obviously extremely difficult to quantify.

As a result, the judgment of the analyst regarding this particular feature of the proposed spatial activity is extremely important. Some insight into this judgment may be provided by the compatibility of the proposed spatial activity with the immediate neighborhood in which it is located as well as with other types of spatial activity (not necessarily competitive) within that neighborhood or development.

In some larger metropolitan areas or relatively high population density areas, it may be extremely difficult to employ time-distance boundaries or gravity models (discussed below). This is because of competition found in a number of different directions from the subject site and at so many different scales. It may be possible, under these circumstances, to arrive at the boundaries of trading areas for specified spatial activity empirically. Trade areas for existing competitive locations may be mapped, and information derived from these empirically derived trade areas can be transferred to the analysis of trade area for the subject site. Empirical testing of trade areas is often done by store interviews, automobile registrations, raffles and a variety of other customer-spotting techniques.

It should be apparent that the foregoing techniques of market area delineation are still more art than science. Even what are seemingly more sophisticated techniques also leave a lot to be desired. Obviously, more scientific methods should be used as far as possible, but often the data with which we work is incomplete and therefore not always adequate. In addition, there is a lack of sufficient practical standards for comparative evaluation because of the disinclination of firms to release information regarding the locational criteria of their spatial activity. As a result, the better information of market area delineation often will come from the files of the analyst from studies previously conducted.

Reilly's Law of Retail Gravitation

Reilly's "Law" is based upon Newton's Law of Gravity where population (or another size variable such as square footage of retail space, dollar retail sales or average bank deposits, etc.) is substituted for mass, and distance is measured in miles or in driving time. The original formula (discussed below) reflects a generally held and readily acceptable axiom that the relative drawing power of two competing spheres of dominance from intermediate area(s) is in direct proportion to their population and in inverse proportion to the square of the distance from the intermediate area(s) to each sphere of dominance. The exponent of the distance was determined by an empirical study of some 225 cases of various-sized cities in Texas. From this study, a clear modal value for the exponent of the distance occurred in the range 1.51–2.5.[1]

Reilly's Formula[2]

The formula in its original form identifies the proportion of trade attracted by "City A" relative to the proportion of trade attracted by "City B" from an intermediate town. In effect, then, the formula provides an index number which requires further "adjustment" to determine the proportion of trade from an intermediate point or market area expected to be enjoyed by the two competing spheres of dominance.

Mathematically, Reilly's "Law" is stated as follows:

$$\frac{B_a}{B_b} = \left(\frac{P_a}{P_b}\right)\left(\frac{D_b}{D_a}\right)^2$$

where:

B_a = proportion of trade attracted by City A
B_b = proportion of trade attracted by City B
$\dfrac{B_a}{B_b}$ = attraction of City A relative to the attraction of City B (an index number)
P_a = population of City A
P_b = population of City B
D_a = distance from intermediate town (market area) to City A
D_b = distance from intermediate town (market area to) City B

Alternatively, and with some algebraic manipulation, the formula has been modified in a variety of ways. The most common alteration that appears in the literature is:

$$A\% = \text{attraction of City A relative to attraction of City B} = \frac{P_a/P_b}{D_a^2/D_b^2}$$

where:

If $A\% < 1$, then a *lesser* proportion of trade from the intermediate town will go to City A than to City B

If $A\% = 1$, then *equal* proportions of trade from the intermediate town will go to Cities A and B

If $A\% > 1$, then a *greater* proportion of trade from the intermediate town will go to City A than to City B.

1 William J. Reilly. *Methods for the Study of Retail Relationships*. (University of Texas, Austin, Texas: Bureau of Business Research, 1929) (Reprinted, Austin, 1959).
2 For an expanded discussion of Reilly's "Law" see James E. Suelflow. *Market Potential—Its Theory and Application*. (University of Wisconsin, Madison, Wisconsin: Bureau of Business Research and Service, III (3), August, 1967).

To understand the logic behind the determination of the proportions of trade expected by the two spheres of dominance, assume a situation where the populations of two competing cities are equal and their distance from a third point (intermediate town or market area) is also equivalent. Intuition would suggest to us that in such a situation, the two competing cities would share equally in the trade from the intermediate market area. The ratio of both population and distances squared in the above formulas would be one, and the resulting index

$$\left(A\% \text{ or } \frac{B_a}{B_b} \right)$$

would also equal one. The adjustment necessary then is similar to that required for location quotients in the previous section: the index divided by the index plus one to determine the proportion of trade expected to go to City A from the intermediate market area. Obviously, the complement of this amount would represent the proportion of trade to City B. In our simple example above where

$$A \text{ percent} = 1, \text{ the adjustment would be } \frac{1}{1+1},$$

or 50 percent of the trade from the intermediate town would go to City A and the complement of that, or 50 percent, to City B. This coincides with our intuitive judgment expressed at the outset.

Breaking Point

As indicated previously, there have been a number of modifications made to Reilly's "Law" since its original development. Most involve adjustments for peculiarities in specific markets or for unique problem situations. One modification which has found general applicability and acceptance was developed by Paul Converse. It determines the "breaking point" between two urban areas, or the point where consumers are attracted in opposite directions. This modification is stated mathematically as follows:

$$D_{ab} = \frac{d}{1 + \sqrt{P_a/P_b}}$$

where:

d = the distance between Cities A and B

D_{ab} = the distance *toward* City A from City B (the breaking point in trading area between the two cities).

The breaking point, calculated from the foregoing equation, determines that point at which potential trade should flow in opposite directions to the two spheres of dominance. For example, assume the distance between Cities A and B is 20 miles and that their populations are 150,000 and

100,000 respectively. The limit of City B's trading area would then be:

$$D_{ab} = \frac{20}{1 + \sqrt{150,000/100,000}} = \frac{20}{1 + \sqrt{1.5}} = \frac{20}{1 + 1.22} = \frac{20}{2.22}$$

$$= 9.01 \text{ miles}$$

If, in the example above, distance were measured in driving time (30 minutes) then the breaking point would be expressed as approximately 13.5 minutes toward City A from City B. It should be noted, however, that the proportions remain the same and that mileage can be converted easily to driving time and vice versa.

Applications of the Law of Retail Gravitation

The following simple problem examples are offered to show the flexibility of the Law of Retail Gravitation in a variety of situations:

A. Westbrook Mall is an existing 600,000 square foot shopping center located at a point which is 15 driving minutes due east of Winfield. A proposed shopping center of 900,000 square feet is being considered at a point which is 25 minutes driving time west of Winfield on the same route that Westbrook Mall is located. How much of the available Winfield trade could the proposed center draw potentially?

$$\frac{P_a/P_b}{D_a^2/D_b^2} = A\% = \frac{900,000/600,000}{(25)^2/(15)^2} = 54\%$$

Therefore,

$$\frac{.54}{.54 + 1} = 35 \text{ percent}$$

of the available Winfield trade could be expected to be drawn by the proposed shopping center. Sixty-five percent would be expected to go to Westbrook Mall.

B. The proposed shopping center in A above and Westbrook Mall are located 40 driving minutes apart. Where is the dividing line (breaking point) for their respective trade areas?

$$D_{ab} = \frac{d}{1 + \sqrt{P_a/P_b}} = \frac{40}{1 + \sqrt{900.000/600,000}} = 17.98$$

miles toward the proposed shopping center from Westbrook Mall.

If the distance in the above example were expressed in miles (say 30 miles) then the breaking point would be expressed as approximately 13.5 miles toward the proposed shopping center *from* Westbrook Mall.

C. Assume the City First National Bank wished to locate a branch bank

73

between two existing competitors. Assume further that it wishes to locate at a point which represents the weakest point of each of those competitors as to their respective drawing power. The two competitors are located 3.5 miles apart. One of the competitors has average deposits of $2.5 million and the other $2.0 million. Other things being equal, where should the new branch of City First National be built (located)?

$$D_{ab} = \frac{d}{1 + \sqrt{P_a/P_b}} = \frac{3.5}{1 + \sqrt{2.5/2}} = 1.65 \text{ miles}$$

toward the competitor with $2.5 million deposits from that one with $2.0 million.

D. New Branford is a community of 10,000 population located 25 miles from Hatfield with a population of 90,000. A large community shopping center (approximately 200,000 square feet) is currently proposed for a location five miles outside of Hatfield and toward New Branford. The merchants in New Branford, especially those in a small center six miles outside of town toward Hatfield, are worried and requesting reduced assessments. Should they be concerned? Why?

$$D_{ab} = \frac{d}{1 + P_a/P_b} = \frac{25}{1 + 90,000/10,000} = \frac{25}{4} = 6.25$$

miles toward Hatfield from New Branford represents the existing breaking point between the two communities. Currently, the market for the small shopping center outside of New Branford is rather thin (1/4 mile), at least toward the larger community. The development of the proposed shopping center can only be detrimental to the "sphere of dominance" currently enjoyed by the town of New Branford and certainly to that of the small shopping center. Should the new development take place, then the merchants in the small center would likely warrant some relief in the form of reduced assessments.

Pull Factors

Ellwood provides a rather interesting modification of Reilly's Law in the development of "Pull Factors" derived from the formula:

$$\frac{P_a}{D_a^2} + \frac{P_b}{D_b^2} + \frac{P_c}{D_c^2} \cdots \frac{P_n}{D_n^2}.^3$$

This formula provides the total pull of all retail districts from multiple

---

3 L. W. Ellwood. "Estimating Potential Volume of Proposed Shopping Centers" *The Appraisal Journal*, XXII (October 1954) pp. 581–589.

market areas. The proportionate share of retail volume (either in dollars or in population) from each market area to each retail district is determined as a percentage by dividing the pull factor for each district by the total of all pull factors.

Reilly's Law represents a melding of two extremes that requires careful consideration before attempting any wholesale application. On the one hand, it is represented by a mathematical formula producing a mathematical result which would be approximately correct all other things, save distance (time) and size, being equal. On the other hand, the formula requires considerable prudence and judgment in its application according to the particular circumstances that arise in specific cases. In other words, Reilly's Law may provide the analyst with a good "first approximation" of the delineation of trade areas, but should be utilized in conjunction with, not exclusive of, other methodology.

Capture (Penetration) Rates

The concept of capture rates is relatively simple, although their determination, particularly for proposed new facilities, is not simple, nor does there exist any formal methodology by which capture rates can be determined with any degree of precision.

There are three circumstances which produce three separate forms of capture. The first and easiest to comprehend and measure is the capture rate for existing facilities. The other two circumstances evolve from proposed facilities where, in one case, both proposed use and site are known and in another where only proposed use is known. Use does not have to be singular as perhaps implied here, but in order to derive a capture rate, use is generally broadly categorized such as GAF (general merchandise, apparel, furnishings); office space; residential rental; etc.

The capture rate is defined as market share either existing or anticipated. An existing capture rate is that percentage of total potential market currently retained by existing competition (existing use and site). In the case of a proposed new facility, it is that share of market potential represented by the excess of demand over supply as determined in market analysis. To the extent that the existing capture rate is less than 100 percent for a particular spatial activity, there exists the potential opportunity for the development of additional spatial activity of the same type. The mere presence, however, of a capture rate of less than 100 percent does not necessarily imply the justification for additional spatial activity without considerable further analysis.

It is not uncommon (particularly in the analysis of retail activity) to see markets designated as primary, secondary and tertiary trade areas with a rather arbitrary application of capture rates applied to each on the basis of the analyst's experience elsewhere with that particular form of retail activity. For example, it is rather typical to see capture rates of 60–75 per cent for primary trade areas (however defined), 15–25 percent for secondary trade areas, and the residual portion of the required level of retail sales assigned to the tertiary trade area. While this particular form of allocation may have been observed from empirical study of trade areas and market penetration of existing stores, it has been used inappropriately when applied to proposed new developments. The presumptions of this particular methodology are too limiting (given an existing facility at a given location) for direct application in the analysis of new opportunity within a particular market.

Certainly, insight is provided by capture rates for existing facilities of a type similar to those which are being proposed, and this provides us with a particularly good starting point for the analysis of capture rates.

Determination of Existing Capture Rates

Determining existing capture rates is just a matter of enumeration of sales for a particular type of activity and relating that to the total potential for the market area. In effect, existing capture rates provide us with some indication as to the potential opportunity for new development to the extent that those capture rates are less than 100 percent. Existing capture rates of less than 100 percent indicate that consumers of that particular type of activity are either importing or traveling outside of the market area in order to acquire the service or spatial activity.

There is a tendency for analysts to "back into" capture rates by first determining the dollar volume of sales necessary for a specified size of spatial activity and then relating that to potential demand (or rather the excess of demand over existing supply), and then testing rather superficially for the reasonableness of achieving these capture rates. In the case of retail spatial activity, it is commonplace to concentrate on a general category or categories (e.g., GAF) of retail activity, and make capture rate projections based upon this form of analysis.

If, for example, capture rates were to be determined for a regional shopping center utilizing this particular methodology, the analyst would first establish the potential amount of GAF expenditures that could be originated within the trade areas. Adjacent areas would be analyzed in much the same manner along with the calculation of regional ratios of GAF to EBI (Effective Buying Income) for comparison purposes. To the extent that the market area figures are below those of adjacent areas or regional figures, there is presumed to exist opportunity for additional spatial activity within the market.

The GAF percentages adjusted and accepted by the analyst for incorporation into his study are converted to per capita GAF expenditures and combined with population projections in order to establish potential GAF sales in the future. This would, of course, be done for each of the trade areas as delineated. Then, in order to ascertain the percentage of total GAF expenditures which must be captured at a particular site, a series of total center sales estimates would be determined and then related to potential trade area sales expenditures. These percentages would then be related to the existing and projected levels of GAF to EBI computed earlier and assessed as to the reasonableness of achieving these levels.

A variation of this technique would find the analyst looking at a number of competitive facilities within the market area considered and assigning equal percentage capture rates to all including the proposed new facility. Then by concentrating on a series of questions dealing with traffic flow, street patterns, transportation factors, parking and various locational advantages or disadvantages, he would begin to adjust the percentages for each competitor either upward or downward depending upon how each relates to the proposed new facility and in light of their respective relation to the general categories of questions proposed. Finally, after a series of iterations, the analyst would refine the percentage capture rates among the proposed development and the competitive facilities. From that point, it is a matter of multiplying the capture rate times the personal consumption expenditures available for type of activity, thus providing an estimate of sales which can be captured by the proposed store at a particular location.

Estimating Capture Rates for New Facilities

Perhaps the best means of obtaining some estimate of capture rates for a particular market area for a proposed new facility is to conduct some primary research in the market among the consumers to determine the level of demand for a particular product or spatial activity. This could be accomplished either by personal interviews or mail questionnaires. An example of a mail questionnaire was presented earlier. In fact, the results of that questionnaire were utilized to determine potential capture rate by simple enumeration of those surveyed responding positively to a question regarding the development of a new shopping center in the market area.

The strength of the capture rate derived from this particular method can be determined by the magnitude of the positive responses in relation to the magnitude of negative responses to the same question. Similarly, capture rates also were developed from responses to questions on the questionnaire which dealt with current shopping patterns within the market area. For this estimate both unadjusted and adjusted capture rates were determined, the latter being weighted by the percentage of the total sample that was represented by respondents from different market segments. This was considered to be more realistic than the "unadjusted capture rate." In any event, total emphasis should not be placed upon a singular estimate of capture rates, but rather on a variety of methods of determining that rate and establishing a range of capture rates within which the reasonableness of their magnitude can be assessed more effectively.

Chapter 7

Feasibility Studies

7

Key Terms

Feasibility Study A study to determine if a project or use is a "go" or "no go" situation at a specific site, given certain economic (financial) criteria and client objectives.

Highest and Best Use Study A study which determines that use, from which among reasonably probable and legal alternative uses, found to be physically possible, appropriately supported, financially feasible, and results in highest land value.

Investment Analysis A process by which the attractiveness of an investment is determined by analyzing the costs and benefits utilizing time, value of money and/or various ratios.

Locational Criteria The economic requirements of the use or users for their space.

Market Segmentation The separation of markets into submarkets which may be defined by parameters such as income and consumer tastes.

Non-Economic Feasibility How successful a project will be in terms of being physically possible.

The term "feasibility study" is probably the most misused and abused term in the general framework of the analysis of real estate markets. The term has been confused with or used interchangeably with all of the other forms of analysis or studies that have been discussed thus far in this book. As indicated previously, each of these forms of analysis or study answers very specific questions posed by the problem at hand. Often, the investor, developer, or owner uses the term feasibility study when, in fact, he means or needs an appraisal or marketability study. In a discussion of what went wrong with feasibility studies in more recent times, John Robert White suggests the following:

> . . . the developer treated these studies as a necessary evil required for financing purposes and expected the analyst to deliver the most optimistic forecast possible. The mortgagee did not have the available staff to analyze the feasibility report properly and decide its credibility. The analyst assumed that he had been engaged to support the

developer's concepts and often considered himself an advocate rather than an independent observer of the market scene.[1]

Characteristics of Feasibility Studies

As noted above, there is a need to define precisely the term feasibility study. Webster defines feasible as "capable of being done or carried out, or capable of being used or dealt with successfully." A synonym given for the term is "possible." Webster's *Dictionary of Synonyms* suggests that which is feasible is ". . . not only highly possible but also to all appearances practicable."

In the context of apartment projects, the following definition is offered:

An apartment project is economically feasible when its projected future net income affords an investor an appropriate rate of earnings on capital, and provides for its recapture. In other words, he must be satisfied with the carefully forecasted "bottom line." In each case, what constitutes a satisfactory rate of earnings is a question the appraiser resolves after intensively studying many factors including attendant risks, forecasts of local and general economic conditions, earnings, prices of comparable properties, and yields available from competitive investment opportunities. The feasibility study is generally one of two types. The problem might be to examine prepared plans of an apartment project and judge its ability to show attractive earnings and adequately recapture capital. Or he may have to determine an improvement program which represents highest and best use of a particular parcel.[2]

In the *Real Estate Appraisal Terminology* handbook, the following more general definition is offered:

A real estate project is "feasibile" when the analysis indicates that there is a reasonable likelihood of satisfying explicit objectives and when a selected course of action is tested for fit to a context of specific constraints and limited resources. The context defines the problem. Feasibility of a real estate project is normally related to its probable economic potential.[3]

The foregoing definition is the same as that offered by Graaskamp in his book, *A Guide to Feasibility Analysis*.

---

1 John R. White, "Non-Feasence with Feasibility = Failure: Improving the Quality of Feasibility Studies," *Urban Land*, October, 1976, p. 6.
2 James E. Gibbons, "Apartment Feasibility Studies," *The Appraisal Journal*, July 1968, p. 326.
3 Byrl N. Boyce, Editor, *Real Estate Appraisal Terminology* (Cambridge, Massachusetts: Ballinger Publishing Company, 1975), p. 86.

John Robert White suggests that feasibility ". . . is the estimation of the relative profitability of a project arrived at by analyzing the relation between the total development cost and the estimated after-tax net income."[4] Further, he suggests:

> . . . the feasibility study usually requires the analyst to make suggestions for the improvement of an already devised land use masterplan. If such a plan has not yet been physically drawn, the analyst must then decide what the best site utilization would be and recommend an investment land use plan that will set forth the various types of land use, the general location of the uses, the density, the number of units, the coverage or floor area ratio, the parking requirements, the quality and probable cost of the improvements, the utilities, the direct and indirect development costs, and the rent levels or sales price. The investment land use plan is not in any sense a physical site plan. Instead, it represents the investment assumptions by which feasibility is tested. In many instances, land use assumptions are changed because it was determined after analysis that the plan was unprofitable. When a final investment land use plan is decided, it can then be translated into an illustrative physical site plan by a planner or architect.[5]

Obviously, the definition of feasibility study has evolved and been expanded over time. Perhaps the most important concept added to the definition is that of after-tax analysis. It has been recognized for some time that for most investors (who are tax liable), the funds invested in any project represent after-tax dollars. The recovery of invested capital and true return on invested capital is therefore necessarily in the form of after-tax cash flows also.

These definitions of feasibility and their evolution also would suggest that a complete feasibility study would incorporate the general framework of a highest and best use study. Even though the investor may not choose the highest and best use, the study should still be carried out.

Meeting Client's Objectives

The initial question that is basic to any feasibility study is "Will it work?" That is, will the proposed course of action, in probability terms, produce the results required by the decision-maker's objectives? In real estate analysis, a feasibility study must be undertaken and expressed in terms of the client's objectives. Without a clear-cut, explicit statement of client objectives, with which the client must concur, the real estate analyst cannot apply a systematic problem-solving process to the feasibility study.

---

4 John R. White, *op. cit.*, p. 5.
5 *Ibid.*, pp. 5 & 6.

The framework within which a feasibility study is conducted evolves from a series of questions to be answered by the analyst and emanating from the question posed above: "What are the client's objectives?" Other questions that emanate from a clear and concise statement of client objectives deal with such items as resources available to the client to achieve those objectives; the courses of action proposed to achieve the objectives, within the limitations established by available resources; external and internal constraints which exist to influence and/or limit the achievement of objectives; and, finally, consideration of the likelihood that the objectives can be achieved by proposed actions within the framework of resources and constraints given.

Among a variety of uses that may be tested for feasibility, it may be found that all, some or none of the uses under consideration are, in fact, feasible. Those that are found to be feasible will require further analysis to determine which best fits the client's objectives. For those uses that have been deemed infeasible, questions should be raised by the analyst regarding the changes in constraints, resources, and/or proposed courses of action that would be required to make the objectives achievable. In other words, a further question is asked regarding infeasible projects: "What can be done to make it work?" The reasonableness of the changes must be assessed and their impact on feasibility determined before a project can be determined infeasible with finality.

A Note On Non-Economic Feasibility Studies

A distinction must be made, at this point, between economic feasibility and physical, technical or engineering feasibility.

Architects and engineers have been conducting "feasibility studies" for a long period of time. Generally, their studies: (1) have primarily a physical orientation; (2) assume a maximum market; and (3) offer, at best, crude comparisons of costs and revenues. Frequently, the only constraint to the market considered in architectual or engineering studies is the zoning; then developments are planned to maximize the zoning.

A few years ago in Hampton Roads, Virginia, one general cargo pier was converted to containerization and was doing approximately 250,000 tons of business per year. The engineering firm retained to study the feasibility of converting two more piers *assumed* that each new pier would handle 250,000 tons of cargo, and using this basis calculated the revenues and costs and compared the two. Their basis of feasibility was to estimate how many years it would take until the bonds financing the project would be paid off under the assumption of an additional 500,000 tons of cargo per year. However, no study was conducted of either the amount of cargo the market might support or the price structure that might be required to attract it.

Feasibility Format

As has been noted before, the proper approach to any form of study or analysis is a team approach. The economist or real estate analyst is more skilled in looking at the economic feasibility or economic capability of the property or proposed use in terms of its market environment. Other experts such as architects, engineers, planners, transportation consultants, ecologists and/or appraisers also may be needed. Obviously, there needs to be someone (e.g., a commercial broker) to coordinate all of these activities. Once each expert has completed his task, the coordinator must then balance the cost factors against market acceptance. In this way, other problems are explored and through the synergism of the team approach, optimum solutions can be sought.

The feasibility study incorporates information provided from market analysis and a marketability study and proceeds to consider the specifics of a particular use at a site; it includes the factors of income and expense, financing and yield within market parameters. The **first** step in estimating the feasibility of a project is to assess the physical capabilities of the site. Architects, engineers and planners are usually more capable in estimating the physical capabilities of a site in terms of zoning, sewer, water, subsoil, rail, highway, etc.

The **second** step in estimating the feasibility of a project is to establish its initial concept. This means discussion at the outset with the developer, investor or owner. If the project represented is simply a property for sale, then the analyst is concerned with the present market; if it is a property for rent or development, then the analyst is concerned with a future market. The different problems identified, obviously, give rise to different types of analyses. For example, in estimating occupancy of an apartment or office project, a comparison approach to occupancy may be utilized. But a motel on the same site requires a built-up type of occupancy rate. It should be reiterated that at this point, the analyst should also define the client's goals and financial capabilities. Any conflicts or problems regarding these latter two items should be resolved at the outset.

Third, the demand side of the equation must be analyzed in terms of users. In determining just who the users are, a profile of the consumer of spatial activity is required. In addition, the analyst is very much concerned with what the consumer of spatial activity can afford to pay. In housing, for example, relevant information regarding this latter point would include, among other things, the income levels of occupants. In retail, gross sales estimates and rental income as a percentage of those gross sales are of considerable value in subsequent analysis. This obviously provides an indication of what similar consumers are paying at present locations.

Amenity requirements of consumers, in addition to their basic space requirements, also must be identified. These include schools, playgrounds, railroads, public transportation, parks, room sizes, layouts, closets, loading docks, etc. depending upon the type of development. Locational criteria, including such elements as convenience, accessibility, services and taxes, must also be identified. The consumer profile should consider when consumers will require the property and over what time periods they anticipate using it. Further questions would include: Where are the consumers of space likely to be coming from? How large a universe of users is there and how stable is it? How competitive is the proposed development likely to be to this consumer in light of his commitments to existing space?

Fourth, the supply side of the equation must be studied in terms of competition. The market area must be delineated using locational criteria; for example, factors of transportation, shopping facilities, housing, school districts, zoning, physical boundaries and driving-time analysis. The competition must be weighted by inventorying and evaluating the present supply. Once competition has been inventoried and evaluated, rents or price levels and amenities associated with competition must be identified.

Probable future expansion of competitive space must be estimated in terms of volume, size and type. This should be evaluated in terms of how it either may aid the proposed use and its development, or hurt it.

Fifth, together with other members of the feasibility team (particularly architects, engineers and planners), the analyst should arrive at a specific development scheme. This follows the completion of the marketability phase. With the identification of a specific development scheme, the feasibility or final phase of the feasibility study is begun.

Sixth, the costs of both construction and operation must be estimated.

Seventh, the financial package relevant to the proposed development must be analyzed in terms of such elements as mortgage loan ratios, cost of money, terms of borrowing and the equity position (including the tax status) of the client/investor.

Eighth, the observed estimates arrived at under marketability must be refined to consider such aspects as phasing and rates of absorption.

Finally, the estimate of economic feasibility determines the rate of return on and of the investment. At this point, income, expenses, and rate of return are identified in terms of who gets what and when. The return of the investment may be included with expenses such as in the case of a land development for sale, housing or industrial, or may be considered when the property is sold. Risk factors are incorporated both in interest and in yield rates.

In summary, all steps in the feasibility study set themselves up for probability analysis and model building in the context of client objectives and capabilities as well as those of the development team. Potential markets must be divided into segments and areas of appeal precisely defined. In addition, the ultimate user of the property should be identified in terms of what he wants and what he can afford to pay. Finally, an estimated schedule of capital expenditures as well as a schedule of financing inputs and income flows should be analyzed and measured against alternative investment possibilities.

Feasibility Studies, Analysis of Highest and Best Use and Investment Analysis

It is difficult, if not impossible, to separate the framework of highest and best use analysis from feasibility analysis. Highest and best use has traditionally been defined in an appraisal context. An example of this is the definition with some explanatory comment that is offered in the *Real Estate Appraisal Terminology* handbook, as follows:

> That reasonable and probable use that will support the highest present value, as defined, as of the effective date of the appraisal.

> Alternatively, that use, from among reasonably probable and legally alternative uses, found to be physically possible, appropriately supported, financially feasible, and which results in highest land value.

> The definition immediately above applies specifically to the highest and best use of land. It is to be recognized that in cases where a site has existing improvements on it, the highest and best use may very well be determined to be different from the existing use. The existing use will continue, however, unless and until land value in its highest and best use exceeds the total value of the property in its existing use.

> Implied within these definitions is recognition of the contribution of that specific use to community environment or to community development goals in addition to wealth maximization of individual property owners. Also implied is that the determination of highest and best use results from the appraiser's judgment and analytical skill, i.e., that the use determined from analysis represents an opinion, not a fact to be found. In appraisal practice, the concept of highest and best use represents the premise upon which value is based. In the context of most probable selling price (market value) another appropriate term to reflect highest and best use would be most probable use. In the context of investment value an alternative term would be most profitable use.[6]

Also in an appraisal context, Paul Wendt reviews the definition of the term:

---

   6 Boyce, *op. cit.*, pp. 107–108.

The use of residual methods and split rates is inextricably related to the classical determination of highest and best use. Babcock described this as "that available use and program of future utilization of a parcel of land which produces the highest present land value." Dorau and Hinman described it as "that use which brings the largest net return in money and amenities over a period of time." More recently, Fisher and Fisher define it as "a designated use of a spatial unit which will allegedly produce the largest net income over a given period of time." Authors of the *Appraisal of Real Estate* define it as "that use which will develop fully the potential utility of the site . . . the highest and best utilization program . . . which will produce the greatest future benefits to the owner of the land." Babcock's definition of the term appears to be not only the simplest, but also the most valid of those considered, since the other definitions fail to consider explicitly the importance of the timing of the receipt of future returns which is the essence of Babcock's present value of land concept.

Agreement with Babcock's definition of concept of highest and best use, however, in no way diminishes the difficulty of applying this concept in a specific case. To estimate the present value of vacant land it is necessary to hypothesize an improvement scheme, estimate the future returns to the property over some time period, assign a portion of these returns to amortization of the building investment by applying an assumed building rate to the estimated value or cost of the improvements, and, finally, capitalize the residual returns to land as a perpetuity by applying some "land rate."[7]

Wendt continues, however, by identifying the fact that after-tax analysis represents a major refinement in techniques for determining highest and best use. He notes that although the price of land should reflect the competition among users, the market is notably imperfect and, with changes in land utilization, prices and values are also noted to change rapidly and abruptly. It is for these reasons, Wendt suggests, that the investor tests going market prices by hypothesizing various improvement schemes.[8]

In reference to after-tax analysis, Wendt further states the following:

It has already been argued that the investor is primarily interested in maximizing his after-tax cash flow as a percentage of any required equity commitment. Assuming that a parking lot or agricultural use does not represent the best economic use of the property, the investor is faced with the decision as to that combination of land and improvements which will maximize the difference between the discounted value of his after-tax cash flows and the necessary outlays. . . .

7 Paul F. Wendt, *Real Estate Appraisal Review and Outlook*, (Athens, Georgia: University of Georgia Press, 1974), p. 160.
8 *Ibid.*, pp. 160–161.

The use of after-tax flows to determine highest and best use also assumes that highest and best use will differ among investor types. After some reflection, it will be seen that this is logical and consistent with price theory and with the principle of competition of uses. This means, in effect, that in competition among users for individual sites, that investor will prevail whose investment calculus satisfies the equation above. Investors for whom tax shelter is highly important will bid for sites matching their needs.[9]

Investment analysis really requires the result of feasibility analysis as one of its points of departure. Feasibility analysis identifies the expected results of one or more proposed courses of action and compares these expected results with the client's objectives and standards of acceptability. It can also identify those changes (in constraints, resources, objectives) that are necessary and possible to achieve desired results and what the costs of effecting such changes most probably will be. Feasibility analysis is more reportorial than evaluative or action-oriented. It can deal with the qualitative as well as the quantitative objectives and constraints.

Investment analysis, on the other hand, is entirely quantitative. It deals in dollars as measurable quantities. It is concerned with *selection* from among alternative courses of action (including the possibility of no action) to achieve the "best" results in terms of the client/investor's objectives. For example, while highest and best use identification may emerge from a feasibility study, the selection of the use program to follow is the result of investment analysis.

---

     9 *Ibid.*, pp. 161–162.

Chapter 8

Formulating Investment Alternatives

8

Key Terms

Absorption Rate The rate at which a market can absorb space with a specific use (i.e., office space).

Acquisition Loan A loan to finance partially the purchase of a project, usually to acquire the land for a development project.

Appraised Value An opinion of value (market, investment, or other) made by an appraiser based upon facts and judgment and processed into an estimate as of a certain date.

Debt Coverage Ratio The ratio of net operating income to annual debt service: $\left(\dfrac{NOI}{ADS}\right)$.

Internal Rate of Return That rate at which *all* future cash flows will be discounted so the net present value will equal 0.

Adjusted IRR That rate which will discount future cash in-flows to equal cash out-flows that have been discounted at a specified rate.

Loan Points A charge as a percentage of a mortgage principal made by the lender. (One point is equal to one percent of the loan principal).

Mortgage Release The document that relinquishes the encumbrance of the mortgagee (lender) due to a mortgage debt.

Sell-Off Period The time estimated to sell out a project.

In the preceding chapter, the purpose and process of conducting a feasibility study were outlined. In actual practice, this process begins with a detailed market study and proceeds through estimates and projections of after-tax cash flows for one or more development plans. This chapter will illustrate the total process by using an actual market study and then demonstrating how these market data are used to formulate several possible investment alternatives. These alternative development plans will then be analyzed in terms of after-tax cash flows and their related rates of return.

The market study used as the basis for this illustration was aimed primarily at determining the rate of absorption for office space at a particular site. The "Office Condominium Market Analysis—Inventure Plaza Study" is contained in its entirety as an appendix to this chapter. The "Inventure Plaza" study was commissioned by Developmental Services

Group, a division of Daniel Crow Interests, 4200 S. Bellaire Circle, Englewood, Colorado, and is used with the permission of Daniel Crow.

Three possible office uses were formulated and projected for the site so that the resulting after-tax cash flows could be used to calculate rates of return. Using a combination of rate of return and risk estimates, the developer/investor could then decide which of the alternative plans would best meet his investment objectives, if indeed any would meet his minimum required return.

The three projected uses were: (1) office subdivision with a sell-off of four lots, with profits taxed as ordinary income; (2) office condominiums with sell-off of individual units, with profits from the sale of the units also taxed as ordinary income; and (3) rental office to be held as a long-term investment.

The process of analysis used for the three alternative plans was to refine demand and cost projections to after-tax cash flows (both positive and negative) at the times they were estimated to occur. The sell-off and/or rental revenues were based on the absorption rate estimates presented in the "Summary of Conclusions and Recommendations" on the first page of the market study. More specifically, the study provides detailed estimates of demand per unit of time, and the entire study is designed to support these estimates (see pages 103 to 160).

Project Cash Flows

The following tables provide a summary of the cash flows relating to each of the three development plans. All assumptions used in formulating these cash flows are provided on the table or on attachments.

The table headings may require some explanation, provided below:

Explanation of Headings for Cash Flow Projection Work Sheet

1. End of Period. The time periods used in the cash flow projection. The office subdivision reflects three-month time periods; the office/condominium cash flow projection reflects six-month time periods; and the rental office use reflects one-year time periods. End of Period 0 is simultaneous with beginning of Period 1, and is used to reflect beginning cash flows.

2. Land Costs. This column reflects the total cost of land and when it was paid. Another column could be added to the work sheet to reflect an additional land loan if applicable.

3. Development Costs. The total cost of development, reflecting when the money is actually paid out. There is an itemized list of total costs for each use.

88

4. Acquisition and Development Loan Payments and/or Draws. This column reflects the draws received from the lender as positive cash flows and the release payments made to the lender as negative cash flows. In some cases they occur simultaneously and only the net figure is shown.

5. Mortgage Balance. This column is used to reflect the mortgage balance outstanding at the end of each of the time periods of the projection.

6. Interest Payments. The amount of interest paid at the end of each time period.

7. Sales. This column is the total proceeds of all sales during the time period indicated.

8. Cost of Sale. The total cost of sale, including broker fees, transfer costs, and, in some cases, promotion and advertising costs, etc.

9. Cash Flow Before Tax. The cash flow, either positive or negative, reflecting all cash flows except the income tax paid or the tax savings. This column is the total of Columns 1, 2, 3, 5, 6 and 7.

10. Taxable Income. This column is calculated for a full taxable year. The taxable income is the profits from sales minus the deduction of interest and/or loan points. The profit from sales is calculated by deducting the cost of sale, land cost, and the development cost from the sales price. This column is used to calculate the amount of income tax paid and is not totalled with the other columns.

11. Income Tax. This is the actual amount of tax paid, calculated by applying the percentage of the marginal tax bracket against Column 10, taxable income.

12. Cash Flow After Tax. This is the critical "bottom line" reflecting all cash flows, both positive and negative, at the time they occur. It is calculated by adding Columns 9 to 11.

Office Park Subdivision Plan

Under this plan, the 3.8 acre site would be developed with streets, water, sewer, etc. and sold off as four lots to builders and/or users. Each lot would be approximately 40,000 square feet. The retail price for fully developed office use land should be between $5.50 and $6 per square foot, based upon comparable sales and available land in the area (see Table 1).

It is difficult to estimate a rate of sale for the subdivision, and the market study did not address itself to this specific problem. For purposes of this illustration, the estimate is based on the rate of absorption for completed office space, but accelerated because there would be four different owners/developers promoting the project. Therefore, the sell-off of the four lots is projected at a rate of one every six months after they are developed.

Table 1 Cash Flow for Subdivision Plan

(Quarters)

(1) End of Period	(2) Land Cost	(3) Development Costs	(4) Acquisition & Development Loan Payments and/or Draws	(5) Mortgage Balance	(6) Interest Payments	(7) Sales	(8) Cost of Sales	(9) Cash Flow Before Tax	(10) Taxable Income	(11) Income Tax	(12) Cash Flow After Tax
0	(550,000)		330,000	330,000				(220,000)			(220,000)
1		(25,000)	15,000	345,000	(8,250)			(18,250)			(18,250)
2		(50,000)	30,000	375,000	(8,625)			(28,625)			(28,625)
3					(9,375)			(9,375)			(9,375)
4			(140,625)	234,375	(9,375)	235,000	(23,500)	61,500	19,625	(9,813)	51,687
5					(5,859)			(5,859)			(5,859)
6			(140,625)	93,750	(5,859)	235,000	(23,500)	65,016			65,016
7					(2,344)			(2,344)			(2,344)
8			(93,750)		(2,344)	235,000	(23,500)	115,406	94,094	(47,047)	68,359
9								-0-			-0-
10						235,000	(23,500)	211,500	55,250	(27,025)	183,875

Assumptions Used for Projection
1. Development cost are $50,000
2. Planning and engineering costs $25,000
3. Acquisition and development loan is 60% of cost @ 10% annual interest payable quarterly
4. 3 months to plan and engineer
5. 3 months to develop
6. Total of four (4) lots
7. 1 sale each six months after development
8. Taxable income and tax paid figured each year
9. Mortgage releases are 150% of original loan per lot
10. 50% tax bracket

SALES PRICE PER LOT	$235,000
LESS: COST OF SALE [10%]	23,500
LAND COST [550,000/4]	137,500
DEVELOPMENT COST [75,000/4]	18,750
PROFIT PER LOT	$ 55,250

The estimated time to plan and engineer the project is three months, as is the estimated development time. Because of the relatively short time period of development and sell-off, the cash flow projections are based on three-month time periods, but the related rate of return is annualized.

Table 2 shows the cash flow's relation to this development plan.

Office Condominium Plan

Under this plan, the site would be developed into a 90,000-square foot office condominium to be sold off as 1,000 square-foot units. The rate of sale would be the approximate absorption rate for rental space for the site established from the market/feasibility study. This sale rate would be 10,000 square feet presold during construction and the sale closed at the end of the construction year. Projected sales for the subsequent year would be 20,000 square feet per year until the entire 90,000 square feet is sold off.

A detailed description of the project follows, and Table 2 provides the complete cash flow worksheet.

Description of the Development

Inventure Plaza at Buckingham is an innovative office development designed to accommodate medical, dental and professional occupants. With a total of 90,000 square feet, there is approximately 35,000 square feet allocated to medical and dental use, which is segregated from the approximately 55,000 square feet of professional and general commercial space. Because of the various tenant needs for both the present and the future, the physical design of the building has been based on a 1,000 square-foot (32 feet by 32 feet) structural module. This allows office suites to be assembled in various sizes, both horizontally and vertically as required by the tenants. Thus, flexibility is produced and an unlimited design tool is created to develop greater effect in massing and layout of the building, forming courtyards, open spaces between structures, immediate roof terraces and unobstructed natural lighting from exterior exposure to all suites.

In keeping with the general area, the masses of the buildings in the development have been designed on a village scale to create a "park-like" office atmosphere. This has been accomplished architecturally by the interplay of one, two, and three-story elevations, richly landscaped common area, courtyards and roof gardens. The enduring design has been accented with an elegant earth-toned masonry exterior and shadow-set windows in anodized frames. The clere-story roofs add to the low profile atmosphere, with cedar shingles to bring out a professional crispness in

Table 2　Cash Flow for Office Condominium Sales Plan

(Semi-annual Periods)

(1) End of Period	(2) Land Cost	(3) Development Costs	(4) Acquisition & Development Loan Payments and/or Draws	(5) Mortgage Balance	(6) Interest Payments	(7) Sales	(8) Cost of Sales	(9) Cash Flow Before Tax =2,3,4,6,7,8	(10) Taxable Income	(11) Income Tax .50×10	(12) Cash Flow After Tax =9, 11
0	(550,000)	(160,710)	543,939	543,939	(77,000)*			(243,771)	-0-	-0-	(243,771)
1		(1,512,483)	1,361,235	1,905,174	(27,197)			(178,445)	-0-	-0-	(178,445)
2		(1,512,483)	743,126	2,648,300	(95,259)	620,000**		(279,616)	(144,756)	72,378	(207,238)
3			(431,700)	2,216,600	(132,415)	500,000	(35,000)	(99,115)	-0-	-0-	(99,115)
4			(431,700)	1,784,900	(110,830)	500,000	(35,000)	(77,530)	(133,845)	66,923	(10,607)
5			(431,700)	1,353,200	(89,245)	500,000	(35,000)	(55,945)	-0-	-0-	(55,945)
6			(431,700)	921,500	(67,660)	500,000	(35,000)	(34,360)	(47,505)	23,753	(10,607)
7			(431,700)	489,800	(46,075)	500,000	(35,000)	(12,775)	-0-	-0-	(12,775)
8			(431,700)	58,100	(24,490)	500,000	(35,000)	8,810	38,835	(19,418)	(10,608)
9			(58,100)	-0-	(2,905)	500,000	(35,000)	403,995	-0-	-0-	403,995
10						500,000	(35,000)	465,000	(106,495)	(53,248)	411,753

Column 10 is profit, as figured below, less interest expense [including points] for the previous year, or 2 six-month periods

SALES PRICE PER SQ. FT.	$50.00
LESS: COST OF SALE	3.50
LAND COST	6.11
TOTAL DEVELOPMENT COSTS	34.92
PROFIT PER SQ. FT.	5.47

MORTGAGE RELEASE CALCULATION:
$3,108,000 MORTGAGE ÷ 90,000 SQ. FT. = $34.53 MORTGAGE PER SQ. FT.
125% × 34.53 = $43.17 RELEASE PER SQ. FT.

* Loan Points

residential character. Lighting throughout the landscaped and parking area, as well as accent lighting on the building, has been planned to maintain visual outline and security.

The structural system chosen to accommodate the many and varied needs of the tenants is that of post-tensioned, poured-in-place concrete. Greater efficiency and availability of materials are combined with spacious floor-to-floor heights and maximum fire protection to make this system the most economical and practical.

Inventure Plaza will be afforded maximum flexibility in the final ownership and occupancy of the project. Condominium declarations and governing documents (including three-dimensional air space surveys) will provide an unlimited opportunity for the occupancy of the building to be made up as the tenant needs may require. Both the medical/dental space and the professional areas will effectively accommodate individual or group practices on either an owner/occupied or lessee/occupied basis, in which case, the latter (lessee/occupied) landlord would be the developer and/or independent investor(s).

To provide consistency in title and control of common areas as well as to create additional tax benefits for the building owners, the improvements will be sold with an undivided leasehold interest in the land.

Table 2 Attachment 1

Assumptions Used in Projection

1. 90,000 square feet built.
2. Sales price is $50.00 per square foot
3. Cost of sale including advertising is 7% of sales price.
4. Construction time is one year.
5. 10,000 square feet sold during construction year and closed at end of construction year.
6. 20,000 square feet sold each year following construction year until the entire 90,000 square feet is sold out.
7. Acquisition loan for 70% of the appraised value with no more than 60% of land cost and 90% of other cost being outstanding at any time.
8. The appraised value of the completed project is $4,400,000.
9. Mortgage release are: maximum mortgage annual of $3,108,000 ÷ 90,000 square feet times 125% equals $43.17 per square feet.
10. Contingency of $120,000 is reflected as a positive cash flow at end of period 2.
11. Loan points of $77,000 shown as interest payment at end of period 0.

Table 2 Attachment 2

	Schedule of Cost for Office/Condominium	
End of Period When Expended	Amount	Explanation
0	$550,000	Land
0	4,000	Market/feasibility Study
0	2,250	MAI/Appraisal Report
0	19,770	Architectural Preliminaries
0	4,372	Legal Fees
0	1,938	Social, Engineering, and Surveys
0	4,500	Marketing Materials
0	3,880	Printing, Photos, etc.
0	120,000*	Contingency Fee
0	77,000**	Loan Points
1, 2***	90,000	Project Administrative Fee
1, 2	2,400	As-built Documents
1, 2	6,500	Utility Tap Fees
1, 2	30,000	Additional Parking Costs
1, 2	124,000	Architectural and Engineering
1, 2	15,000	Advertising and Marketing
1, 2	2,757,066****	Building Contract
	$3,812,676	Total Project Cost

* Contingency reflected a positive cash flow at end of construction year if not used. In this projection it was not used.

** Loan points were treated as interest.

*** 50 percent EOP 1 and 50 percent EOP 2.

**** Contract Price from Table 2, Attachment 1.

Table 2 Attachment 3

Schedule of Values

Description	Cost
Earthwork	$ 28,884.00
Foundation	15,600.00
Paving	41,615.00
Landscaping	66,000.00
Concrete	462,843.00
Resteel and Mesh	57,720.00
Post Tensioning	73,451.00
Masonry	245,307.00
Structural Steel	35,131.00
Carpentry	13,783.00
Roofing	28,016.00
Cauking	7,500.00
Patio Membrane	22,128.00
Hardware	8,870.00
Glass and Glazing	34,328.00
Drywall	88,622.00
Painting	12,346.00
Acoustical	45,907.00
Ceramic	9,181.00
Wall Covering	14,654.00
Carpet	9,756.00
Window Covering	10,444.00
Elevators	33,500.00
Mechanical	611,951.00
Electrical	192,000.00
General Conditions	260,448.00
Bond, Insurance	21,081.00
Tenant Finish	306,000.00
	$2,757,066.00

Rental Office Plan

The rental office use was projected as a long-term investment with a ten-year holding period with the first year of the projection being the construction year. The rental office supply in the Denver area, as indicated by the market study, is somewhat overbuilt. This would indicate a conservative rate of fill and a relatively high vacancy and credit factor. The rate of fill estimated by the study was used for this projection.

The mortgage amount projected was derived from using a debt coverage ratio.[1] The following stabilized net operating income was developed:

---

1 For a detailed explanation of this procedure see Messner, Schreiber and Lyon, *Marketing Investment Real Estate*, p. 70.

Income	
90,000 square feet at $7.50	$675,000
Less 10% vacancy and credit	67,500
Gross Operating Income	$607,500
Less: Fixed Operating Expense	
$90,000 × 1.05	94,500
Variable Operating Expense	
$81,000 × 1.40	113,400
Net Operating Income	$399,600

The debt coverage ratio used was 1.2, the interest rate 9.5 percent, and the term 25 years with monthly payments. This calculates a loan of $3,176,160. This would be a construction loan that converts to a permanent loan at the end of the construction year. The interest for the construction year was based on one-half year for the full amount of the loan.

The operating expenses were broken down into two categories: fixed and variable. The fixed expenses per square foot annually are as follows:

Taxes	.70
Insurance	.10
Maintenance	.15
Miscellaneous	.10
	1.05

These were projected to increase at 3 percent per year after the first year. The fixed expenses are calculated on the entire 90,000 square feet.

The variable expenses per square foot are as follows:

Utilities	.50
Janitorial	.55
Management	.35
	1.40

The variable expenses were projected also to increase at 3 percent per year after the first year. The variable expenses are calculated on the square footage occupied. The following is the rate of fill showing the square footage used for the rent and variable expenses:

Year	Beginning of Year	End of Year	Used in Projection
1*	–0–	10,000	–0–
2	10,000	30,000	20,000
3	30,000	50,000	40,000
4	50,000	60,000	55,000
5	60,000	70,500	65,250
6	70,500	81,000	75,750
7	81,000	81,000	81,000
8	81,000	81,000	81,000
9	81,000	81,000	81,000
10	81,000	81,000	81,000

* Year 1 is construction year.

The rental rate used for the projection was $7.50 per square foot annually. This increased 3 percent the sixth year and each year thereafter. The depreciation used in the projection was a 30-year useful life, 150 percent declining balance method.

The projected sale price at the end of Year 10 was based on a capitalization rate of 10.5 percent using the tenth year net operating income. The cost of sale was projected as 7 percent of the sales price. A detailed schedule of costs and a complete cash flow projection follows.

Schedule of Costs

Amount		Explanation
$ 4,000		Market/Feasibility Study
2,250		MAI Appraisal
19,770		Architectural Preliminaries
4,372		Legal Fees
1,938		Soil, Engineering, and Surveys
4,500		Marketing Materials
3,880		Printing, Photos, etc.
90,000		Projected Administrative Fees
2,400		As-built Documents
6,500		Utility Tap Fees
30,000		Additional Parking Costs
124,000		Architectural and Engineering
15,000		Advertising and Marketing
2,757,066		Construction Contract
3,065,676		Total Capitalized Depreciable Costs
	63,523	Loan Points
	1,500	Taxes During Construction
	500	Insurance During Construction
65,523		Total Expendable Costs
120,000		Contingency Fee
550,000		Land Cost
3,801,199		Total Cost of Project
3,176,160		Loan Amount
625,039		Equity Capital Required

Cash Flow Analysis

Date_____

Name _____ Purpose _____

Mortgage Data

	Encumbrances	Amount	Remaining Term	Payment Period	Interest Rate	Payment Period	Remarks
1	1st Mortgage	3/76/160	25 YR	MONTHLY	9.5%	27050	
2	2nd Mortgage						
3	3rd Mortgage						

		(1) Year: 1 *	(2) Year: 2	(3) Year: 3	(4) Year: 4	(5) Year: 5	(6) Year: 6
4	Initial Investment	625039					
5	1st Mortgage	3/76/160	3/43497	3/07592	3068/25	3024740	2977049
6	2nd Mortgage						
7	3rd Mortgage						
8	Total Encumbrances						
9	Principal Reduction	— o —	32663	35905	39467	43385	47691

Ownership Analysis of Property Income: Taxable Income

10	Total OPERATING Gross Income	— o —	150000	300000	412500	489375	585169
11	~~Vacancy & Credit Loss~~						
12	– Operating Expenses FIXED VARIABLE		94500 28000	97200 57600	99900 81400	102600 99180	105300 118928
13	Net Operating Income	— o —	27500	145200	231200	287595	360941
14	– Non-Operating Expense	65523 **					
15	– Interest	150868	300337	297095	293533	289615	285309
16	– Depreciation	— o —	153284	145620	138339	131422	124851
17	Taxable Income	⟨216391⟩	⟨426/21⟩	⟨297525⟩	⟨200672⟩	⟨133442⟩	⟨49219⟩

Cash Flows

18	Net Operating Income	— o —	27500	145200	231200	287595	360941
19	– Princp. & Int. Pymts.	150868	333000	333000	333000	333000	323000
20	– Funded Reserves	⟨120000⟩					
21	– Capital Additions						
22	Cash Flow before Taxes	⟨30868⟩	⟨305500⟩	⟨187800⟩	⟨101800⟩	⟨45405⟩	27941
23	– Income Tax	⟨108/96⟩	⟨213061⟩	⟨148758⟩	⟨100336⟩	⟨66721⟩	⟨24610⟩
24	Cash Flow after Taxes	77328	⟨92439⟩	⟨39042⟩	⟨1444⟩	21316	52551

Analysis of Sales Proceeds   Year:

	Adjusted Basis	Excess Depreciation		Tax on Gain %		
25	Original Basis	Total Depr.		Excess		
26	+ Capital Improvements	S/L Depr.		Cap. Gain		
27	+ Costs of Sale	Excess Depr.		Cap. Gain		
28	Sub-Total			Total Tax Liab.		
29	– Depreciation	Gain		Sales Proceeds		
30	– Partial Sales	Sales Price		Sales Price		
31	AB at Sale	– AB		– Sales Costs		
32		Gain		– Mortgage		
33		– Excess		Proceeds before Taxes		
34		Cap. Gain		– Total Tax Liab.		
				Proceeds after Taxes		

* YEAR 1 IS CONSTRUCTION YEAR
** LOAN POINTS 63,523 ⌐ TAXES DURING CONSTRUCTION 1,500 – INSURANCE 500

Cash Flow Analysis

Date_____

Name _____ Purpose _____

Mortgage Data

	Encumbrances	Amount	Remaining Term	Payment Period	Interest Rate	Payment Period	Remarks
1	1st Mortgage						
2	2nd Mortgage						
3	3rd Mortgage						
		(1)	(2)	(3)	(4)	(5)	(6)

		Year: 7	Year: 8	Year: 9	Year: 10	Year:	Year:
4	Initial Investment						
5	1st Mortgage	2 924 625	2 866 998	2 803 652	2 734 018		
6	2nd Mortgage						
7	3rd Mortgage						
8	Total Encumbrances						
9	Principal Reduction	52 424	57 627	63 346	69 634		

Ownership Analysis of Property Income: Taxable Income

10	~~Total Gross Income~~	644 760	664 200	684 450	704 700		
11	~~Vacancy & Credit Loss~~	108 900	112 500	116 100	119 700		
12	− Operating Expenses	131 220	135 270	139 320	143 370		
13	Net Operating Income	404 640	416 430	429 030	441 630		
14	− Non-Operating Expense						
15	− Interest	280 576	275 373	269 654	263 366		
16	− Depreciation	118 608	112 678	107 044	101 692		
17	Taxable Income	5 456	28 379	52 332	76 572		

Cash Flows

18	Net Operating Income	404 640	416 430	429 030	441 630		
19	− Princp. & Int. Pymts.	333 000	333 000	333 000	333 000		
20	− Funded Reserves						
21	− Capital Additions						
22	Cash Flow before Taxes	71 640	83 430	96 030	108 630		
23	− Income Tax	2 728	14 190	26 166	38 286		
24	Cash Flow after Taxes	68 912	69 240	69 864	70 344		

Analysis of Sales Proceeds END OF Year: 10

	Adjusted Basis		Excess Depreciation		Tax on Gain %			
25	Original Basis	3 615 676	Total Depr.	1 133 536	Excess 213,833	50	106 917	
26	+ Capital Improvements		S/L Depr.	919 703	Cap. Gain 50,000	25	12 500	
27	+ Costs of Sale 7%	294 420	Excess Depr.	213 833	Cap. Gain 1,165,607	35	407 962	
28	Sub-Total	3 910 096			Total Tax Liab.		527 379	
29	− Depreciation	1 133 536		Gain				
30	− Partial Sales		Sales Price	4 206 000	Sales Price		4 206 000	
31	AB at Sale	2 776 560	− AB	2 776 560	− Sales Costs		294 420	
32			Gain	1 429 440	− Mortgage		2 734 018	
33			− Excess	213 833	Proceeds before Taxes		1 177 562	
34			Cap. Gain	1 215 607	− Total Tax Liab.		527 379	
					Proceeds after Taxes		650 183	

The statements and figures presented
herein, while not guaranteed, are secured
from sources we believe authoritative

Prepared by _____

Table 3 After Tax Cash Flow Comparison of Three Alternative Development Plans

Years	(Quarters) n	Subdivision	Office Condominiums	Office Rental
0	0	⟨220,000⟩	(243,771)	(625,039)
	1	(18,250)		
	2	(28,625)	(178,445)	
	3	(9,375)		
1	4	51,687	(207,238)	77,328
	5	(5,859)		
	6	65,016	(99,115)	
	7	(2,344)		
2	8	68,359	(10,607)	⟨92,439⟩
	9	–0–		
	10	183,875	(55,945)	
	11			
3	12		(10,607)	⟨39,042⟩
	13			
	14		(12,775)	
	15			
4	16		(10,608)	⟨1,464⟩
	17			
	18		403,995	
	19			
5	20		411,753	21,316
	21			
	22			
	23			
6	24			52,551
	25			
	26			
	27			
7	28			68,912
	29			
	30			
	31			
8	32			69,240
	33			
	34			
	35			
9	36			69,864
	37			
	38			
	39			
10	40			720,527*
Adjusted IRR		13.8%	0.49%	4.47%
Term of Investment		2½ Years	5 Years	10 Years

* Annual Income plus Reversion.

Summary and Conclusion

As indicated in Table 3, which shows the cash flows and related "adjusted IRR"[2] for each of the three alternative development plans, the subdivision alternative represents not only the highest rate of return potential, but also the only feasible alternative plan. Neither the office condominium plan nor the office rental plan appears to offer a feasible rate of return to the developer under the assumed market conditions presented in the market study.

The subdivision alternative offers a rate of return potential that may be above the required rate of the developer/investor. Although the rate of return is not adjusted for risk differential for the three alternatives, the three are judged approximately equal in risk in spite of the significant differential in the investment time horizon.

The purpose of this exercise was not to show the final rate of return calculations as being representative of the actual market in the Denver area and its potential at this time, but rather to illustrate the process of analysis which could be undertaken based upon a well documented and defensible market study. In this particular case, the final conclusions reflect a substantial difference among the three alternative plans which may not occur in the "typical" case. There was no attempt to create this large differential; rather, data were extracted directly from the study and used within the framework of cash flow analysis to demonstrate the process rather than the result.

---

2 See Messner, Schreiber and Lyon, *Marketing Investment Real Estate*, p. 47, for an explanation of this rate and its calculation. In this case, a "safe rate" of 5 percent was used to discount the negative cash flows in the project alternatives.

Reprinted with permission of
Daniel Crow, President and Owner,
Developmental Services Group
of Daniel Crow Interests,
Englewood, Colorado

Appendix to Chapter 8

Office Condominium
Market Analysis
Denver, Colorado

TABLE OF CONTENTS

LIST OF TABLES

LIST OF ILLUSTRATIONS

Study Area

Denver Hospital Locations

Location of Principle Medical Office Buildings
in the East Denver Area

Location of Medical Office Buildings and Major Developments
in Aurora

Location of General Commercial Office Buildings
in the East Denver Area

Sample Zip Code Areas and Subsectors

These maps, except for "Study Area," are deleted from this copy of the study due to readability problems. This list is included here as an indication of the scope of material in the original study.

I.   SUMMARY OF CONCLUSIONS AND RECOMMENDATIONS

Findings contained in this report are capsulized in the following paragraphs.

1. We have found strong evidence indicating a sizable opportunity area for commercial office condominium space in the east Denver area. Interest in the commercial condominium concept in Denver has been encouraging. Based on the results of our survey of medical professionals and three non-medical professional groups, we see a demand for at least 80,000 square feet of medical office space and approximately 105,000 square feet of general commercial office space in the east Denver area alone.

2. The subject property is in a position to take most of this potential up to the limits of the site itself. In order to do this, however, it will be necessary that:

a. the office space be of exceptionally high design and construction. Purchasers will demand this to a greater degree than lessees.

b. that aggressive marketing begin as soon as possible, as other well-conceived condominium projects could provide competition. It should be noted, however, that none were discovered in the course of our market investigations.

3. An acceptable range of unit sale prices, based on annual rentals in similar rental office buildings, would be from $50 to $60 per square foot with medical office space at the higher end of that range.

4. The potential seen for this project is based on a nearly complete domination of the market for office condominiums and not upon the general market conditions for office space, nor on the inherent strength of the project location.

5. There is potential for leasing general commercial office space and medical office space at the proposed site in addition to condominium sales. Although it would not normally have the potential of a major office location through leasing alone, the potential to lease from 4,000 to 12,000 square feet of medical office space annually and 15,000 to 25,000 square feet of general commercial office space per year only enhances the outlook for this project.

Office Condominium Market Analysis – Denver, Colorado

II.   GROWTH TRENDS IN THE DENVER SMSA

The Denver Metropolitan Area (Standard Metropolitan Statistical Area) was the ninth fastest growing metropolitan area in the United States from 1960 to 1970, growing 32.09 percent during that decade. Like most metropolitan regions of similar size, all of this growth occurred in the suburbs, while the central city grew only slightly. The table below illustrates the substantial rise in population in each of the counties except Denver County and city.

Table 1   1960 – 1970 COUNTY POPULATION

County	1960 Population	1970 Population	Percent Change Since 1960
Adams	120,030	185,788	54.78
Arapahoe	100,524	162,142	61.30
Boulder	74,244	131,890	77.64
Denver	507,181	514,678	1.48
Jefferson	127,344	233,032	82.99
Total	929,323	1,227,530	32.09

Source: Denver Regional Council of Governments

Although the 28 percent compounded annual growth rate during the 60's compares favorably with that of other cities, all indications are that the rate of growth has increased during the early 70's and is not decelerating. Population estimates for the years following the last census indicate growth of 40,400 in 1970; 55,800 in 1971; and 70,600 during 1972.

The momentum of growth during the 1960's favored the west part of the Metropolitan Area (essentially Jefferson County) with the greatest portion of increment. Thirty-five percent of all Denver growth during the 1960's occurred in Jefferson County. Areas to the south and the north also grew rapidly as first tier suburbs, such as Englewood, became saturated. Although growth rates in Jefferson County have not subsided during the 1970's, more of the remaining growth appears to have been deflected toward the eastern portions of the metropolitan area. Freeway accessibility stimulated growth in the suburbs to the north and south during the 1960's.

As Table 2 indicates, growth rates in Arapahoe County, which lies to the south and east of Denver city and county, have almost equalled those of Jefferson County.

Table 2   ESTIMATED RATES OF ANNUAL POPULATION GROWTH

Period	Adams	Arapahoe	Boulder	Denver	Jefferson	SMSA
1960-1970	4.4%	3.6%	6.4%	0.4%	7.1%	2.8%
1970-1973	5.1	7.5	6.6	0.9	8.6	4.5
1970	4.7	3.1	5.2	0.9	6.4	3.3
1971	5.9	7.3	6.2	1.0	7.6	4.4
1972	5.1	9.5	7.6	0.8	10.5	5.3

Source: U.S. Bureau of the Census, DRCOG

109

Office Condominium Market Study – Denver, Colorado

III.   ANALYSIS OF SUBJECT SITE, LOCATION AND ENVIRONS

The parcel under consideration for development lies in the south part of Aurora, a suburb to the east of Denver. It contains a total of 168,313 square feet or about 3.86 acres. It is at the southwest quadrant of Kingston and East Mississippi Street, a wide four-lane traffic artery with turning lanes. Kingston is not yet a paved road but is due for major upgrading in the near future. Contiguous to the south boundary of the tract is a drainage canal which is 100 feet in width.

The northern part of Aurora was the first to be developed as an extension of activity along Colfax Avenue. Municipal offices, commercial offices and a good deal of retailing still exist along this corridor. Although it served as a sort of downtown Aurora, this area was never well organized for that role, and it presently is central to only a fraction of Aurora's population.

Development gradually spread southward and a new commercial and retailing center evolved in the Del Mar Circel area at Sixth Avenue South and Peoria. Hoffman Heights Center, a community-sized shopping center, serves as the focal point for this area. As the residential area spread further south, it too lost its centrality to the major portion of Aurora's population.

Most recent growth has taken place primarily in the south and east portions of Aurora. Commercial development in this area has centered around the Buckingham Square Shopping Center at the southeast quadrant of Havana and Mississippi--two blocks from the subject. The indoor mall center contains 670,000 square feet and is presently the largest shopping center in the east part of the Denver metro area. Strip commercial development has occurred up and down South Havana and to a lesser degree along Mississippi, although much is being held in speculation. A 90,000 square foot office building sits on the south edge of the shopping center at Arkansas and Mississippi.

East Mississippi has full ingress and egress to I-225 about 1.5 miles east of the subject site. Although the interstate freeway has not been the spine of activity up to now, it is expected to be in the future. The construction of the new Aurora Mall Shopping Center will undoubtedly accelerate this process.

Aurora Mall is to be a 1.2 million square foot regional shopping center at the southeast quadrant of I-225 and Alameda Avenue. With the completion of the Cherry Creek reservoir section of I-225, this center will take a regional draw for the entire east portion of the metropolitan area.

The land use surrounding the subject in the southwest portion of Aurora is relatively new upper middle income residential. To the south of the parcel is mostly single-family detached housing. Further to the south and east newer developments have included condominiums and townhouses. This has become the most rapidly growing residential area in Aurora and the subject's propinquity to it is excellent.

The subject site sits at a strategic position relative to the location of expected development in the triangle between Mississippi, Parker Road and Havana. Relatively good accessibility to the Havana Heights growth area is also a valuable locational asset.

There may be certain advantages in having an interstate freeway location. Exposure and visibility is to a larger volume of traffic from a wider section of the metropolitan area. The subject location is less competitive in that regard, particularly concerning its potential for general commercial office space.

The advantages of its location include its exposure on a major feeder to the freeway, proximity to a major shopping facility and immediate access to a higher income residential area.

STUDY AREA

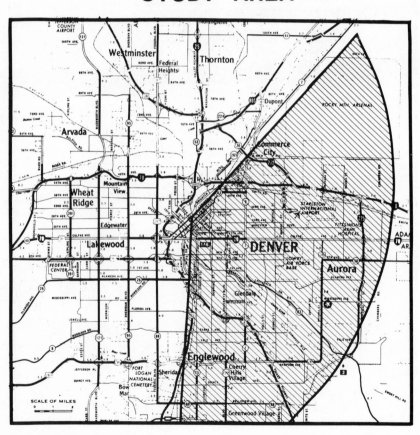

▨ **STUDY AREA**

✪ **SUBJECT**

Map Prepared By: REAL ESTATE RESEARCH CORPORATION

IV.   MARKET ANALYSIS--MEDICAL OFFICE SPACE

Our analysis of the market for medical office space has involved three aspects: 1) an examination of the supply of existing medical office facilities in the study area and, more importantly, in the area of the subject; 2) an investigation into the announced and planned developments in medical services and offices; and 3) a calculation of the demand and projected growth in demand for medical offices.

A.   Supply of Medical Office Space

There is less of a truly measurable market for medical office space than other types of commercial space. One reason for this is the propensity for medical professionals to own their own space--either building new or converting other space for their usage. Another is the potential to convert general-commercial office space into medical office space, thereby making a somewhat flexible supply of space. Nevertheless, to the degree that the typical medical professional desires neither to construct his own building nor lease converted space within a non-medical building, an examination of the inventory of medical professional buildings is worthwhile.

1.   Location of Hospitals in the Denver Metropolitan Area

Most of the hospital facilities in the Denver metropolitan region are located within the central city and much of the inpatient capacity is concentrated in three areas--1) southeast of the central business district around the present Presbyterian Hospital; 2) University of Colorado Medical Center at Ninth Avenue and Colorado; 3) on the west side around Sloan Lake. Very little dispersion of hospitals to the suburbs has taken place. The notable exceptions--Swedish in Englewood, American Medical Center in Lakewood and Lutheran in Wheat Ridge--are all within older first tier suburban areas.

Construction of two hospitals in Aurora represents the first true suburbanization of hospital facilities in the area. The Aurora Community Hospital and the Presbyterian Hospital will account for an additional 328 beds in Denver.

113

Office Condominium Market Analysis - Denver, Colorado

LIST OF HOSPITALS IN DENVER METROPOLITAN REGION

Map Code No.	Name	No. Beds	Location
1	Swedish Hospital	286	Hampden Avenue in Englewood
2	Craig Rehabilitation Center	80	Englewood
3	Porter Memorial Hospital	289	South Denver
4	University of Denver Hospital	335	Southeast Denver
5	Bethesda Hospital and Community Mental Health Center	70	Southeast Denver
6	American Medical Center	85	West Colfax in Lakewood
7	Florence Crittendon Services	12	West Denver
8	St. Anthony Hospital Systems	508	West Denver
9	Beth Israel Hospital	232	West Denver
10	Jewish National Home	156	West Denver
11	Lutheran Hospital and Medical Center	320	Wheat Ridge
12	Denver General	390	South of Central Business District
13	St. Luke's Hospital	465	East of Central Business District
14	Spalding Rehabilitation Center	80	East of Central Business District
15	Children's Hospital	161	East of Central Business District
16	St. Joseph	553	East of Central Business District
17	Presbyterian Medical Center	468	East of Central Business District
18	Mercy Hospital	370	East of Central Business District
19	National Jewish Hospital	225	East Denver
20	Mount Airy Psychiatric Center	82	East Denver
21	University of Colorado Medical Center	450	East Denver
	Colorado General Hospital		East Denver
	Colorado Psychiatric Hospital		East Denver
	Wardenburg Student Health Center		East Denver
22	Veterans Administration Hospital	380	East Denver
23	General Rose Memorial	400	East Denver
24	Rocky Mountain Osteopathic	174	East Denver
25	Valley View Hospital and Medical Center	250	Thornton, North of Denver
26	Spears Chiropractic Hospital		East Denver
27	Booth Memorial Hospital		East Denver
28	Fitzsimmons Army Hospital	850	Aurora
29	Fort Logan Mental Health Center	298	Southwest Suburban Denver
		7,969	
	Proposed		
	Aurora Presbyterian Hospital	128	I-225 and Sixth Avenue
	Aurora Community Hospital	200	I-225 and Mississippi
		8,297	

The illustration above shows the location of existing and
proposed hospital facilities. By 1975 there will be nearly
8,300 rooms in the metropolitan area, discounting Boulder.
Most of the hospital locations shown represent a concentration
or potential concentration of medical office space.

2.   Medical Office Space in the East Denver Study Area

A large portion of the medical office space remains in the
hospital concentration east of the CBD. Generally speaking,
the higher the degree of specialization, the greater the
centrality and proximity to major hospital facilities. The
large concentration of medical offices in the Presbyterian
Hospital area east of the central business district is demon-
strative of this phenomenon, since many of the buildings are
occupied by various types of specialists. On the other hand,
isolated buildings along Yale or Downing, for instance, are
typically groups of less specialized practitioners.

Examination of the inventory yielded several generaliza-
tions about outlying medical office space.

    a.   The buildings are typically under the ownership
        of a corporation comprised of doctors, who
        occupy at least part of the building.

    b.   The buildings are seldom larger than 50,000
        square feet and are usually of low-rise or
        mid-rise construction.

    c.   The buildings rarely have space available.

    d.   Rentals range from $7.00 per square foot to
        $8.50, depending on the degree of remodeling
        necessary and the age and quality of the structure.

That medical office space is in tight supply in most parts of
the study area is evidenced by several indicators: 1) the
number of annexes to larger medical office buildings--often
taking place in converted houses near the medical office
building; 2) the frequent utilization of old and marginal
buildings for medical offices; 3) the frequency of conversion
from other types of structures; 4) the spillover of medical
office usage into general-commercial office buildings, which

Office Condominium Market Analysis – Denver, Colorado

Table 3   MEDICAL OFFICE BUILDING SURVEY

No.	Name	Address	Estimated Size (Sq. Ft.)	Occupancy (Percent)	Description and Comments
1	Belcaro Medical Bldg.	915 So. Colorado	10,000	100	Two-story brick bldg., 10-15 yrs. old
2	Belcaro Medical-Dental Ctr.	925 So. Colorado	5,000	100	Includes pharmacy; similar to above
3	Dental Arts Bldg.	965 So. Colorado	20,000	100	Ownership is by a group of dentists; common area shared
4	Yale Med. Arts Bldg.	5150 Yale Circle	40,000	100	Newer 4-story bldg; fully occupied & spilling into annex; pharmacy
5	University Park Med. Clinic	1919 So. University	15,000	100	Ownership by doctor's corp.; pharmacy
6	1660 University Med. Bldg.	1660 So. University	15,000	100	Garden type entrances at 2 levels; corporate ownership
7	Cherry Hills Medical Bldg.	3535 Cherry Crk. N. Dr.	50,000	99	Corp. ownership by doctors; $7.00/sq.ft. leasing below mkt.; pharmacy & optical co.
8	Medical Office Bldg.	3865 Cherry Crk. N. Dr.	25,000	100	Corp. ownership by doctors; 3-story bldg.; pharmacy & optical co.
9	Left Bank Professional Bldg.	5055 E. Kentucky	4,000	100	Corp. ownership by doctors; good design & landscaping; hexagonal central waiting area.
10	Medical-Professional Bldg.	4900 Cherry Crk. S. Dr.	20,000	100	Corp. ownership by doctors; well designed central enclosed courtyard
11	Professional Bldg.	5800 E. Evans	6,000	100	Two-story bldg; includes dental lab; occupants are general practitioners
12	Southmoor Professional Bldg.	6850 E. Hampden	10,000	100	Newly built; on stilts; x-ray lab for dentists
13	Bevans Bldg.	6740 E. Hampden	15,000	75	Some general commercial space; lease for $6.50/sq.ft.; owned by dr.
14	Park Hampden Med.-Dental Ctr.	Hampden	7,500	100	Tenant mix includes dentists; clinical psychologists; orthodontists; pediatricians
15	Southmoor Park Med.-Dental Ctr.	Hampden	8,000	100	Mix of family doctors and specialists
16	Cherry Hills Medical Arts Bldg.	3535 So. Lafayette	35,000	-	Bldg. over 10 yrs. old; includes pharmacy
17	Denver Skin Clinic	2200 E. 18th	2,500	100	Owner-occupied
18	Eye Association Bldg.	2121 E. 18th	6,000	100	Owner-occupied
19	Medical Bldg.	1855 Gaylord	35,000	-	Originally owned by doctors; now sold and leased back; lease expires April, 1974
20	Medical Bldg.	1801 High	40,000	-	Four-story bldg; pharmacy, optical
21	Medical Professional Bldg.	3705 E. Colfax	50,000	90	Four-story, built in 1950; pharmacy; leasing
22	Medical Bldg.	800 Clermont	20,000	100	Newer 3-story; near CU Med. Center
23	Glendale Prof. Bldg.	4521 E. Virginia Ave.	10,000	50	Owner-occupied bldg. const. by dentists; $6.25-$6.50 sq.ft. for gen'l. commercial; $7.50-$8.00 sq.ft. med.

Source: Real Estate Research Corporation

usually charge above $8.00 per square foot for such space. The following table describes over 300,000 square feet of medical office space. The list does not represent the entire inventory of medical office space, nor does it correspond to all space inspected; however, it is a representative sample which substantiates the points made above.

3. Aurora

Aurora presently has only a few scattered medical office buildings and clinics--none of which are sizable. They are generally owned by the doctors themselves or by an association of doctors, dentists or other practitioners. Most of the practitioners are presently concentrated in three areas:

a. Colfax-Elmira Area

Medical office buildings take a predictable location in this older part of town which has a well-established residential neighborhood. Municipal buildings, schools, commercial activity and other professional offices are in this area. It qualifies as Aurora's original "downtown." Medical office buildings that are included here are:

1. Aurora Medical Arts Building - 1646-66 Elmira

This is actually the largest medical-dental office building in Aurora. It is well located within a residential area with proximity to a school and retail strip. There are presently 21 doctors here and ownership is by a group of practitioners. Some space is available in this 15,000 to 20,000 square foot building.

2. 1590 Florence

This is an older one-story structure which houses three doctors.

3. 1504 Galena

This is a two-story office building containing one medical office among its primarily general-commercial tenancy. Its location is just off East Colfax. No space is available.

Office Condominium Market Analysis - Denver, Colorado

4. Johnson Building - 12128 East Fourteenth

This small one-story building of roughly 1,000 square feet has one doctor's office. It is located one block from East Colfax.

5. 1532 Galena

This relatively new two-story office building is devoted primarily to general-commercial tenants but includes one dentist's office. It is fully occupied.

6. Aurora Medical Clinic - 1480 Kingston

The Aurora Medical Clinic is one block off Colfax further east of Elmira concentration. This is an older one-story building containing 1,500 to 2,000 square feet and one practice.

Other office buildings in that area include:

1. 1544 Elmira Professional Building

This is a two-story building containing about 6,000 square feet. The building is approximately 15 years old. Present tenants include attorneys and realtors.

2. 1550 Elmira

A one-story building of about 6,000 square feet; an attorney's office is on one half, the other half is vacant.

b. Delmar Circle Area

Several medical-dental clinics have clustered around the community-sized retail center at Delmar Circle. These include:

1. Optometric Building - 126 Delmar Circle

It is a small one-story building housing two optometrists. It contains less than 2,000 square feet.

2. <u>Delmar Clinic</u> - 132 Delmar Circle

    About six doctors have their office in this
    one-story building containing less than 5,000
    square feet. Sitting adjacent to the optometric
    building, both have a location on the perimeter
    of the community shopping center, convenient
    to the surrounding residential area.

3. <u>Hoffman Heights Medical Clinic</u> - 821 Quari Court

    This is a one-story building with less than 3,000
    square feet. Ownership is by the doctors within
    the clinic.

c. Chambers Road Concentration

    The Chambers Road concentration is in a fast growing
    residential area east of the I-225 loop between Colfax
    and Sixth Avenue.

1. <u>Altura Professional Building</u> - 1350 Chambers Road

    This is the newest addition of office facilities in
    Aurora. The building contains only two doctor's
    offices, the other tenants being of various non-
    medical professions. A pharmacy is within the
    building. Entrances to each office are separate.
    Net rentable area is about 10,500 square feet.
    It is fully occupied and apparently had no problem
    in immediate absorption.

2. <u>Chambers Med-Dental Clinic</u> - 1390 Chambers Road

    This is actually two buildings - one for dentists -
    which lie adjacent to the Altura Professional
    Building. The buildings date from the mid-1960's
    and are one-story containing about 7,500 square
    feet in all.

There are other buildings in Aurora not included in these three
concentrations. These are all located on traffic arteries which
have some commercial strip development, but their location is
due primarily to their centrality to a residential base. These
small clinics are:

Office Condominium Market Analysis – Denver, Colorado

Table **4**   AURORA MEDICAL OFFICE BUILDINGS

	Building Name	Location	Estimated Size (In Sq. Ft.)	Number of Professionals	Remarks
1	Aurora Medical Arts Building 1646-66 Elmira	Off Colfax near municipal buildings	20,000	21	Ownership is by a corporation composed of doctors
2	1590 Florence	Colfax-Elmira Area	1,500	3	Older one-story building
3	Johnson Building 12128 East Fourteenth	Dayton and Fourteenth	1,500	1	Small building housing one doctor
4	1532 Galena	Colfax-Elmira Area	8,000	1	Two-story raised office building with parking underneath. One dentist's office; fully occupied
5	Aurora Medical Clinic 1480 Kingston	One block off Colfax	1,500	1	Old one-story building
6	1504 Galena	One block off Colfax	7,500	1	Two-story building with only one doctor's office now there
7	Optometric Building 126 Delmar Circle	Delmar Circle	2,000	2	One-story building on edge of shopping center
8	Delmar Clinic 132 Delmar Circle	Delmar Circle	4,000	6	One-story building on edge of shopping center
9	Hoffman Heights Medical Clinic 821 Quari Court	Delmar Circle	3,000	5	Ownership by group of doctors
10	Altura Professional Building	Chambers Road	10,500	13	Mix of general-commercial with medical; lease; newest modern building in Aurora
11	Chambers Medical-Dental Clinic	Chambers Road	7,500	9	Mostly owner-occupied
12	1390 Peoria	Between Colfax and Sixth	1,500	3	Small one-story; two MD's; one doctor
13	897 South Havana	On Havana between Mississippi and Alameda	2,500	1	Converted house
14	11631 Montview Boulevard	Off Moline, four blocks north of Colfax	2,000	3	One-story raw building; occupied by three dentists
			73,000	70	

Source: Real Estate Research Corporation

897 South Havana

This is a converted house holding one practitioner.

1390 Peoria

Three doctors have offices in this small one-story building. Each have outside entrances.

11631 Montview

This is another small one-story row building adjacent to a retail strip.

In addition, there are some doctors within the Camelot Office Building and some offices are opening in Buckingham Square Shopping Center.

The space described above amounts to a total of over 70,000 square feet of medical office space. Anticipated additions to the supply represent more than a 100 percent increase in that inventory.

B. Estimate of Demand for Medical Office Space

We have attempted to estimate the total demand for medical office space in the community of Aurora. From this estimate we have arrived at projected absorption figures for the subject property under the assumption that it is to be leased at a rate competitive with other buildings. These figures are not only to be contrasted to our projections for the project as a condominium, but may also represent additional potential for the subject.

Our demand estimations for medical office space in the community of Aurora will be based on 1) projected growth in the number of medical doctors in the metropolitan area and 2) projected movement or relocation of medical professionals to Aurora. We have dealt with Aurora as an entity since it is small enough to consider most variables (e.g. competition, relevant developments) yet large enough to serve as a data base and source.

1. Growth in the Number of Physicians

The Denver metropolitan area has been above the national average in physicians per capita population for some time.

Table 5   NUMBER OF PHYSICIANS IN THE DENVER SMSA 1963–1970

Year	Total	Total Patient Care	Patient Care Office Based				Hospital Based	Other Professional Activity	Inactive
			General Practice	Med. Spec.	Surg. Spec.	Other Spec.			
1970	2,898	2,374	289	419	514	357	768	364	160
1969	2,765	22,361	281	384	520	335	609	356	–
1968	2,657	2,143	290	382	499	295	677	348	166
1967	2,505	2,162	328	368	498	283	685	228	115
1966	2,388	2,053	354	348	476	269	606	219	116
1965	2,354	2,025	345	344	471	264	601	205	124
1964	2,260	1,957	347	343	455	250	562	181	122
1963	2,091	1,808	349	322	431	238	468	155	128

Source: American Medical Association, Distribution of Physicians

In 1963, Denver had 1,808 practicing* physicians, or about 1 physician per 563 people. By 1970, the total number of doctors had risen to 2,374--an increase of 566 or about 80 additional doctors per year and a ratio of 513 people for every doctor.

Population increases during this time averaged about 30,000 annually, so that a physician was added for every increase of 375 people. This ratio was markedly above existing physician/population ratios at that time and indicates a very favorable physician influx for Denver.

Assuming a population increase of 157,500 since 1970 and a growth in the number of physicians comparable to the rate of increase during the 1960's (1 physician/375 people) an estimate of the total number of physicians for 1973 is 2,800. The current ratio of physicians to population in the Denver metro area is, therefore, 1/496. This ratio is not only above the national average, but more favorable than most SMSA's of comparable size.

2. Distribution of Physicians in the SMSA

In order to project demand in a specific locale, it is helpful to examine trends in the existing distribution of physicians. Table 6 shows that nearly 80 percent of the physicians in the Denver SMSA in 1963 were within the city of Denver itself, while Denver's population was only 50 percent of metropolitan area. The reasons for discrepancy are clear enough:

a. Centrality needed for specialization of medical professionals

b. Centrality needed for larger hospital facilities

*patient care only; teaching, administration not included

123

Table 6   DISTRIBUTION OF PHYSICIANS IN THE DENVER SMSA

County	1970 Distribution	% Distribution	1969	1968	1967	1966	1965	1964	1963	% Distribution
Adams	67	2.8	63	65	62	58	62	42	19	1.1
Arapahoe	165	7.0	131	121	112	106	102	117	127	7.0
Boulder	179	7.3	152	136	131	124	118	110	104	5.8
Denver	1,812	76.3	752	1,687	1,722	1,630	1,606	1,558	1,444	79.9
Jefferson	156	6.6	138	134	135	135	137	130	114	6.3
Total	2,374	100.0	2,236	2,143	2,162	2,053	2,025	1,957	1,808	100.0

Source: American Medical Association; Real Estate Research Corporation

Another factor is the inertia of existing locations of medical offices. Aside from the capital invested in buildings, it is simply a difficult process to uproot a practice. As population increases at the edge of the metropolitan area, a greater concentration results, at least initially, in the central areas. Table 7 below portrays numerically this phenomenon in Denver. Although only 2.5 percent of the population increase occurred in Denver, the city proper took 368 of the 566 physicians added during that time--65 percent. The central city increased its physician/population ratio from 1/352 to 1/283 during that period of suburbanization.

Table 7   POPULATION TO DOCTOR RATIO IN DENVER SMSA
                          BY COUNTY: 1963-1970

	1963	1970
Adams	7,355	2,731
Arapahoe	937	975
Boulder	880	747
Denver	352	283
Jefferson	1,377	1,480
SMSA Average	563	513

Source: American Medical Association

As suburban areas continue to add persons on their fringes, as they continue to develop their own patterns of services, solidifying at least partially their own economies, we would expect the ratios to even out over the metropolitan area. It is the rate and degree to which this equalization process will take place that will determine the demand for medical offices in Aurora.

Office Condominium Market Analysis – Denver, Colorado

C. Projection of Demand for Medical Office Space in Aurora

There are currently 49 physicians with offices in Aurora. (MD's only; osteopaths have not been included for the purpose of remaining consistent with data for the entire metro area. Adjustment for office space needs for osteopaths and dentists will be made after projections of MD space demands.) Using estimates of the current population, a ratio of 1 doctor for every 2,500 people is derived. This is much less than the city of Denver, Arapahoe County, as well as the average for the metropolitan area as a whole (1/496).

With the construction of two hospitals, the development of the largest regional shopping center in the metro area, the continued rapid growth rate of Aurora, and, in general, the maturation of its economy, it is not at all unlikely to expect a dispersal of doctors to Aurora and an equalization of the doctor to population ratio to be more consistent with the total metropolitan area averages.

Although the concentration of physicians will probably never be as great as in the central city, Aurora should be somewhat above the median (not mean) concentration for the SMSA. Assuming continuation of the trends witnessed in the last decade, Aurora should see a doctor/population ratio of 1/750 to 1/1,000.

Current population projections for Aurora in 1978 are at 242,000 people. Based on conversations with planners and recent reductions in building activity in 1973, we feel a more reliable estimate is 230,000.

If an equalized distribution of medical doctors does occur by 1978, there will be an additional 180 to 255 doctors practicing in Aurora. Aurora will be accepting an average of 35 to 50 doctors' practices per year in the next five years.

In translating this to a demand for additional office space, it has been necessary to make two adjustments. First, only about 75 percent of the additional medical doctors will be office based. Secondly, dentists have not been included thus far in our analysis of medical office space demand. Their inclusion will be based on data retained from the American Dental Association* for Denver SMSA counties, showing that 850 dentists practice in Denver at

*Distribution of Dentists by Region, State, District and County, American Dental Association

a dentist/population ratio of 1/1,444. Arapahoe County, Adams and Douglas had ratios of about 1/2,400. A reasonably conservative estimate for Aurora by 1978 is 1 dentist to 2,000 people. We have found a total of 29 dental practices in Aurora; thus, an addition of about 85 dentists will be likely by 1978--or about 17 per year.

We have used a range in office space utilization per doctor of 600 square feet to 1,000 square feet and a 500 to 750 square foot average office size for dentists. This is based on responses made in the survey sent to study area medical professionals. Projected demand for medical-dental office space develops as follows:

Office Condominium Market Analysis - Denver, Colorado

Physicians

Given

1)   A 1978 population of 230,000
2)   50 existing practices in 1973
3)   A ratio of 1 doctor/750 people to 1/1,000 by 1978
4)   75 percent of practicing physicians office based

Then	Minimum	Maximum
Additional MD's	180	255
x .75 Office Based	135	190
Office Space per Physician	x 600 square feet	x 1,000 square feet
Total 5 Year Space Demand	81,000 square feet	190,000 square feet
Annual Demand	16,200 square feet	38,000 square feet

Dentists

Given

1)   29 existing practices
2)   A dentist/population ratio of 1/2,500 by 1978

Then	Minimum	Maximum
Additional Dentists by 1978	63	85
Office Space per Dentist	x 500 square feet	750 square feet
Total 5 Year Space Demand	31,500 square feet	63,750 square feet
Annual Demand	6,300 square feet	12,750 square feet

Grand Total Medical-Dental Office Space Demand   132,750 - 253,750 square feet

Annual Demand   26,550 - 50,750 square feet

D.   Potential Capture of Subject Site

With projections of demand established for the community of Aurora, it is necessary to examine prospective developments which will have a direct impact on the potential for medical office space at the proposed site assuming it were a typical lease project.

Most significant to the future of medical activity in Aurora is the establishment of two new acute care facilities. The Presbyterian Hospital will be at the northwest quadrant of I-225 and Sixth Avenue. The hospital will have a 128 bed capacity. It is presently under construction and should be ready by late 1974.

The Extendicare Hospital or Aurora Community Hospital is privately developed by a hospital developer from Louisville, Kentucky. It will have a bed capacity of 200. It is also under construction and scheduled for completion in 1974.

The movement and growth of hospital facilities in the east suburban area is in itself a positive force affecting the demand for medical office space in the area. However, these additions also change the surface on which the potential for medical office space is most suitable.

Expectedly, medical office buildings in the immediate proximity to the hospital are by far the most successful and desirable. In the case of Aurora, both hospitals are incorporating medical office facilities.

The Presbyterian Hospital is leasing a three-story medical office building, containing a total of 40,000 square feet plus basement. Leasing has apparently begun and rentals will be at $7.50 per square foot. Floor plans are laid out in 800 foot modules. An estimated 40 to 50 doctors will have their offices here upon full absorption.

The Extendicare Hospital will also include an undetermined amount of medical office space. Most reliable estimates, based on foundation size and information in the community are about 50,000 square feet. Rental rates have not yet been projected. An absorption of 55 to 65 medical professionals should be realized when the project is completely filled.

Office Condominium Market Analysis – Denver, Colorado

Assuming that other aspects of the subject development were similar to the developments proposed for the hospitals (i.e. that the subject were a lease project, with rents, quality of offerings, design, etc., similar to the other medical offices), the potential draw of the project would be relatively low among MD's for at least the next two years and possibly for the next four years.

By minimal, we mean approximately 5 percent of the total Aurora demand generated among MD's, equivalent to an annual absorption of 1,000 to 2,000 square feet or two to five practices.

We would expect that the draw of the hospital locations is less pronounced for dentists. Assuming competitive rentals and design, we project an annual absorption of 20 percent to as much as 50 percent of the total demand. Osteopaths, optometrists may account for additional absorption, which may reach as high as 12,000 square feet per year.

A breakdown of demand from the various medical groups appears as follows:

Group	Annual Absorption (Leasing)
Physicians, MD's	1,000 – 2,000 square feet
Dentists	1,000 – 6,000 square feet
Other	2,000 – 4,000 square feet
	4,000 – 12,000 square feet

As a lease project, therefore, the subject could expect to absorb from 4,000 to 12,000 square feet annually. As a condominium office project, this lease potential provides for built-in flexibility in the marketing process.

V.   MARKET ANALYSIS - GENERAL COMMERCIAL OFFICE MARKET

In the course of our study, Real Estate Research Corporation undertook an extensive examination of the market conditions for general-commercial office space in the East Denver study area. The purpose of such research was to determine the potential for office space at the subject location with normal leasing as the marketing arrangement. The survey included over two million square feet of suburban and central city (excluding Central Business District) office space. Efforts were concentrated on buildings erected since 1970, although occupancy, rentals and size of other significant buildings were also noted.

A.   Overall Market Conditions

Since 1970, average growth in the office supply in the study area has been around 600,000 square feet annually. Our research found that about 2.5 million square feet of office space has been built in the study area since 1970. Rentals ranged from $5.00 per square foot net rentable area in smaller inexpensive buildings to $7.50 in some of the newest buildings.

Our occupancy survey found an average occupancy rate of 88 percent in 2.037 million square feet of existing space; i.e., not including space under construction or proposed. Considering the amount of semi-competitive average quality space included, this is a relatively high occupancy. Slightly less than 250,000 square feet is presently available. Although this is, in quantitative terms, enough space to handle additional demand for more than six months in the future, much of the vacancy is in less competitive locations and buildings. In areas of greatest demand (e.g., the Cherry Creek area, South Colorado Boulevard and Hampden Avenue) little space is presently available for occupancy.

B.   Character of Supply

As in most metropolitan areas, Denver did not develop major concentrations of outlying suburban office space until well into the 1960's. In fact, the major portion of suburban office growth appears to have occurred in the last four years.

Three primary geographic pressures have been exerted on the location of suburban office space:

1.   Proximity to freeways and high traffic arteries
2.   Proximity to major retail-commercial centers
3.   Proximity to higher income residential areas

131

Office Condominium Market Analysis – Denver, Colorado

A brief examination of the distribution of office buildings in the study area will provide a geographic context for the subject's development and render a clearer understanding of the nature of competition as well as the locational needs of the tenants.

The Cherry Creek Area is the largest and oldest outlying concentration* of office space in the study area. Its evolution is a result of the coexistence of several factors: high income residential sector; an outlying regional shopping center; reasonable proximity to high traffic arteries of University and Colorado Boulevards and Cherry Creek Drive which leads into the Central Business District.

The high concentration of office space that has evolved here has led to many of the same problems confronting office tenants in the CBD--namely, parking, congestion and higher rentals per square foot. Although the concentration maintains its prestige (as evidenced by the continued demand for office space here), it has lost a good deal of its functionality in accessibility to the entire metro area. As the surrounding residential areas lose their status to more distant suburbs, a decline in the importance of this area can be expected for the future.

The character of office space users is geared to professional services rather than corporate management. As noted in the previous section, there is a large concentration of medical professionals. Other professions are in significant numbers--presumably a result of the surrounding high income residents.

Spinoff from the largest of the region's shopping centers, Cinderella City in Englewood, has created another major concentration of office space. This concentration is located strategically with respect to growth to the south, southeast and southwest, but it too suffers from congestion and parking problems and a lack of immediate accessibility to an interstate freeway. Little additional intensification of the existing concentration is expected. The two largest banks in the area, First National Bank of Englewood and Continental National Bank, offer larger amounts of general-commercial office space. Unusual is the office space included within Cinderella City Shopping Center. The Texaco Corporation has their regional office there. A special area is devoted entirely to real estate and is geared to the walk-in traffic from the retail area.

*The term "outlying" here is used as the area is technically not suburban but part of the city of Denver proper. Our previous use of the term "suburban" refers to areas of new growth--not to municipal entities.

The implementation of an interstate freeway system has created new pressures on certain areas which now have greater accessibility to the entire metropolitan region. Most significant among these is at the intersection of I-25 and South Colorado. There is a concentration of about 900,000 square feet existing or under construction. High-rise construction, larger and more elaborate buildings predominate in this area. South Colorado presently takes a large amount of the north-south traffic on this side of the metropolitan area, resulting in a growing problem of congestion. Office users range from large corporations (Gulf Oil) to local professionals.

Another growing concentration is evolving along East Evans Avenue near its junction with I-25. In contrast to the South Colorado concentration most of the buildings here are smaller and lower in quality. Tenants are smaller and have a more local business flavor. A large amount of frontage as yet undeveloped suggests an intensi-fication of the office space in this concentration. Further south on I-25 another feeder, Hampden Avenue, is developing as perhaps the fastest growing concentration of office space in the study area-- resulting primarily from the growth in the surrounding residential areas and in southeast Aurora, combined with interstate proximity and accessibility. The character of most of the office space along this corridor is of high quality, although generally in smaller office buildings. Office tenants reflect a more local orientation, as witnessed by the number of medical professional buildings.

At I-25 and Belleview the first and largest office parks in the Denver metropolitan area have been developed, Denver Technological Center and Greenwood Plaza. Denver Technological Center has been developed along rigid quality controls on landscaping and architecture. Most of the buildings are owner-occupied, although some are multiple-tenant general-commercial offices, such as in the Executive Park on the north side of Belleview. Extensive landscaping and modern architecture are also a trait of the Greenwood Plaza Office Park on the west side of Valley Highway across from Denver Technological Center. Seven large office buildings are presently constructed, containing from 350,000 to 400,000 square feet of office space with more under construction.

Despite the peripheral location, this executive office space is some of the most expensive in the area beginning at $7.00 per square foot. Small executive suites for one or two people are offered, complete with answering and secretarial service at a much higher price, but this has been relatively unsuccessful. The office park setting, amenities and location appears to have most appeal to the larger corporations. Regional headquarters of Kodak, IBM and Xerox are all in Denver Technological Center. Phillips Petroleum Company occupies most of an entire building in their executive park. Johns-Manville moved its national headquarters from New York to occupy three buildings of Greenwood Plaza.

With the completion of I-225 to I-25, accessibility to this area will increase, thereby enhancing the position of these two office parks. Ongoing and planned construction is indicative of the expectation for continued demand in this area.

Yet further south on I-25, at the intersection with Arapahoe Road, several office buildings have been erected. Stearns-Rogers occupies a large building with options on a good deal more space. Other buildings are smaller--of the sub 15,000 square foot variety-- and house mostly real estate and insurance professionals. Rent levels are somewhat lower than other parts of the metro area and demand from small tenants appears high.

The Rocky Mountain Arsenal has provided an effective barrier to development in the northeast. In an exceptional position, however, is the Montbello development which includes 67 acres earmarked for an office campus among 525 acres of industrial land, residential development, a motel and a shopping center. Thus far, two buildings have been erected containing in all less than 75,000 square feet with one under construction and several more planned.

Montbello office space is reasonably priced and reasonably attractive. With interstate freeway proximity and accessibility to the airport, several large space users (International Harvester, Montgomery Wards) have been attracted to this location.

C. Supply of Office Space in Aurora

Aurora has had very little office space development in the last four years. The Camelot Building, near the subject in the Buckingham Square area, has been the only sizable building in Aurora. It has only 1,000 of its 60,000 square feet available at this time, although it reportedly encountered slow absorption after its opening in 1971. Rentals are at $6.50, but remaining space is more costly. The regional headquarters of Oldsmobile recently moved into the Camelot Building from their downtown location. Much of the tenancy has a real estate orientation.

The Altura Professional Building on Chamber's Road is the only other newer general-commercial building in the area. As its name implies, its tenancy is geared to local professionals who provide service to the surrounding, growing residential base.

D.   Ongoing and Anticipated Developments

A primary thrust of our research into the general commercial office market has been to compile data on future developments and plans for developments. In this way, we are able to predict market conditions under which the proposed subject development will enter and operate in the market.

Although suburban office market conditions are presently reasonable, proposed developments will change the situation substantially within the next 16 months. The following table presents those office developments which we have been able to discover. It is probable that more exist, but this is believed to be a nearly complete survey of proposed developments and probably represents a conservative estimate of additions to the supply through the first quarter of 1975.

Because of prior mortgage commitments, construction of office space is adding to the supply at a faster rate than has been the case in the last four years. Firm commitments exist for an addition of 1,600,000 square feet of office space by the first quarter of 1975 (16 months).

This represents an average monthly increase in the supply of office space of 100,000 square feet in the study area alone. This does not include other parts of the metropolitan area, especially the central business district, which has three major buildings under construction at this time. In terms of suburban office space, however, this does represent a major portion of the entire metropolitan area.

Assuming the demand for additional new suburban office space to remain similar to its behavior in the last four years (i.e., that turnover from old space, movement from the CBD and influx of office users from outside the area proceed at the same rates) office market conditions should evolve in the manner described below:

Table 8   <u>FUTURE DEVELOPMENTS IN THE OFFICE MARKET</u>

No.	Name	Location	Projected Date of Completion	Size Sq.Ft. NRA	Price/ Sq.Ft. NRA	Remarks
1	Camelot Office Bldg. II	So. Havana & Arkansas	1-75	98,000	$7.50	Prestige office space; 2nd of a planned six bldg. complex
2	Empire Office Bldg. II	Arkansas & So. Colorado Blvd.	10-74	140,000	$6.75	Second high-rise bldg. at complex
3	Greenwood Plaza - Plaza Marin I	Belleview & I-25	2-74	150,000	$7.00	First of 3 add'l. bldgs. in Greenwood Plaza, reportedly for Johns Manville use
4	Montbello Campus IV	No. I-70 in Montbello Dev.	3-74	48,000	$6.25	Third office bldg. in Montbello office campus
5	240 St. Paul	Cherry Creek Area	1-74	18,500	$6.50	Three-story bldg. with most space committed
6	Hampden Exec. Office Plaza	Hampden & Tamarac	4-74	110,000	$7.00	Includes health spa and rec. facilities
7	Executive Terrace Club	Hampden	10-74	30,000	$7.50	Luxury office space with central atrium area
8	Pennants at the Park	Hampden	-	-	-	Hal Krause Development
9	Fountainhead Project	3000 So. Havana	12-74	100,000	-	A build to suit project which will include commercial, residential and 500,000 sq.ft. of office space
10	Stapleton Plaza - Howard Johnson Complex	Quebec across from airport	1975	176,000	-	Nine-story office bldg. in complex containing 11-story motor lodge, health club, shops, theatres
11	Titan Const. Bldg.	36th - Quebec	1975	±100,000	-	Have not yet broken ground
12	Hera Inv. Bldg.	Cherry Creek - Ellsworth & Steele	-	100,000	-	Not yet under construction; will be luxury space
13	Blue Cross Bldg.	Speer & Broadway	1974	110,000	$7.50	Luxury office space in proximity to CBD
14	Writer's Tower II	South Colorado	9-74	110,000	$7.50	Second high-rise bldg. in complex
15	Arapahoe Bank & Trust	Arapahoe Road	1-74	30,000	-	Bank bldg. under construction
16	Nottingham Bldg.	Evans Avenue	3-74	20,000	$6.50	Two-story bldg. with 2,000 sq.ft. committed
17	Columbia Sq. Office Bldg.	West Littleton	1-75	32,000	-	Planned - no construction yet
18	Cherry Creek Towers	Cherry Crk. Area-E. Virginia Ave.	4-74	30,000	$7.25	High rise bldg. off So. Colorado
19	Twin Towers	Cherry Crk. Area-So. Colorado	1-75	133,000	$7.50	First of 2 towers with retail, entertainment, etc.
20	231 Milwaukee	Cherry Crk. Area	4-74	± 25,000	-	Bldg. under construction
21	Denver Tech. Ctr.	Belleview & I-25	3-74	-	$7.50	Bldg. under construction
22	Valley Plaza Office Park	Hampden & Yosemite	12-73	14,800	$7.00	About 60% owner occupied
23	Plaza 6000	East Evans	4-74	40,000	-	To be sold as condominium; 1st or 3 bldg. complex
				±1,665,300		

Source: Real Estate Research Corporation

Office Condominium Market Analysis – Denver, Colorado

	t_1	t_2
Supply	2.5 mil square feet	4.11 square feet
Demand	2.2 mil square feet	2.92 square feet
Vacancy	.3 mil square feet	1.19 square feet

Where supply refers to the total inventory of office space constructed since 1970, demand to the total occupancy of new office space, $t_1 = 10/73$ and $t_2 = 3/75$.

To summarize, while supply will be increasing at a rate of 100,000 square feet monthly, demand for new office space will remain at 45,000 square feet a month. Vacant space will increase from 240,000 square feet to 1.19 million square feet. Average occupancy rates will drop from 88 percent to nearly 70 percent.

Projected rent levels will increase as a result of increasing construction and operating costs to over $7.00 per square foot for new buildings. A median projected rental is $7.50 for developments surveyed. In light of competition with slightly older buildings leasing at $1.00 per square foot less, absorption of most proposed developments is expected to be extremely sluggish.

E. Application to Subject Site

It is necessary to quantify the expected performance of an office building at the proposed subject location under the market conditions stated above. We have assumed for this purpose an office space similar in most respects to existing and proposed buildings, i.e., that the project is to be leased, the structure similarly equipped and priced to others in the market. By eliminating marketing variables, the subject can be judged on the strength of its location, which serves as a basis for its inherent marketability.

Based on comparison with a number of similarly situated office buildings, we estimate that annual absorption of good quality office space at the subject location would be from 15,000 to 25,000 square feet annually under a leasing arrangement in addition to condominium space offered. A total potential for the site would be approximately 60,000 square feet.

137

Office Condominium Market Analysis - Denver, Colorado

Under market conditions projected for the next one and one-half years, however, the amount of available new first-class office space will equal nearly two full years of demand. The degree to which space availability will affect the absorption of office space at the subject site can only be estimated, but all indications are that it will be substantial. We estimate a diminution of about 30 percent is most reasonable.

We project the absorption of 10,000 to 17,000 square feet annually in addition to space sold as condominium. This is assuming the production of first-class office space at a rental rate comparable with other new buildings in the area.

VI.   SURVEY OF PROFESSIONALS

The market for condominium office space has not yet been established.
Traditional methods of measuring the office market are thus only a
preface to the central question of "How many people are willing to
buy commercial office space?"--a question which can actually only
be answered by posing it to a group of potential purchasers. Our
projections for the degree of success of the project therefore rely
most heavily on the results obtained from our mail survey questionnaires
sent both to medical professionals and non-medical professionals.

A.   Methodology

We limited our survey geographically to zip code areas within the
study area as illustrated on the following map. Such a geographic
delineation implies an assumption that professionals outside the
study area would have no interest in the proposed office space due
to its location. That assumption accepted carte blanche is of course
incorrect; however, the percentage frequency of interest certainly
declines with distance from the primary study area and "falls off"
radically as the sectional orientation changes. That is to say, it
is entirely unlikely that a professional presently with offices in
Wheat Ridge would be interested in owning offices in Aurora,
although it is not impossible. The geographic delimitation was
designed primarily to incorporate efficiency into the sampling
techniques to elicit the highest frequency of response given the
number of surveys to be sent.

Within the study area three subsectors were identified. These
corresponded to existing locations of doctors classified as
1) Inner City – Central Business District, 2) Central City, and
3) Suburban. Each survey was coded according to its subsector
location; in this manner, further identification of the geographic
source of the demand could be made, and marketing efforts could
be made in a direct relationship to the interest encountered in a
specific area.

For example, if an inproportionate amount of interest was elicited
from Central Business District-located professionals, marketing
efforts should give that area high priority.

The survey was conducted in two phases. The first phase encompassed
medical professionals--mostly M.D. physicians, but also O.D.'s,
dentists and optometrists.

139

Office Condominium Market Analysis - Denver, Colorado

A decision was made to implement a Phase II survey which would include non-medical professionals. Phase II included attorneys, insurance agents and Certified Public Accountants. These professions were chosen in consultation with the client under the assumptions that
1) these professions would constitute the bulk of demand and
2) it is desirable to limit or control the professions allowed to purchase within the buildings. It was hypothesized that other acceptable professions would constitute a relatively minor portion of overall demand and that our selections would lend a reasonably conservative inclination to the projections.

B. Phase I Survey - Medical Professionals

1. Sampling of Medical Professionals

About one out of five medical professionals within the study area was surveyed. There are a total of 1,314 medical professionals within the study area. Physicians total 957, dentists 302, and optometrists 49. This represents the "population" from which our sample was taken. Two hundred fifty surveys were sent or a sample size of about 20 percent.

The percentage returns from each area did not radically differ. Suburban returns were somewhat higher at 9.6 percent than central city (6.7 percent) and inner city (5.7 percent). This may have been due to the interest expressed by several Aurora practitioners.

Results of the survey have been presented numerically on the survey form. To summarize briefly, the respondents were usually from an individual practice; they usually leased their office space, which was likely to be between 500 square feet and 1,500 square feet. They more often paid a lower price for their space (below $6.00 per square foot) than a high rental (above $8.00), although half of them paid between $6.00 and $8.00.

The respondents usually had none of the services mentioned. Only three had a pharmacy within their present building, three had laboratories and two had accounting services. Nevertheless, 50 percent of the respondents were happy with their present space; only three rated their space as inadequate. Over half of the respondents plan to move within the next two years.

Ten of eighteen respondents saw some degree of segregation of medical from non-medical professions desirable. Half of these felt segregation by building was the best method. Only two were negative about the inclusion of non-medicals within the entire complex.

Apparently, segregation of the various medical professionals is not needed or wanted by the doctors themselves. Only one comment was made of the incompatibility of osteopaths and MD's.

Unexpectedly, as many respondents favored multi-story structures (high-rise or mid-rise) as garden level offices. Relatively few (3 of 18) favored one- to two-story buildings with entrances off hallways. This is in light of the fact that most of the medical office buildings are currently of this type. This may represent an openness to innovation in the design of medical office structures or a general lack of enthusiasm for the typical one- to two-story medical office building.

The services listed for the respondents' ranking were generally rated either "desirable" or "unnecessary." Accounting services found no solid support, but half of the answers rated it a desirable feature. Pharmacies appear to be most important of the services mentioned and general medical laboratories next. Only five of sixteen respondents felt a medical library was unnecessary, but only one rated it as important.

Generally, the doctors approved of the simple amenities of landscaping and design, while health spas and recreational facilities appeared to be frivolities.

Nearly all of the respondents expressed interest in condominium ownership for their own use. Fifteen of eighteen answered positively to our direct question. This led us to a conclusion that the respondents represented that portion of the sample which would be willing to purchase, or at least willing to consider purchase, of a condominium unit. Furthermore, the percentage of positive respondents to the entire sample is equivalent to the percentage of the "population," or sum total of medical practitioners in the study area who would seriously consider purchase of a condominium office. Fifteen of 250 is

Office Condominium Market Analysis – Denver, Colorado

six percent. Six percent of the study area population, 1,314, is about 79. Thus, we see the potential for about 80,000 square feet of medical office space in condominium offices in the study. Understandably, not all people who express interest are certain purchasers. On the other hand, the complete elimination of all those who did not respond was a conservative assumption. In the long run, those factors will balance out, leaving a relatively accurate estimate of marketability. Existing current plans call for a total of about 35,000 square feet of medical office space. If marketing is begun immediately, if concerns for professional mix and protections for the owner are resolved promptly, we see no reason why the building cannot presell.

Our projections have not considered the probability that many professionals would be willing to purchase more space than they need--strictly as an investment in income property. Exactly half of those surveyed expressed this inclination.

We conclude, therefore, that the chances for completely and successfully marketing the medical office space within your project are excellent. We suggest that a diversification of medical types be attempted whenever possible. Extra effort in including a pharmacy, a medical lab or radiology lab should be made. Accounting services do not appear to be a necessity, although it is probable that accountants will be tenants in the complex. The idea for a medical library should be planted in the minds of the buyers as a project for their owners' association rather than something you should deal with. In marketing, it should be emphasized that those types of innovations are possible for the association. A consciousness of that degree of flexibility could be a strong selling point.

FACTUAL INFORMATION

1. Which of these most closely approximates the arrangement of your present practice?

    1   (11)   Individual practice
    2   (3)   Partnership with one other practitioner
    3   (2)   Parternship with two or more associates
    4   (3)   Corporate practice with _____ associates

2. Approximately how much office space do you presently occupy? (If you have more than one office, list only the one you would most likely move.)

    1   (2)   Less than 500 square feet
    2   (13)   500 – 1500 square feet
    3   (2)   1500 – 5000 square feet
    4   (1)   Over 5000 square feet

3. Do you currently lease the office space which you occupy?

    1   (15)   Yes
    2   (3)   No

4. If you lease your space, approximately how much do you pay per square foot per year? (optional)

    1   (6)   Less than $6.00
    2   (3) $6.00 - $6.99
    3   (5) $7.00 - $7.99
    4   (2) $8.00 and up

5. Does your present office facility include

    1   (3)   Pharmacy
    2   (2)   Laboratories
    3   (2)   Accounting service

        Other   1 optician _____
        (15)   None
6. How well does your present office space suit your needs and the needs of your patients?

    1   (9)   Very satisfactorily
    2   (7)   Adequately
    3   (3)   Inadequately
                    Negative: aesthetically poor; too small
        Comments   Positive: well planned _____

7. Do you plan to expand or move to a new office within the next two years?

    1   (11)   Yes
    2   (8)   No

ATTITUDES

8. Since it may be necessary to include more than one type of profession within the complex, to what degree should these professions be segregated? (rank according to desirability)

    1 (8) No segregation by profession
    2 (3) Segregation of medical and non-medical professions by sectors within buildings
    3 (5) Complete segregation of medical and non-medical by buildings
    4 (2) Inclusion of no non-medical professions within the complex

    Other suggestions? _____

    _____

9. Is segregation of the various medical professions necessary?

    1 (2) Yes
    2 (17) No

    If yes, to what degree? No osteopaths with MD's; dentists with doctors O.K.

    _____

10. What type of structure do you consider most preferable among the three basic types?

    1 (7) Multi-storied structure using elevators and hallways for internal circulation
    2 (3) One- to two-story offices with hallways for circulation
    3 (8) Garden level offices with individual entrances

    Other suggestions? _____

    _____

11. What services would you consider most desirable in a new medical office complex?

		Very Important 1	Desirable 2	Unnecessary 3
1	Accounting Services	( )	(8)	(8)
2	Pharmacy	(7)	(7)	(3)
3	General Medical Laboratory	(6)	(7)	(4)
4	Dental Laboratory	(2)	(5)	(9)
5	Medical Library	(1)	(10)	(5)

    Other ideas?   X-ray laboratory _____

    _____

12. What amenities do you consider most desirable?

		Very Important 1	Desirable 2	Unnecessary 3
1	Health Spa	(0)	(7)	(8)
2	Recreational Facilities (e.g. handball courts) if cost is not passed on to tenant in sale price or rent level	(0)	(8)	(9)
3	Pleasant Landscaping	(13)	(5)	(0)
4	Attractive Interior and Exterior Design	(14)	(4)	(0)

Other Ideas? _____ Common meeting room for classes _____

13. Would you be at all interested in condominium ownership of your office space?

1 (15) Yes
2 (3) No

14. Would you be interested in condominium ownership as an investment?

1 (9) Yes
2 (9) No

We have no means of identifying you as a respondent; however, if you have a special interest and would like to have our client contact you with further information about this planned project, please furnish your name and address below.

_____

_____

_____

Office Condominium Market Analysis – Denver, Colorado

2.   Questions on Phase I Survey

The medical professional questionnaire was divided into
two sections, one devoted to factual information regarding
their present situation, the second intended to investigate
the individual's thoughts on new space, including design,
services and condominium ownership. The illustration above
is a copy of the questionnaire. Questions on the first page
are directed towards their present space needs. How much
space do they occupy and how much do they pay for that
space? What services are included, and are they satisfied
with their present arrangement? Finally, is an expansion
or relocation in their plans for the near future?

The attitudinal questions centered around various design
and marketing aspects of the client's project. To what
degree should the various professions be segregated?
What type of building structure is typically preferred?
It was necessary to know the degree of importance of
including services such as accounting, pharmacy, labs
or library in the complex. A question concerning amenities
was posed in order to differentiate what was most important
in the minds of potential buyers from what was simply
desirable or unnecessary. The best indication of interest
or acceptance of the condominium ownership concept was,
we felt, a positive answer to a direct question. We posed
that question regarding interest in ownership for use and
ownership for investment. Finally, in order to assist the
client in actual contacts, an opportunity was given to the
respondent to identify himself.

3.   Results of Phase I Survey

A total of 19 of the 250 surveys were returned answered.
(Three surveys were returned because of a change of address,
thereby lowering the total sample size to 247.) The percentage
of return was thus about 7.7 percent of the sample. Nearly
half of the respondents were from suburban offices (nine),
seven from central city areas and three from inner city (central
business district and proximal areas).

C. Phase II Survey - Non-Medical Professionals

1. Sampling of Non-Medical Professionals

The total number of professionals within the three professional groups selected, Attorneys, Insurance Agents and Certified Public Accountants, with offices within the study area amount to a population of 1,227. Our sampling parameters for this population are described in the following table:

Table 9   SAMPLING DISTRIBUTION OF NON-MEDICAL PROFESSIONAL GROUPS

	Population	Sample	% Total
Insurance Agents			
Inner City (CBD)	272	31	51.7
Central City	171	19	32.5
Suburban	83	10	15.7
	526	60	
Attorneys			
Inner City (CBD)	151	83	59.2
Central City	39	21	15.3
Suburban	65	36	25.5
	255	140	
CPA's			
Inner City (CBD)	264	118	59.2
Central City	116	52	26.0
Suburban	66	30	14.0
	446	200	
Total			
Inner City (CBD)	687	232	58.0
Central City	326	92	23.0
Suburban	214	76	19.0
	1,227	400	100.0

FACTUAL INFORMATION

1. Do you presently own or lease your office space?

    1 (9) Own
    2 (19) Lease

2. About how much space do you or your firm presently occupy?

    1 (2) Less than 500 square feet
    2 (14) 500 to 1,499 square feet
    3 (9) 1,500 to 5,000 square feet
    4 (3) Over 5,000 square feet

3. About how many employees are within your office?

    1 (1) Just yourself
    2 (4) One besides yourself
    3 (7) Two to five
    4 (16) More than five

4. If you lease your space, approximately how much do you pay per square foot per year? (optional)

    1 (12) Less than $6.00
    2 (5) $6.00 to $6.99
    3 (1) $7.00 to $7.99
    4 (1) $8.00 and up

5. Do you plan an expansion of your office in the next year and a half?

    1 (13) Yes
    2 (16) No

6. Do you plan to relocate your office from its present location?

    1 (4) Yes
    2 (23) No

7. Rank your present office facility in the following qualities:

		Very Good 1	Adequate 2	Problematic 3
1	Location with respect to business clients	(18)	(10)	(0)
2	Location with respect to your residence and those of your employees, if any	(16)	(10)	(2)
3	Traffic congestion on roads leading to it	(14)	(10)	(3)
4	Convenience and expense of parking	(20)	(7)	(1)
5	Price or expense of office space	(19)	(8)	(1)
6	Availability of services (including restaurants, shops, etc.) nearby	(18)	(9)	(1)
7	Adequacy of the office space itself in such matters as lighting, soundproofing, and temperature control	(14)	(12)	(2)
8	Attractiveness of exterior and interior design	(13)	(13)	(2)

Other facets you wish to comment on _____

_____

8. What do you consider important in the location of your office space?

		Very Important 1	Somewhat Important 2	Relatively Unimportant 3
1	Accessibility to your clients	(19)	(5)	(4)
2	Proximity to your residence or those of your colleagues or employees	(10)	(15)	(3)
3	Proximity to downtown	(7)	(5)	(16)
4	Proximity to a major shopping center	(1)	(9)	(18)
5	Access to interstate freeway	(9)	(11)	(8)

		Very Important 1	Somewhat Important 2	Relatively Unimportant 3
6	Accessibility to a variety of services (including restaurant, office supply shops)	(9)	(15)	(4)
7	Proximity to other offices and office buildings	(5)	(12)	(11)
8	Visibility to a large amount of traffic	(2)	(4)	(22)
9	Proximity to bus lines	(2)	(10)	(15)
	Other; specify: _____			

9. Which of the following office building types do you prefer?

1 (7) High-rise (7 stories and up)
2 (4) Mid-rise
3 (18) Low-rise (3 stories or less)

10. What physical and structural characteristics do you consider important in an office building or complex?

		Very Important 1	Desirable 2	Relatively Unimportant 3
1	Availability of underground or covered parking	(6)	(12)	(10)
2	Large and attractive common areas	(4)	(13)	(11)
3	Attractive and pleasing view	(8)	(15)	(4)
4	Attractive landscaping	(4)	(22)	(3)
5	Individual temperature control	(18)	(8)	(2)
	Other ideas: _____			

11. What services do you consider important in an office building or complex?

		Very Important 1	Desirable 2	Unnecessary 3
1	Copying Service	(8)	(9)	(11)
2	Secretarial and Stenographic Services	(6)	(8)	(14)
3	Travel Agency	(0)	(1)	(26)
4	Personal Services (barbers, beauty salon)	(0)	(9)	(19)
5	Recreational Facilities, Health Spa (if at no cost to you directly or indirectly)	(0)	(13)	(15)
6	Informal eating facility (lounge with vending)	(6)	(16)	(6)
7	Cafeteria or Restaurant	(1)	(22)	(8)
8	Conference Rooms	(8)	(11)	(9)
9	Stationery, Office Supplies and News	(1)	(15)	(11)
	Other suggestions: _____			

12. Is it important that your office be segregated from offices of other unrelated professionals?

1 (13) Yes
2 (15) No

13. Aside from the intention of fitting the design to the needs and desires of the potential tenants, the most unusual aspect of this project is the opportunity for condominium ownership. Does this concept appeal to you for your own office space needs?

1 (21) Yes
2 (7) No

14. It will also be possible to buy office space over and above one's own office space needs. This could serve as an investment while it is leased to another tenant. Would the purchase of condominium office space as an investment interest you?

1 (17) Yes
2 (11) No

If you wish to be contacted for further information regarding the office complex, leave your name, address and/or phone number below.

_____

_____

_____

Office Condominium Market Analysis - Denver, Colorado

The sample represented nearly one-third of the population in the study area. Each profession was alotted a certain portion of the total of 400 surveys sent out. It was hypothesized, based on observations thus far, that CPA's would generate most interest. Two hundred surveys were sent to CPA's, 140 (35 percent) to attorneys, and 60 (15 percent) to insurance agents.

From this alottment by profession, our sample was distributed geographically just as the professionals themselves were distribured. For instance, 59.2 percent of the CPA's work in the CBD or surrounding areas; 59.2 percent or 112 of the 200 surveys alotted to CPA's were sent to the CBD offices. Greater percentage returns from any one area would indicate direction for marketing strategy.

2. Results of Phase II Survey

The percent return of Phase II was similar to that of Phase I-- 8.1 percent. Distribution of the respondents was similar to the distribution of the professionals, with 19 of 29 (65 percent) respondents having offices in the CBD. No geographic bias appears in the returns.

An unusually high rate of response was received from insurance agents, while attorneys seemed to exhibit less interest than average. Response from CPA's was not as high as expected.

	Sample Size	Return	% Return
CPA's	200	12	6
Attorneys	140	8	5.7
Insurance Agents	60	9	15
	400	29	7.25

Three-fourths of the responses (21 of 29) expressed interest in condominium ownership for their own use. This is substantially less in ratio than that of the medical professionals, yet high enough to justify an assumption that non-responses are equivalent to lack of interest.

3. Information on Present Office Facility

Two out of every three of the respondents lease their
office space. In all but two cases the rental was at
less than $7.00 and usually less than $6.00 per square
foot. Size of office space usually was between 500
and 1,500 square feet, and the number of employees
usually over five.

About half said they planned an expansion in the next
year and one half, but very few planned to relocate.
The returns generally indicated a high level of satis-
faction with their present space. Traffic congestion
scored highest in the unfavorable ranking and it was
considered a problem by only three of the respondents.

4. Information on Attitudes Toward Office Space

Accessibility to clientele was by far the highest ranked
feature in the location of office space. Proximity to
services, residences of employees, and interstate freeway
also ranked highly. Visibility to traffic, proximity to
bus lines and location near shopping facilities were
least important in the answers given by respondents.

Low-rise structures were preferred by a majority of the
professionals. They felt most structural features mentioned,
such as large common areas, covered parking, pleasing
view and attractive landscaping were desirable, but only
a small number ranked them as very important. Individual
office temperature control was ranked as very important in
18 of 28 responses.

Response to the services mentioned in Question 11 indicated
that most were desirable, but few felt they were absolutely
necessary. Copying services and conference rooms came
closest to "very important" status with eight rankings in
that classification.

About half of the respondents felt a need for segregation
of professions within an office building.

Office Condominium Market Analysis – Denver, Colorado

5.   Market Conclusions

Condominium ownership of office space interested 21 of
28 respondents for their own use. As an investment, 17
of 28 (60 percent) expressed interest. Our conclusion as
to the marketability for condominium office space is that
about 5 percent of the population of those three professional
groups in the study area would be candidates for condominium
ownership for their own use. Approximately four out of every
five of those will be open to the purchase of space over and
above their own needs.

This would indicate that about 60 firms would be willing to
buy, rather than lease, their office space. Average office
space utilization is estimated to be around 1,250 per firm.
We can find a justification for about 75,000 square feet of
condominium office space. The amount of additional space
demanded for investment is less clearly determined; however,
some plausible assumptions can be made. Judging from
experience, much of the investment office space sold in
a situation like this is sold to tenants who anticipate
expansion. Anticipated expansion of an office is unlikely
to be more than 50 percent of present size. It seems
reasonable to expect that those 80 percent of the buyers
who are interested in investment space could justify an
additional 30,000 square feet, calling for a total of
105,000 square feet.

VII.   THE OFFICE CONDOMINIUM CONCEPT IN THE DENVER AREA

A.   Advantages and Disadvantages of Condominium Ownership

This report has uncovered ample market for office condominiums for the proposed project. This has been based on positive interest encountered in our survey and is in light of soft office market conditions in the study area in the next two years.

The marketability of office condominiums derives from actual cost advantages to the purchaser. These advantages are by no means unmitigated by other disadvantages to some purchasers, yet, to a definite segment of the market, the advantages appear to outweigh disadvantages.

Among the advantages are:

1.   Lower total annual payments as a result of favorable financing.

2.   Tax deductions resulting from interest on mortgage and depreciation on real property owned.

3.   An annual equity buildup in real estate which is likely to appreciate through time.

4.   Savings on services and maintenance through the elimination of the landlord as middleman.

5.   More complete control over one's own space.

The disadvantages should also be recognized:

1.   Inflexibility for changing space requirements.

2.   Lack of an established retail market and the consequent lack of liquidity in equity.

3.   Lower profitability relative to other investment opportunities.

4.   The necessity of a sizable down payment.

5.   Input of some time and effort in management decisions.

Office Condominium Market Analysis – Denver, Colorado

Clearly these points may not apply in every case. For instance, inflexibility may not be a problem to a firm whose space requirements remain stable. A purchase of more space than needed at the time of purchase can also circumvent the problem to a certain degree.

The points seem to indicate that the typical purchaser of office condominium space will have certain predictable characteristics. We anticipate that the purchaser will have the following characteristics:

1. An income somewhat unrelated to his space needs

2. Stable space needs over time

3. Stable location needs over time

4. A well-established income at time of purchase

We have prepared a table which compares the costs of leasing versus condominium ownership. Leasing figures of the new Presbyterian Hospital medical office building ($7.50 per square foot) were compared to the maximum projected costs per square foot of the proposed project, $55.00 per square foot.

Office Condominium Market Analysis – Denver, Colorado

Assumptions

1. 1,000 square foot office unit

2. Unit rental at $7.50 per square foot

3. Unit sale price of $55.00 per square foot

4. Mortgage terms available
    a. 20% downpayment ($11,000)
    b. 8-3/4% interest
    c. 30 years

5. Operating costs (including maintenance, janitorial and other condominium association expenses, real estate taxes) of $2.25 per square foot

6. Land costs of $0.50 per square foot in the form of a leasehold interest

7. Accelerated depreciation schedule of 150% declining balance and 33-1/3 year estimated life

8. Equivalent increases in operating costs and rental rates

9. No appreciation in the value of the real estate

Office Condominium Market Analysis – Denver, Colorado

Table 10   ANNUAL AFTER TAX COMPARISON
                                      RENTING VS. BUYING
                                1,000 SQ. FT. MEDICAL OFFICE

		Rent ($7.50/Sq. Ft.)	Buy ($55.00/Sq. Ft.)
A.	Annual Cost (Before Taxes)		
	Rent	$7,500.00	
	Mortgage (Principal & Interest)		$4,153.60
	Estimated Operating Expenses		2,280.00
	Land Costs		500.00
	Total Costs	$7,500.00	$6,933.60
B.	Less		
1.	Annual Income Tax Saved		
	Annual Tax Deductions		
	Rent	$7,500.00	
	Interest on Mortgage		$3,850.00
	Estimated Operating Expenses		2,280.00
	Depreciation		2,475.00
	Land Lease		500.00
	Total Deductions	$7,500.00	$9,105.00
	Income Tax Saved (50% Bracket)	$3,750.00	$4,552.50
2.	Annual Equity Buildup		303.60
C.	Net Annual Costs (After Taxes)	$3,750.00	$2,077.50
D.	Net Annual Cost Per Square Foot	$ 3.75	$ 2.08
E.	Savings		
	Per Square Foot		$ 1.67
	Per Unit		$1,670.00
	Total Cash Savings First 10 Years		$15,090.00

Source: Real Estate Research Corporation

Office Condominium Market Analysis – Denver, Colorado

Table 11   ANNUAL AFTER TAX SAVINGS FIRST 10 YEARS
OFFICE RENTAL VS. CONDOMINIUM OWNERSHIP (1,000 SQ. FT.)

Year	Rental Net Cost Per Square Foot	Ownership Net Cost Per Square Foot	Annual Savings $
1	3.75	2.08	1,670
2	3.75	2.12	1,630
3	3.75	2.22	1,530
4	3.75	2.29	1,460
5	3.75	2.23	1,520
6	3.75	2.25	1,500
7	3.75	2.28	1,470
8	3.75	2.30	1,450
9	3.75	2.31	1,440
10	3.75	2.33	1,420
			15,090

Source: Real Estate Research Corporation

The comparison shows a clear advantage and financial savings to the purchaser of a condominium office. Several items should be pointed out, however. The cost of the downpayment is not included in the analysis. It can be assumed that the value appreciation of the office unit would tend to cancel both the cost of the downpayment and the loss of the earning power associated with the payment. Also, a certain loss will occur upon the sale of the office unit in the form of capital gains tax.

Nevertheless, the comparative analysis reinforces the competitiveness of the proposed office condominium and its marketability to a significant segment of the office market.

B. Condominium Developments in the Denver Area

The business or office condominium concept has been introduced to Denver only recently--so recently that it is too soon to tell the degree of momentum it is generating. Although the office condominium concept was used formally as early as 1969 in a Fort Collins office-bank building, this was more a matter of practicality than intentional marketing. It was, nevertheless, successful, preselling its entire 22,000 square feet of office space.

The old Rocky Mountain Bank Note Building on Bannock outside the central business district is presently being converted to an attorney's condominium, equipped with a legal library costing $40,000 to $50,000. The building is one-story and is in the process of extensive renovation. Prices for the space range from $48 to $54 per square foot. Marketing has proceeded, although total absorption remains undisclosed.

Another conversion project at Eleventh and Bannock contains 12 walk-up type units. Marketing has not yet begun. Conversion costs were $34 to $35 per square foot and land costs were $10 per square foot. The developers expressed anguish over legal problems and IRS difficulties.

Another office-condominium in the hospital district near the downtown area has sold out at rates of $55 to $60 per square foot. The building is pitched to medical professionals but has attracted diverse professions.

Of greatest import is an office condominium project presently under way along East Evans Avenue in the southeast Denver suburban area. Plaza 6000, as it is named, will consist of a three-building complex with a total of 96,000 square feet net rentable area. The first building is under construction. The developers of Plaza 6000 are evidently well known in the Denver area, having been involved in successful residential condominium projects.

The physical design of the buildings is ordinary--three-story brick with a garden level and a penthouse. The complex will offer 422 spaces of surface parking and 33 underground spaces, or 11 per building. (Parking space/Building area ratio = 1/211 square feet.)

Prices of space range from $35.00 per gross square foot ($41.18 per square foot NRA) for garden level space to $55.00 per gross square foot ($64.70 per square foot NRA) for penthouse space. A complete price schedule is given below:

	Per Gross Square Foot*	Per Square Foot Net Rentable Area*
Garden Level	$35	$41.18
First Floor - Plaza View	$47	$55.29
First Floor	$45	$52.94
Second Floor - Plaza View	$47	$55.29
Second Floor	$45	$52.94
Third Floor - Plaza View	$49	$57.64
Third Floor	$45	$52.94
Penthouse	$55	$64.71

Underground parking--$1,500 per stall

No restrictions have been placed on the type of office user which would be permitted. Conversation with the sales department revealed about 50 percent of total interest was by CPA's.

A conference room, exercise area, sauna and lunch facility will be incorporated in each building.

*Published rates were in gross square feet. As this is not common practice, they have been changed to reflect rentals of net rentable space. An efficiency of 85 percent was assumed, although this may be low for particular areas.

Office Condominium Market Analysis - Denver, Colorado

Although they have experienced favorable marketing response and a good deal of interest, Plaza 6000 is similar in design and marketing operations to a typical lease project. It lacks sensitive attention to detail that an office condominium will need to a greater degree than a typical speculative office building. There has been no explicitly stated orientation or purpose to the building--another factor more important in condominium office marketing than in leasing.

The location of the building is similar in many ways to the subject. It is situated on the south side of a high traffic artery leading within one to two miles to an interstate freeway. There is generally denser development in the East Evans - I-25 area and certainly more office activity, but there is no shopping center or focal point in the area, as there is near the subject. No turn lane is provided on East Evans, making ingress from the east difficult at certain times of the day.

A prototype sale of space within Plaza 6000 with typical mortgage and including taxes, management and services, the cost of $45 per square foot space within the building would be comparable to an expenditure of $6.76 per square foot per year. This does not include other considerations such as tax shelter and equity growth.¡ There is little, if any, direct cash savings on this project and its success may depend on the acceptance of the condominium concept itself and the importance of those indirect benefits.

Section III

Financing and Leasing

Chapter 9

Financing Real Estate Development

Key Terms

BOY Beginning of year.

Discount Rate The interest (risk) rate at which cash flows are discounted.

EOY End of year.

Equity The value of the owner's interest in a property in excess of all claims and liens.

Equity-Debt Ratio The ratio of the equity value in a property to the amount of debt incurred by that property.

Exchange A procedure of trading equities in certain types of properties, usually done to defer capital gains tax liability incurred from an outright sale.

Financial Structure The financial arrangements (equity and/or debt) that have been made to obtain control of an asset or assets.

Floor Loan A permanent mortgage loan arrangement that is based on occupancy. The lender disperses a base or "floor" amount and continues to disperse loan proceeds up to the committed amount as occupancy increases.

Gap Financing A short-term loan to meet obligations created between the construction loan phase and permanent loan phase of a project.

Interim (Construction) Financing Short-term loan to finance construction of a project, paid with permanent financing proceeds at the completion of the project.

Lease Financing The acquisition of property rights via a lease rather than by purchasing the property.

Leverage The use of fixed cost funds to acquire an income-producing asset in the expectation of a higher rate of return on the equity investment.

Limited Partnership A partnership arrangement that limits liability to nonmanaging partners to the amount they have invested.

Loan Package A presentation for acquiring financing that explains the project, its feasibility and the borrower's credit background as well as the procedure the borrower will employ to successfully complete the project.

NOI (Net Operating Income) Annual net income after deducting fixed costs (debt service is not included) and operating expenses.

Opportunity Cost An implied cost of foregoing an alternative investment.

Overall Rate The ratio of net operating income to the sales (or purchase) price. It may also be determined via mortgage-equity analysis.

Permanent Financing The long-term mortgage loan to finance a completed project.

Present Value The discounted value of all future cash flows.

Private Placement A loan that is made without the use of a financial intermediary.

Purchase Money Mortgage A loan given by the seller to finance the purchase of a property.

Sale/Leaseback An arrangement whereby the owner/occupant of a property sells his interests and then leases the same property with the intention of liquifying equity.

Tax Saving A reduction of tax liability on other earned income as a result of a negative taxable income from an investment.

Tax Shelter Tax savings from non-cash tax deductable expenses (i.e., depreciation).

The Role of Financing

Financing has a primary role in the real estate development and investment process and thus represents one of the most important elements of feasibility analysis. From the investor/developer's standpoint, as well as that of the lender, proper interim and permanent financing in terms of the amount, timing of loan proceeds and repayment, and interest charges is fundamentally important to the "success" of the proposed project. It is rare indeed to find a real estate development that does not have as a major source of financing debt capital secured by a mortgage. The reasons for this are well-known.

First of all, the developer uses short-term construction loans because he lacks the necessary equity capital for the entire project and/or he desires to shift a portion of the risk to the lender. When the developer is able to borrow an amount that equals (or often even exceeds) *his* cost of construction, there seems to be little meaning in the concept of "leverage" since technically he has advanced no capital. In reality, his true investment is his time and skill as a developer plus his organization of capital and human resources that will be used to complete the project.

The longer-term investor (if he is not also the developer) may also lack the necessary capital for the purchase of the property on a strictly cash basis, although there are occasions when an investor or a group of investors use equity capital entirely. For example, during periods of relatively high interest rates and unattractive loan terms, investors with the necessary capital may choose to finance new or even existing real estate purchases exclusively with their own capital. Here, as in the case of the developer borrowing for only short periods during construction, the reason for borrowing may be either to take advantage of positive leverage or to spread the risk of the equity investment over several investments rather than to put all the required dollars into a single investment—or perhaps a combination of both.

Business firms and other *users* of income producing property may purchase the property from funds available within the firm, but even here some form of debt financing typically is utilized. Since the acquiring firm is in all probability capitalized with bonded indebtedness, the purchase of real estate with internal funds has an implicit equity/debt ratio associated with the cash used for purchase. Some user firms also borrow directly from mortgage lenders, but these are usually the smaller firms that cannot, because of their size, approach the bond markets for debt capital. Still others may prefer private placement as a means of acquiring debt funds to use in real estate purchases. Not-for-profit users of real estate such as government agencies, educational institutions and public service organizations most often finance their use of real estate through leases and/or direct loans from mortgage lenders.

Generally speaking, investors examining the feasibility of real estate developments or analyzing the relative desirability of existing properties must include the key variable of financing in order to measure appropriately the relative desirability of the proposed development or purchase. Market prices and rates of return are based upon the "typical" buyer, and that buyer generally borrows. Thus, overall capitalization rates (net operating income divided by sales price) reflect this financing structure and tend to establish market norms or standards.

The lender, on the other hand, bases his decision to lend or not on the market and feasibility studies which focus on predictions of net operating income for the projected project or existing property.[1] Such studies must then assume a particular pattern of financing in arriving at a final conclusion as to feasibility. Thus, financing is an integral part of both the study itself and the decisions of both the investor/borrower and the lender concerning the desirability of proceeding with the planned project.

Meaning of "Financing"

"Financing" refers to the process of obtaining funds or capital, generally for the purpose of supporting a development and/or investment by gaining control over assets. Under this definition, the scope of financing is quite broad and includes not only mortgage loans as a source of funds, but lease financing as well. The ownership and/or control of an asset may be acquired for a number of reasons. In this chapter we will focus on real estate to be used in a trade or business or acquired as an investment.

By definition the term "asset" includes much more than just real property, even though this book deals primarily with real property. However, the principles and techniques can be applied to practically any form of asset that may be used or controlled.

The economic system of this country is such that the sources of capital funds and their requirements are constantly changing. Recently, the pace and nature of change has been much more dramatic than in prior years. Since the early 1970s, record inflation rates were fought with monetary policies that caused the rise in the cost of long-term funds needed to finance real estate investments. Lendable funds became in short supply at just the time when developers most needed additional funds for extended time periods.

In this chapter we deal with various means of acquiring control and use of an asset. We explore the various sources of capital and their particular requirements.

---

1 For a more complete discussion of lending practices and techniques see Stephen D. Messner, Irving Schreiber and Victor L. Lyon, *Marketing Investment Real Estate* (Chicago: REALTORS NATIONAL MARKETING INSTITUTE® 1975), p. 70.

Equity Financing

Single Ownership

All or part of the funds needed to acquire the control of an asset may be furnished by one or more owners who obtain, in addition, the rights of possession, enjoyment and disposition. The equity buyer may be an investor who invests for the right to enjoy all of the cash flows that may be generated by the investment. In this instance, the motivation for purchase is the "return on investment" that the property offers as compared with other types of cash flow streams with similar risk and of similar duration.

The equity buyer may also be a user of the property who utilizes the asset to conduct his trade or business. He then may look at the purchase more as a cost of doing business rather than making an investment on which he seeks a return, even though there may be considerable investment potential in the asset. This chapter will explore how an equity buyer/user should view his purchase when the asset is used in his business and may increase in value during use.

Group Ownership

Many investors may not have the funds necessary to meet the minimum equity requirements of a real estate investment, or they may simply wish not to concentrate their capital in a single or a few investments. Group equity financing is possible and has grown in use in recent years. There are several types of entities that may be created to acquire group equity ownership for investment buyers. Limited partnerships are a popular vehicle to acquire an equity interest in an asset. Such vehicles have certain built-in safeguards to the limited partners, with the major advantage being that the liability is usually limited to the loss of the actual amount of capital invested.

With proper structuring, the limited partners can derive additional benefits through depreciation losses in excess of their actual capital contributions. The following is an example of one-year tax benefits from such structuring.

Office Building with Price of $100,000
    Mortgage of $85,000, 9% interest, 25 years
    Monthly Payments of $713.32
    Equity of $15,000
    Percentage of Property Value Represented by Improvement is 80%
    Net Operating Income of $11,000
    Method of Depreciation—Straight-line
    Economic Life—25 years
    Investor Tax Bracket—50%
    In this example for illustration purposes, the $15,000 limited partner equity
    investor represents 100% of the ownership.

Pro Forma Statement

Year 1

Net Operating Income	$11,000
Less: Annual Debt Service	8,560
Cash Flow Before Taxes	2,440
Less Income Tax*	95
Cash Flow After Taxes	$ 2,345
*Net Operating Income	$11,000
Less Interest	7,610
Less Depreciation**	3,200
Taxable Income	$ 190
× 50% = Income Tax	$ 95

**$100,000 × 80% Building Allocation $80,000
$80,000 ÷ 25 yrs. = $3,200 Annual Depreciation

The mortgage in the foregoing example must be a non-recourse loan with no personal liability, and the property must serve as the sole security for the loan in order for the limited partners to obtain the tax advantages.

The following illustrates the same example with the limited partner's basis being limited to his capital contribution:

Net Operating Income	$11,000
Less: Annual Debt Service	8,560
Cash Flow Before Tax	2,440
Less Income Tax*	1,455
Cash Flow After Tax	$ 985
*Net Operating Income	$11,000
Less Interest	7,610
Less Depreciation**	480
Taxable Income	$ 2,910

× 50% Tax Bracket = $1,455
Building Allocation 80% × $15,000 basis = $12,000
$12,000 ÷ 25 yrs. = $480 Annual Depreciation

There is a dramatic difference in the cash flow after tax under the two types of structuring. As indicated in the example above, the cash flow after tax for first year with the non-recourse loan is $2,345, or 2.4 times greater than the comparable figure for the same property structured with a personal liability loan. The foregoing example illustrates that structuring mortgages in a limited partnership purchase of equity can make the difference between a feasible or infeasible project—that is, an adequate after tax return to the invested capital.

It is also possible to design partnership agreements that allocate profits and losses disproportionately to ownership interests. This form of partnership can be especially advantageous in situations where there are significant differences in the tax brackets of the equity partners. The Tax Reform Act of 1976 makes it more difficult to accomplish the structuring of the foregoing examples. As always, competent tax council from your CPA and/or tax attorney is vital in structuring any purchase.

There are various other entities that can be created to acquire equity ownership in an asset: regular corporations, general partnerships, and land trusts to name just a few. Each has its own distinct advantages and disadvantages that should be fully explored before making a decision on which to use.

Another means of acquiring an equity ownership in an asset is by exchanging an existing equity ownership into another equity ownership. When certain conditions are met, the exchange of equity from one asset to another may qualify for a Section 1031, IRS code exchange. If the exchange qualifies under Section 1031, all or part of the tax that would be incurred under a sale and purchase may be deferred. The exchange of equity may represent a means of acquiring control of an asset with little or no capital outlay.[2]

There are forms of equity ownership other than those discussed. In the broad sense of acquiring equity for investment purposes, the equity investor is concerned with his return on investment. The question of feasibility always arises. Is the projected return on investment sufficient to compensate the invested capital? Are there alternative investment opportunities for capital with greater potential return with no higher degree of risk? Rates of return requirements for equity capital fluctuate with the money market and general economic conditions of the country.

Risks and Returns to Equity

In traditional real estate literature, real estate investment positions are divided into either equity or debt. The nature and variety of equity positions were discussed above. In contrast, mortgage debt interests are typically portrayed as both more secure and predictable than equity positions. However, the evolution of mortgage lending over the past decade has changed the respective positions of both borrower and lender.

There are many times the lender or mortgagee assumes two roles in financing the acquisition of ownership of an asset. In addition to furnishing the mortgage funds, he may also invest capital to acquire an equity

---

2 The mechanics and tax treatment of a Section 1031 exchange are covered in detail in Ibid., Chapter 11.

position. The lender attempts to enjoy the best of both worlds by wearing two hats. He enjoys a competitive rate of return on his mortgage investment, and an even higher return on his equity investment. On the investment he makes in the mortgage, all of his return is interest income and is completely taxable. On his return on the equity investment some of the income he receives may be sheltered by his participation in the depreciation basis. There are also instances when the lender acquires his equity position solely as the basis for making the mortgage investment, without any incremental capital outlay.

The money and capital are responsible for determining markets and how a lender acquires his equity position if, in fact, he does. In terms of financial feasibility, an equity position acquired with or without a capital outlay may make the rate of return acceptable to the lender for his multi-roles in the acquisition of the asset. When acting solely as a lender, his return on the simple mortgage investment may not be adequate to entice him to make the loan when he considers alternative investments.

Rate of Return

Generally speaking, the rate of return to the equity owner should be higher than the rates of return to mortgage capital invested. The reason for the typical differential is that there is usually a higher degree of risk associated with the equity position. This is brought about by the priorities of income and the right of transfer of ownership rights (title) if default on the repayment of the debt or associated interest occurs. The priorities of the property income are usually as follows, with the rank of priorities going from bottom to top:

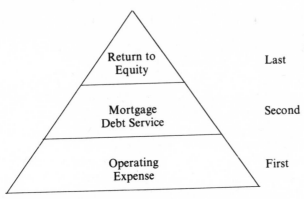

The first dollars of income go to the operating expenses; the next dollars of income go to the mortgage investor in the form of debt service; and the last dollars of income go to the equity investor.

The risk associated with the before-tax-return on equity investment may be illustrated in the following example:

169

Property Value or Price	$100,000

Operating Information:

Gross Effective Income	$18,000
Less: Operating Expenses	− 7,000
Net Operating Income	$11,000

Financing Information:

Loan Amount	$80,000
Annual Interest	9%
Annual Debt Service (Interest Only Loan)	$ 7,200

If this property were held for five years and experienced *no change* in either income or value over the holding period, the respective cash flows from the investment would look like this:

Initial Investment: $20,000
Cash Flow per Year: $ 3,800
(NOI minus ADS, $11,000–$7,200)

n	Cash Throw-Off	Reversion	Cash Flows	Present Value at 19%
1	$3,800		$ 3,800	3,193
2	3,800		3,800	2,683
3	3,800		3,800	2,255
4	3,800		3,800	1,895
5	3,800	$20,000	23,800	9,974
				$20,000

At a discount rate of 19 percent, the "present value" of the future cash flows is exactly equal to the initial investment of $20,000, and thus the before-tax IRR of the investment is 19 percent.

If it is assumed that the sales price of a property is a multiple of the NOI, then the overall rate of capitalization (ORC) in this example is 11 percent, or $11,000 divided by $100,000 (NOI ÷ selling price). As a multiplier, this may be expressed as the reciprocal of the overall rate, or 9.09 percent (1 ÷ 11). In the first example, NOI is assumed to remain constant, and thus the value also remains constant. If, however, NOI is forecast to change or the actual NOI is different than the forecast while the overall rate of capitalization is assumed to remain constant, value will be affected as a direct function of annual income. For example, assume that the actual gross income in the example above was 5 percent below the level forecast even though the forecast of operating expenses was accurate.

Then,

Gross Income		$17,100
Less: Operating Expenses		−7,000
Net Operating Income		$10,100
Less: Annual Debt Service		−7,200
Cash Throw-Off		$ 2,900
Sales Price, EOY 5		$91,818
($10,100 ÷ .11)		
Less: Mortgage Balance		−80,000
Reversion, EOY 5		$11,818

n	Cash Throw-Off	Reversion	Present Value at 7.45%
1	$2,900		$ 2,699
2	2,900		2,512
3	2,900		2,338
4	2,900		2,175
5	2,900	$11,818	10,276
			$20,000

Since a discount rate of 7.45 percent reduces the sum of all future cash flows to $20,000, the amount of the initial investment, the IRR is then approximately 7.5 percent. Note that the drop in gross income of 5 percent reduced the return on investment to the equity investor from 19 percent to 7.5 percent. In essence, this points out the significance of cash flow projections and their importance to the equity investor. An "error" of only 5 percent in the gross income resulted in a drop of over 11 percentage points (or a drop of over 60 percent) in rate of return to the equity investor.

Return to Mortgage Investor

The return to the mortgage investor would remain intact even if gross income were to drop to as little as $14,200, or by 21 percent. It is apparent that because the priorities of property income leave the last dollars of income to the equity investor, his position is riskier than the mortgage investor and must offer a potentially higher rate of return to compensate for the higher risk.

It also becomes apparent how crucial accurate forecasting of income is to estimates of return on investment and the related investment decision-making process. The supply and demand measurement from the market or feasibility study determines the accuracy of the forecast. The above illustration indicates how dramatically the return on equity is affected by a seemingly slight forecasting error.

171

Mortgage Financing

As indicated earlier, the major portion of the total capital necessary to acquire control of an asset is usually furnished by the mortgage lender (investor). This is true whether the buyer is an investor who has no personal interest in the property except for the cash flow it can generate, or a user whose primary interest is the direct services the property can provide. The user acquiring the control of an asset through purchase will use mortgage financing because the property can serve as security for a loan that has a cost less than the rate of return he can earn through his business operations.

There are many types of mortgages utilized by mortgage investors. The choice of a mortgage depends on the needs of the borrower, the specific role of the lender, and general economic conditions which affect the demand for and supply of loanable funds.

Construction Loans

Construction loans are used when the mortgage investor furnishes the capital necessary to construct a project. Generally the lender will phase the investment of his capital into the construction mortgage as work on the project is completed. Construction lenders protect their investment of funds by ensuring that the work for which they are advancing money has actually been done. This protection is provided by frequent inspections of the construction site.

Lenders also are concerned about possible liens placed on the project by labor and suppliers who have worked on or supplied construction materials, since such liens can often take a superior position to the construction loan. The lender wants assurance that liens will not be placed on the property; he usually accomplishes this by having lien waivers signed by labor and suppliers before he advances his periodic sums of money.

Permanent Loans

The construction lender is vitally concerned with repayment of his loan as well as a return on his investment. Funds for repayment are generally guaranteed through a permanent loan commitment. This is accomplished through a mortgage investor who wants a long-term investment. The permanent lender issues a commitment that says upon the satisfactory completion of construction a long-term mortgage loan will be issued on the project and the dollars advanced will be used to pay off the short-term construction lender.

Floor Loans

This type of loan is another form of permanent loan commitment which obligates the lender to make a loan for a base amount of money referred to as the "floor," with an agreement to provide additional funds once a certain level of occupancy has been achieved in the project. This type of loan is usually structured for the safety of the mortgage investor since the lender will increase the amount of money he will invest in the project only as the occupancy goes up. When a project attains the projected level of occupancy, the lender will have funded the full amount he committed to invest in the project.

Gap Commitment or Guarantee

Floor loans can create a problem for the developer/investor in that the floor amount guaranteed is not sufficient to fund the project. It creates a gap between the funds needed and the funds made available by the mortgage investor. This gap is often provided for by a gap lender. The gap loan commitment is somewhat riskier than the permanent floor loan and usually requires a higher rate of return. The gap lender's repayment of his loan is largely dependent on the occupancy increasing to the projected level so the permanent floor lender will fund the total amount he committed for, thereby repaying the gap lender.

Purchase Money Mortgage

Another type loan often utilized in providing funds to acquire an asset is a purchase money mortgage created by the seller of the property. This type of loan occurs when a seller converts a portion of his equity to a mortgage investment.

An example of purchase money mortgage financing by a seller is as follows:

Sales Price	$100,000
First Mortgage	40,000
Sellers' Equity	$ 60,000
Terms of Acquisition by Equity Investor:	
Equity Investment (Down Payment)	$ 20,000
Existing First Mortgage	40,000
Purchase Money Second Mortgage	40,000
	$100,000

The seller has in fact provided the buyers with $40,000 to acquire the property he is selling, although he did not actually advance the $40,000. Instead, he converted $40,000 of his equity to a purchase money mortgage investment. Since he did not really lend the $40,000, this is sometimes called a soft money mortgage.

There are many variations to the purchase money mortgage. The seller of the property, by varying his return on his purchase money investment, can make a property salable that would not be otherwise.

Even though purchase money mortgages are often second mortgages, the interest rates may be equal to or lower than the first mortgage interest

173

rate. This is largely due to the fact that these are soft money mortgages and are used to facilitate the sale of a property that would not otherwise be feasible. A lower rate of return on the purchase money second mortgage often elevates the rate of return to the equity investor sufficiently to attract his capital.

Loan Package

One of the most important ingredients in the mortgage loan process is the "loan package." This represents all of the background information needed to appraise the potential of the project proposal and to evaluate both the property and the borrower as credit risks. Mortgage investors are concerned with the safe return *on* their investment as well as the return *of* their investment. A mortgage investor wants and needs answers to a wide variety of questions before he will risk his investment. The preparation and presentation of the loan package is a vital step in securing a mortgage loan to finance a major portion of a development project.

The following outline on preparing and presenting a loan package is an excellent check-list for use in organizing information and exhibits for presentation to a mortgage investor for any type of project.

Preparation and Presentation of Loan Package

Without effective "packaging" of the loan application to the lender, all of the hard work of planning, analysis and coordination may be in vain. It is critical to know what the lender expects in the way of information, how he will react to certain requests and requirements in the loan package, and what format will best satisfy his needs and loan criteria.

A. Three Steps in Preparing a Loan Package

1. Primary Application
    a. Survey of potential lenders and prevailing rates
        (1) Informs lenders that the project is underway
        (2) Used as a means of gaining information on the competition
    b. Make application in writing to several of lenders surveyed
        (1) Indicate nature or concept of the project
        (2) Estimate rents anticipated and other general data
        (3) Show the plan of timing for the project
            (a) When to start
            (b) Completion and final funding
        (4) Estimate amounts needed and when

2. Interim Submission
    a. Submit to those lenders showing an interest
    b. Update *all* information presented in preliminary application

    c. Provide more accurate estimates of amounts of funds needed and timetable of needs

3. Final Submission
    a. Submit in sequence of most favorable lender first
        (1) Advantages of "priority" submission
        (2) Alternative of simultaneous submission
    b. Allow sufficient time for adequate review and evaluation by lender
        (1) Research needed to confirm and/or supplement analysis
        (2) Appraisals will be required
        (3) Time needed to pass through organizational structure
    c. Provide multiple copies in appropriate sizes
        (1) Find out from each lender how many members are on the loan committee
        (2) Standard vs. special size—uniformity of page size if possible

B. Contents of Final Loan Application

1. Concept of Project—Overview
    a. Use architectural renderings when possible
    b. Use any other visual aids to help convey the idea

2. Market Studies to Indicate the Need or Demand for the Project
    a. See that these are completed by others, if possible, to ensure objectivity
    b. Get list of acceptable researchers from key lenders
    c. Hold tight on deadlines for study—market may be gone by the time the study is completed

3. Feasibility Study

4. Site Location
    a. State or regional map with general area of property indicated
    b. City or metropolitan area map with property indicated
    c. Exact site location

5. Site Studies
    a. Engineering
        (1) Sewer line—size, capacity, etc.
        (2) Water line—size, capacity, etc.
        (3) Other utilities
        (4) Topography and soil condition
    b. Legal
        (1) Photographs of site
        (2) Roads
        (3) Copy of survey
        (4) Zoning—copy of exact ordinance with complete definitions
        (5) Title policy

6. **Plan for Building**
   a. Renderings
   b. Scale model (if available)
   c. Complete plans and specifications for those who request them
   d. *Key point:* Simple presentation for a layman
      (1) Floor plan—floor and details of typical space
      (2) Elevations
      (3) Perspective
      (4) Unique details, such as entry lobby

7. **Cost of Project**
   a. Need for breakdown by item or component
      (1) Bids for projections; indicate firm bids
      (2) Profits
      (3) Costs
         (a) Advertising
         (b) Commissions
         (c) Open house
         (d) Lease costs

8. **Management Plan for the Project**
   a. Rent-up procedures
   b. Copy of typical lease
      (1) Performance clause
      (2) Cash flow projections
   c. Management profile—experience, qualifications, etc.
   d. Schedule of lease prices
      (1) Concessions
      (2) Commissions
      (3) Tenant allowance
      (4) Copy of lease to be used
   e. Available money to carry project

9. **Sponsorship Information**
   a. Legal name and type of organization of borrower
   b. Record of mortgagor—experience (what other projects?); resumes
   c. Current financial statement (not more than 90 days old)
   d. Credit report—Dun & Bradstreet rating
   e. Management team: copy of contract outlining responsibilities
   f. Who signs mortgage?—co-makers vs. guarantors
   g. GLIC—mortgage or lease guarantees

10. **Details on Loan Requested**
    a. Amount
       (1) Source of equity
       (2) Profits retained
       (3) Syndication
       (4) Joint venture

b. When needed
  (1) Future delivery
  (2) Date of closing
c. Source of construction money—bank, rent, interim, etc.
d. Description of security

C. Negotiation of Mortgage Contract

1. Term of the Mortgage
  a. Length of term
  b. Balloon payment

2. Method of Payment

3. Default Procedure and Conditions Constituting Default
  a. Time to cure
  b. Notice provisions
  c. Responsibility for expenses and fees necessitated by default
  d. Control in event of default

4. Insurance Required—Amounts, Types, Type of Insurance Company

5. Tax and Insurance Escrows

6. State Laws Under which Lease Will Be Interpreted

7. Assignment of Rents
  a. Conditions under which assignment will take place
  b. Notification procedures for both mortgagor and tenants

8. Exculpatory (Hold Harmless) Provisions
  a. Liability may be limited to property only
  b. Personal liability may continue for some time into term of loan
  c. Personal liability may be affected in event of failure of property to meet minimum standards of occupancy, etc.

9. Assumption and Assignment
  a. After what time period may note be "paid off?"
  b. Declining penalty schedule for early prepayment
  c. Penalties for partial prepayments
  d. To what are prepayments applied? Principal or interest?
  e. Fees for assumption

10. Permission for Sale or Transfer to a Controlled Entity

11. Permission for Junior Lines

12. Permission for Partial Conversion or Sale at Later Date

13. Condemnation
  a. Portion of award to be applied to mortgage
  b. Award to be applied to principal, interest, or both

177

14. **Title Insurance**

15. **Contingencies Based on Inspections by Municipal Authorities** —

16. **Lawyers to be Employed to Effect Closing**

17. **Assignment of Commitment Prior to Closing**

18. **Periodic Financial Statements Required**

19. **Final Settlement Date**
    a. Period during which closing permitted
    b. Acceptable justifications for an extension

20. **Stages of Payout and Basis for Same**

21. **Considerations to the Lender (Publicity, Signs, etc.)**

22. **Inspections Required During Construction, and by Whom**

23. **Participation Provisions**

D. **Request Permission to Make Personal Presentation to Loan Committee**

Lease Financing

The control and use of an asset is all that is necessary for many users of real estate. Most users acquire control and use through the traditional method of purchase with borrowing. Expansion of many businesses is limited because of the lack of necessary capital to acquire ownership of assets needed to expand. Lease financing is one alternative solution to the capital shortage problem.

Leasing vs. Owning

Many businesses, when comparing the alternatives of leasing vs. owning view the leasing alternative in terms of their cost of capital. This is illustrated in the following example:

Acquisition Cost of Real Estate $100,000
Annual Rent $ 12,000

Their analysis would be that their cost of capital ($100,000) would be 12 percent. If they could borrow capital at anything less than 12 percent, they would be better off borrowing and purchasing than leasing.

Let's assume the asset they are considering purchasing or leasing has a 15-year life. If the asset is actually declining in value and will have a zero value at EOY 15, their cost of capital has been approximately 8.4 percent and not 12 percent. That is, the present value of a $12,000 level annuity for 15 years is $100,000 when discounted at 8.44 percent; thus, the IRR of this "investment" is approximately 8.4 percent.

The opportunity cost of money that a business has must be considered in making the decision to buy or lease. Opportunity cost in this instance refers to the "cost" of not investing capital in the operations of the business firm; that is, the rate that could be earned if invested in the business operation rather than in the real estate used in the business.

Regardless of the cost of capital, if the opportunity exists to invest capital in excess of that which the business is capable (or desirous) of borrowing, the leasing alternative is preferable if the opportunity cost of money is greater than the cost of capital.

The following example illustrates the analysis process that may be used to evaluate the decision to buy or lease:

> Cost of Asset $100,000
> $12,000 Annual Rent, paid in advance
> Value of Asset, EOY 5: $100,000
> Opportunity Cost of Money: 15 percent

The process first requires reducing both alternatives to annual cash flows. In this example we will assume the asset is to be purchased free and clear. We will analyze before taxes.

Cash Flows

	Leasing		Owning
EOY	$'s	EOY	$'s
0	(12,000)	0	(100,000)
1	(12,000)	1	0
2	(12,000)	2	0
3	(12,000)	3	0
4	(12,000)	4	0
5	0	5	100,000
Total Outlay	60,000		0

Both of the alternatives represent outlays of cash at different periods of time. To compare and evaluate the two obligations, we need to compare them at the same point in time. One useful time to compare the two alternatives would be EOY 0 which is simultaneous with EOY 1, or the present. We bring these two obligations together at EOY 0 by discounting the cash flows to EOY 0 at the opportunity cost of money of 15 percent. **179**

		Leasing
EOY	$'s	

EOY	$'s	
0	(12,000)	$+(10,435)+(9,074)+(7,890)+(6,861)=(46,260)$
1	(12,000)	
2	(12,000)	
3	(12,000)	
4	(12,000)	
5	(–0–)	

The negative present value of leasing is $46,260.

	Owning
EOY	$'s

EOY	$'s
0	$(100,000)+49,718=(50,282)$
1	0
2	0
3	0
4	0
5	100,000

The negative present value of owning is $50,282.

The comparison can now be made between an outlay of $50,282 for purchase at EOY 0 and outlay of $46,262 at EOY 0 for leasing. This indicates that with investment opportunities available to yield 15 percent, the leasing alternative is better than owning. This is true even though the total outlay for leasing over the five-year period is $60,000 and the total outlay for owning is 0. The $100,000 at EOY 5 under the owning alternative represents the value of the asset at EOY 5.

It is clear that the key element of comparison between the two alternatives is the opportunity rate of return used to discount the respective cash flows. Note that while leasing appears the more profitable alternative *if* the firm has investment opportunities available that yield 15 percent or more, at 10 percent the situation is reversed:

Leasing	Owning
($50,038)	($37,908)

Net Present Value Profile

Thus, there is a whole range of comparisons that may be viewed in the form of a net present value profile, as follows:

Net Present Value Profile

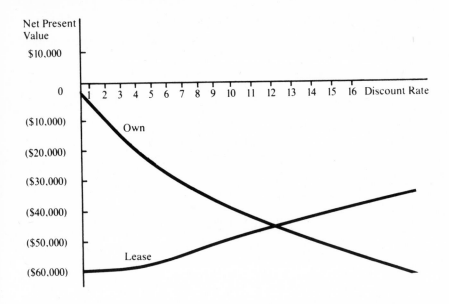

From the exhibit above, it may be seen that the ownership option has a lower cost at any rate below 13 percent plus; at any rate above this point the leasing alternative has a lower cost. This observation suggests an alternative approach to the own/lease decision problem.

Another approach to making the decision whether to lease or own is the cash flow differential method. This method calculates exactly the rate of return on the dollars invested in the ownership of the asset. The following is an example of this method using the same assumptions as above:

EOY	A Owning	B Leasing	A-B Difference
0	$(100,000)	$(12,000)	$(88,000)
1	–0–	(12,000)	12,000
2	–0–	(12,000)	12,000
3	–0–	(12,000)	12,000
4	–0–	(12,000)	12,000
5	100,000	–0–	100,000
			13.7%

Owning the asset in the foregoing example means an outlay of $100,000 at EOY 0, but it means a savings of $12,000 at EOY 0 also by not having to make the lease payment. In other words, owning instead of leasing means a *net* outlay of $88,000 at EOY 0, reflected in the "A-B" Column.

Years 1 through 4 of ownership also means a savings of $12,000 annually by not having to pay rent. In other words, owning vs. leasing has a $12,000 annual cash flow benefit to the net investment of $88,000 at EOY 0.

The fifth year positive cash flow of $100,000 of ownership reflects the value of the asset at EOY 5. The zero cash flow of leasing at EOY 5 reflects the rent having been paid in advance. The $100,000 at EOY 5 in the "A-B" Column also reflects a benefit to the net investment of $88,000 at EOY 0. The calculation of the rate of return is the five years of cash flow benefits in the "A-B" Column related to the investment amount of $88,000 in the same column at EOY 0.

The conclusion is that the rate of return on the investment is 13.7 percent. The question now is, is there an investment opportunity available for an investment of $88,000 that will yield greater than 13.7 percent? If the answer is no, the ownership alternative is less costly.

These examples were simplified to illustrate the process for making the decision whether to acquire control and use of an asset by ownership or leasing. The same process can be used whether the asset is mortgaged or is owned free and clear.

It would be more realistic to do the comparison after taxes. To do this, reduce both alternatives to cash flow after taxes from EOY 0 through all the years of the proposed lease term, then make the rate of return calculation of the "difference" column as illustrated. The logic for making the decision is exactly the same.

Investment Base

Another dimension of lease financing occurs when an asset is already owned and the owners/users are considering selling the asset and leasing it back. In this instance, an understanding of investment base theory is necessary to make the decision.

The concept of "investment base" is based upon the notion that to calculate a return on investment, you must know the investment amount. At the time of purchase of a property, the investment base is the amount of the cash outlay necessary to make the purchase. For a property that has been owned for sometime, the investment base would be the after-tax cash proceeds of sale as if you had sold it. If you turn down an offer to sell an asset, you have, in fact, at that moment in time invested what would have been the proceeds of sale if you had accepted the offer. By rejecting an offer you are giving up the opportunity to use what would have been the proceeds of sale in an alternative investment. Therefore, you are investing that amount in your own property.

Assume that in the foregoing example the prospective owner was not considering the purchase of an asset for $100,000 but had already owned it and could sell it for $100,000 and lease it back for $12,000 a year for five years. The framework of analysis is the same as in the previous example.

We will use the same example with the same assumptions but make the comparison on an after-tax basis. Assume a 40 percent tax bracket for the existing owner, and assume that the $100,000 asset is real property and has an 80 percent building allocation. The building is estimated to have a remaining economic life of 25 years; straight-line depreciation will be used in calculating net income.

EOY	A Owning	B Leasing	A-B Difference
0	$100,000	($7,200)**	($92,800)
1	1,280*	(7,200)	8,480
2	1,280	(7,200)	8,480
3	1,280	(7,200)	8,480
4	1,280	(7,200)	8,480
5	1,280+95,200***	–0–	96,480
			IRR=9.6%

* $80,000 depreciable base ÷ 25 years = $3,200 annual depreciation expense × 40 percent tax bracket = $1,280 annual tax saving.
** $12,000 annual rent which is fully deductible × 40 percent tax bracket = $4,800 tax credit. $12,000 annual rent minus the $4,800 tax saving equals a net rent of $7,200 per year.

*** Sales Price EOY 5	$100,000
Adjusted Basis at time of sale	84,000
Capital Gain	$ 16,000
× 30 percent = tax on sale	$ 4,800
Sales Price EOY 5	$100,000
less Tax on Sale	4,800
Proceeds of Sale after Tax	$ 95,200

The conclusions are based on the same logic as before. The question becomes: "Is there an alternative investment opportunity to invest the $92,800 reflected at EOY 0 in the difference column to yield greater than 9.6 percent after tax return?" If the answer is yes, the leasing alternative (sale/leaseback) is better. If the answer is no, the ownership alternative (continuing to own) is better. In other words, the rate of return on the investment of $92,800 invested in the current ownership of the asset is exactly 9.6 percent.

Sale/leasebacks can be advantageous to the seller/lessee in that he can reinvest capital at a higher rate of return and still maintain control and use of the asset which is all he needs for his trade or business. Sale/lease-backs can be very good for the buyer/lessor because he has acquired what is practically a management free investment upon which he earns his required rate of return. His return requirement is based on the strength of the seller/lessee.

In sale/leasebacks, the buyer/investor often can obtain a better mortgage than the existing owners can by having a lease contract income stream to pledge toward repayment of the debt.

Sale/leasebacks can be used with practically any type of asset: real property, equipment, etc. The process of analysis is basically the same for any asset.

Chapter 10

Leasing

10

Key Terms

Bundle of Rights The collection of rights relating to the ownership of property (i.e., occupancy, use, right to bequeath certain or all rights).

Lease Clause A condition that is specified in a lease agreement.

Lessee The tenant or renter of rights pursuant to a lease agreement.

Lessor The owner, or landlord, of the rights being rented in a lease agreement.

Sandwich Lease A lease agreement whereby the tenant rents his/her rights obtained by a lease agreement to another party.

Silent Lease Clause A lease clause that is left out of the lease.

Standard Form Lease A rhetorical title for lease agreements.

Sublessee The party that rents rights from a leasee (i.e., the tenant in a sandwich lease).

Sublessor A leasee who rents his rights to a sublessee.

Fundamental to the analysis of the market in which an existing property or a proposed development is located are the specific lease and rental terms which exist in that market area. In essence, these represent the benefits (as well as the conditions) of property ownership.

In the earlier chapters, tools and techniques were discussed which could identify and analyze the existing structure of rents for given market areas and even project such rents over future time periods. In this chapter, we will go beyond the single variable of price per spatial unit and discuss the fundamental lease clauses that can influence the nature of the development and the return on investment. To the financial analyst, the primary consideration in conducting a market analysis is the dollar rent per unit of space that is related to the existing or proposed development.

To the broker, however, the dollar price per unit of space may be of secondary concern when he takes into account the many additional conditions specified in clauses connected with the contract to lease the space. Thus, this chapter undertakes a discussion of those lease clauses that may have a significant economic impact on the property and therefore its owner and/or user, beyond the simple dollar price paid for the right to use the property in some manner for a specified length of time.

185

The legal treatment, and thus the economic impact of lease clauses, will vary from region to region and from state to state. Indeed, even within a single state different metropolitan areas will have unique leasing practices because of a variety of zoning, construction and other market factors. This chapter makes no attempt to differentiate practices geographically, but rather cites the most general treatment of a particular clause with a special emphasis on the economic impact and importance of this clause in the negotiation process.

Property Rights

Our system of ownership was inherited from the English and has its roots in the Norman Conquest. William the Conqueror was the greatest English property owner of all time. He claimed ultimate ownership of all real estate. He gave his generals, known as lords, a franchise to reap some of the benefits from estates assigned to them. In exchange, the lords pledged their loyalty to the king and part of the spoils from the land (taxes), and agreed to provide fighting men for the king's army. The lords divided their estates among underlords who, in turn, further divided the land. In each case, the overlord got a pledge of loyalty, a part of the spoils (taxes), and some fighting men. The lowest estate owner was the knight and the smallest franchise was the knight's franchise.

Changes in the English economic system have not resulted in changes in the theory that the ultimate source of ownership rights in land is the sovereign (state). This theory still prevails. It is the *state* which ultimately determines *who owns what* and *what* is ownership.

Ownership is a collection of rights relating to an object. Ownership has been described as a "Bundle of Rights." For example, if you own income property, you have the right to keep the rent as long as you pay your taxes and carry out your other obligations to the state. Within limits, you have the right to decide who will be your tenant, whether that space will remain vacant, etc. However, the state can impose taxes against the property or take it from you for a public purpose in exchange for fair compensation.

In a sense, an income property owner shares "property" rights with the state. He also shares property rights with his tenants, lessees, and his mortgagee. All of these parties can be said to have rights in the real estate.

Finally, keep in mind that a right is only a right to the extent that the state is willing to enforce it by punishing the people who might encroach on that right.

What Is a Lease?

A lease is a contract for a portion of the "Bundle of Rights" on a piece of real property for a consideration over a given period of time.

The question is often raised as to whether a lease is a lessor's lease or a lessee's lease. In general, a lease is considered to be a lessor's document for various historical and economic reasons. Originally, all property rights were in the hands of the landlord (although most subsequent laws have been for the benefit of the tenant or lessee). Consequently, the lease, as a contract for the use of a portion of the "Bundle of Rights" inherent in real estate, is transferred to the lessee for a consideration.

Another reason that leases are considered to be lessor's documents is that leases are a matter of economics. A lessee wants to pay as little as possible, and a lessor wants to receive as much as possible. Since lessees are paying for a portion of the "Bundle of Rights," it is generally considered good business to have the lessee purchase only those rights which are necessary for the economic operation of this enterprise or for the lessee's use of the property.

In some situations, a lease may be considered a lessee's document. In such cases, the lessee has paid for a larger portion of the "Bundle of Rights" than he would have paid in a lessor's lease.

The Broker's Role in Leasing

In an ordinary lease negotiation there are several parties involved. First, there are the lessor and the lessee who have the most vital interest in the lease document. Next are the attorneys representing the lessor and the lessee. The attorney's role should be to draft the document and to make sure that the agreement between the parties has been written in a legally binding fashion.

Finally, there is the broker. The broker's role in leasing is sometimes quite confusing. It should be most clearly explained before the lease negotiation commences. The broker acts as a consultant *to his client* in matters pertaining to the economic impact of the lease clauses on the value of the real estate. His function is to protect the highest value of the real estate. His duty is to make sure that the lease does not devalue the real estate, or, in any event, that the client is aware of the impact of the lease clauses on the value of the property.

Economic Impact

The broker involved in leasing must clearly understand that each and and every lease clause has an economic impact. The lease must be considered as a whole. Clauses not only have an individual impact, but they also have an impact on each other. Therefore, it is not always possible to assign a specific economic value to a particular clause. Each clause must be considered as it relates to the whole lease, as well as individually. **187**

If all the roles of the various parties are clearly defined from the beginning of the lease negotiation, and each of the persons involved understands his respective function, many of the difficulties which occur when the roles are unclear will be avoided.

A lease negotiation is a delicate matter. The broker cannot address himself to the legal matters in the lease even if he is aware of them. Under the circumstances, how then does the broker raise legal questions concerning the lease in areas which are of a sensitive nature without engaging in the practice of law?

One method which has proved useful is sometimes called the "what if" approach. When a problem arises the broker asks the question "what if." For example, the condemnation clause is left out. The broker does not say, "Where is the condemnation clause?" Instead, he asks, "What if the property were to be condemned or a portion of the property taken for public use? What if the building is destroyed by fire?" etc.

The "what if" question also gives the broker the opportunity to raise the questions involved in lease clauses which have been left out of the lease. Clauses that are left out of the lease are sometimes referred to as "silent lease clauses." Remember, all rights in the land traditionally were in the hands of the state. The state has permitted certain of the rights to go to the landlord. As the landlord made contracts with tenants, the landlord could dictate terms at will. Over time, the state has written and passed laws to protect tenants from landlords. If the lease contract does not cover a matter, the law would govern. Most of the time the law would work in favor of the tenant.

A good example of a law which works in favor of the tenant is the condemnation clause. In California, for example, the only award that can be paid by a condemning agency is the fair market value of the real estate at the time of the taking. In a leased property, there is no separate award for the lessee. In a lease, it is customary to have a clause which states that in the event of condemnation all of the proceeds from the condemnation shall go to the lessor and that the lessee shall not be entitled to anything.

If there is no condemnation clause in the lease the law states that the tenant is entitled to the present value of the difference between the contract rental and the fair market value rental for the remaining term of the lease.

Without a condemnation clause the lessor's position could be changed considerably, and this clause certainly could have a material effect upon the lessor's value.

Different Kinds of Leases

Gross Lease

In this type of lease, the lessee pays a single rental and the lessor pays all or a part of the operating expenses of the real estate, such as taxes, insurance and maintenance.

Net Lease

This is the exact opposite of the gross lease. Here, the lessee pays rent and also pays all of the expenses of the operation of the real estate. Sometimes net leases are referred to as *net* leases, *net net* leases, or *net net net* leases (occasionally called triple net leases). These variations evolve out of who paid for taxes—one net; insurance—two nets; and maintenance—three nets.

These latter terms are considered synonymous with "net" lease and their use is redundant. It has been the objective of the commercial-investment division of REALTORS NATIONAL MARKETING INSTITUTE® to establish the phraseology of either "gross lease," as described above, or "net lease." Any lease in between would be considered, at best, a modified gross lease.

Percentage Lease

A percentage lease is one in which the tenant pays a minimum rental and, as a further rental, pays a percentage of the volume of the business done on the demised premises, whichever is greater. The percentage paid differs according to the type of business.

Definition of Gross Sales Volume. In a percentage lease it is necessary to define "Gross Sales Volume" against which the percentage will be applied. It is very important that "Gross Sales" be clearly defined so that the items which are included are clearly described as well as those items or circumstances that are *excluded*. Excluded items might be exchanged merchandise, merchandise between stores, goods that are returned to the shippers or manufacturers for defects, etc.

Radius Clause. In a percentage lease it is customary to have a clause which indicates the distance from the subject property that a competing store from the same chain may be located. This is usually a distance sufficient so that two stores from the same chain are not in the same trade area. This may be done by miles or by some other definitive geographical description depending upon circumstances.

Stay Open Clause. In a percentage lease it is common practice to have a "Stay Open Clause" which states the store hours in the lease. This may be defined either as hours of the day and/or hours as customary for the particular trade area in which the demised premises are located.

Owner Not a Partner. In leases where percentage rent is a strong influence in the rental terms and particularly in leases where the entire rent may be based upon a percentage of the sales of the lessee, an important declaration is that no partnership does, in fact, exist between the lessor and the lessee. It would be extremely hard to use the provisions of the lease to force the lessee's performance if you were declared partner in his business. In these cases it should be stated in the lease that sales volume is the criterion for determining the value of the property location and is also the determinant of the amount of rental payments. Obviously, if this provision is necessary in the lease, it is equally important in the conduct of the relationship between the lessee and the lessor in order to substantiate the fact that they are not in the partnership.

All of these clauses have a definite economic impact on the real estate. Imagine a lease with a percentage rent, where one of these clauses were missing from the lease.

Graduated Lease

In this lease, the rent is adjusted on some regular basis, either annually or every two or three years, etc. For example, the lessee may start out with a lease for a store at $100 per month; the second year it may be $105 per month; and then the third year, $110 per month; and so on.

Adjusted Lease

An adjustment might be based on some index, the most common being the Wholesale Price Index or the Retail Price Index (published by the Department of Commerce), depending upon the nature of the business. The adjustments are usually made not less than annually and not more than every five years.

Ground Lease

In this situation, the lessee pays rent for the ground and usually pays all taxes, maintenance, etc. He improves the property at his own expense and uses the ground for whatever purposes are permitted in the lease.

Standard Form Leases

Most leases start out with the title *Standard Form Lease*. As a practical matter, however, there is no such thing as a "standard form lease." This language is generally used to make the parties feel more comfortable. It is doubtful whether all persons who have the statement, *Standard Form Lease*, on their leases use the same lease form.

Determining the Rental

In a lease negotiation, first the premises to be leased are described, and the rental is determined, as well as the term.

In a negotiation, there are two points of view: the lessor's point of view and the lessee's. From the lessor's point of view, the setting of the rental is all of the costs involved in a project. These costs would include, but are not limited to, the following: the *value* of the land, building contract costs, site work, soil tests, architectural and engineering fees, insurance during the course of construction, finance charges, brokers' commissions, and all other costs incidental to the construction of the building.

An oversimplified view of this might be that all of the costs involved in taking the property from its present state to its rentable state are considered as costs. In existing property, the costs involved are generally the value placed on the present improvements plus any costs of bringing the improvements to a rentable condition.

From the lessee's point of view, rental is an entirely different matter. A lessee looks at the rental from the standpoint of what comparable space is being rented for in the same general area. In the case of commercial property where location is so important, rental is based on the volume that a merchant lessee can expect to do. All rent in a commercial property is considered as a percentage of the volume, even in the case of a nonpercentage lease. The applicable percentage is generally available from any percentage lease book.

The Urban Land Institute publishes a book called *Dollars and Cents of Shopping Centers*. This book includes volumes and the percentages generally attributed to these volumes, depending upon the type of business. Examples of the type of information available from that publication are shown in Tables 1 and 2. These examples only scratch the surface of the wealth of information available, however, and perusal of the source is strongly urged.

State Laws

Obviously laws vary from state to state. An attorney should be consulted in the various states for the appropriate laws and the ways they might apply to the particular situations mentioned. As an example, some states have a law which indicates that unless there is a holdover clause in the lease and a tenant remains on the demised premises after the expiration of the lease, then the lease term is automatically renewed unless the lease specifically states the contrary. In many states, there is no such stipulation. This is just one example of how state laws may vary.

Dates

In a lease it becomes obvious that there are a number of dates that are specifically required, each of which has a different significance. Generally, the first date has to do with the day on which the lease was first drawn. The second will generally note the commencement date of the lease term. The third may be the termination date of the lease term.

The lease term date and the date that rental commences are not necessarily the same. For example, in a retail store building, a period of time is usually allowed for the tenant to take possession prior to the commencement of the lease term itself, to fixturize and stock the store prior to opening. Generally, this is covered in a paragraph which will indicate that all of the terms and conditions of the lease are in full force and effect except rent: "Rent will commence on _____ (date) and end on _____ (date). The total rental shall be as follows . . ." Then the total rental is given and divided up according to the way the rental is to be paid.

Table 1   Tenants Most Frequently Found in Community Shopping Centers

Tenant Classification	Rank	Median GLA	Median Sales Volume per-square-foot of GLA	Median Total Rent per-square-foot of GLA
Food and Food Service				
Supermarket	2	20,519	$135.22	$1.74
Restaurant without liquor	17	2,350	64.09	4.17
Restaurant with liquor	20	2,522	60.82	3.00
General Merchandise				
Junior department store	6	30,000	51.97	1.64
Variety store	13	18,000	33.67	1.51
Clothing & Shoes				
Ladies specialty	14	1,617	62.08	3.90
Ladies ready-to-wear	1	2,940	61.83	3.68
Menswear	7	3,000	65.55	3.87
Family shoe	5	3,200	52.37	3.00
Dry Goods				
Yard goods	11	3,767	43.19	3.03
Furniture				
Radio, TV, hi-fi	19	2,000	67.45	3.02
Other Retail				
Drugs	8	8,530	78.95	2.59
Jewelry	12	1,806	77.93	4.38
Cards and gifts	10	2,000	48.90	3.71
Financial				
Bank	16	2,863	—	3.35
Insurance	18	650	—	4.06
Other Offices				
Medical and dental	3	800	—	4.47
Services				
Beauty shop	4	1,200	50.54	3.77
Barber shop	9	677	43.70	3.62
Cleaners and dyers	15	1,980	31.31	2.75

Source: Urban Land Institute, *Dollars and Cents of Shopping Centers:* 1975, p. 122.

Table 2 Community Shopping Centers' Composition by Tenant Classification

Tenant Group	Percent GLA	Percent Sales	Percent Total Charges	Percent Tenants
Food	15.7	33.2	31.1	10.4
Food Service	3.7	3.8	6.0	8.5
General merchandise	35.8	30.1	27.0	9.9
Clothing and shoes	7.8	7.6	10.6	9.6
Dry goods	3.0	2.0	3.6	6.6
Furniture	3.7	3.6	3.6	6.9
Other retail	14.5	15.5	18.2	10.8
Financial	2.5	0	3.6	9.2
Offices	2.2	0	3.0	6.0
Services	3.6	1.8	5.0	10.1
Other	4.3	2.4	6.3	5.8
Vacant space	3.3	0	0	6.2
TOTAL	100.0	100.0	100.0	100.0

Source: Urban Land Institute, *Dollars and Cents of Shopping Centers:* 1975, p. 298.

In summary, various dates are required in a lease: the date the lease is drawn; the date of possession; the date the lease commences; the date rent commences; and the date of the termination of the lease. Finally, at the end of the lease, there is the date which indicates when the lease was executed by the parties.

Legal Description (Lessor and Lessee)

The next section of the lease is a full description of the lessor and the lessee. It is necessary to know the actual lessor and lessee of the property and whether the lessor or lessee is a corporation, partnership, or an individual. In the case of a corporation or partnership, it is advisable to have an authorization from the corporation or a resolution indicating that the party who signed the lease has the authority to sign it.

Demised Premises Description

The property to be leased is commonly referred to as the "Demised Premises." It is very important to have a full description of the demised premises. This is especially true in multi-tenanted buildings. In consideration of liability and responsibility, the property must be clearly defined with respect to the physical part of the building where the liability and responsibility shall rest for the lessor and the lessee.

Term and Possession

The term of the lease notes the commencement date and the termination date. The economic impact of this particular paragraph is obvious since **193** the time of possession of the premises indicates the period in which rent will be applied. As observed in the section on dates (above), however, possession of the premises and rental term may differ.

Rental

In a rental clause, the total amount of the rent to be paid during the lease term is generally provided, as well as the method by which the rent will be paid. For example, "the total rental shall be 'X' thousand dollars during the term of the lease and shall be paid as follows: so much payable in advance and then so much on the first day of each and every successive month until the total rental shall have been paid." This particular paragraph has the most obvious economic impact on the lessor and the lessee.

Use of the Premises

The use of the premises clause deals with the nature and type of activity which may take place upon the premises. This is of particular concern in multi-tenanted buildings and in shopping centers. For example, if the lessor had a neighborhood shopping center and was depending upon a supermarket as his major attraction, the use clause should be restricted to a supermarket. If, some years hence, the supermarket decided to sublet (an example of clauses depending upon each other for their total economic impact), and the sublessee were not restricted to a supermarket, consider the economic impact on the shopping center. The whole economic structure of the shopping center could be destroyed.

Without the restriction on use, the lessor would find it difficult to protect the tenant mix and the economics of the shopping center. This clause is interrelated not only to the subletting clause and assignments clause, but also to other tenancies within the same structure or shopping center.

Acceptance and Surrender of the Premises

Acceptance and surrender deals with the way the premises are to be accepted upon the commencement of the lease term. It is based on the fact that the premises are assumed to be in a rentable condition when the tenant takes possession. The *surrender* of the premises deals with the fact that, when the premises are returned to the lessor, the lessor will get them in the same condition as they were when accepted by the lessee, less ordinary wear and tear. The economics here deal with the problem of the cost of preparing the premises for a new tenant. If the property were in a state of disrepair, the lessor's costs would be greatly increased and his interest in the property devalued.

Repair of the Premises During Term of the Lease

Obviously there is a great economic impact on the real estate if the lessor must make all the repairs for the interior as well as the exterior of the building. This certainly has an effect on the net income. If the tenant has to take care of the interior and the lessor takes care of the exterior (which would be limited to the roof and the exterior walls), the economic impact on the lessor is limited. The nature and the kinds of repairs and the responsibility for making such repairs, of course, are negotiable. It is very important in any lease to indicate clearly who is responsible for the repair of what.

Alterations

The difference between an alteration and a repair should be clearly defined. Generally speaking, a repair is the maintenance of something that was in existence at the time of the acceptance of the leased premises; whereas an alteration is a material change either in the interior or the exterior of the structure. An alteration deals with the structural integrity of the building.

Liens

Any time a lessee is permitted to make an alteration or repair on the premises, the lessee should first give notice to the lessor as to the nature and types of repairs or alterations and must obtain the permission of the lessor in writing to make such alteration or repair. This procedure is necessary in order to solve two problems: one is that the lessor wants to know the nature of alterations; secondly, the lessor wants an opportunity to file a notice of non-responsibility so that, in the event that the bill is not paid for the repair or the alteration, all contractors are on notice that the lessee, not the lessor, is responsible for payment of the bills. Unless a notice is legally posted, the responsibility ultimately becomes the lessor's. The economic impact of this arrangement is obvious.

Utilities

It is normal for the lessee to pay all of the utilities. These include water, electricity, heating, garbage pick-up, etc. However, depending upon the nature of the tenancy, some of these services may be provided by the lessor. In any event, any services or utilities which are provided by the lessor will obviously be reflected in the rental paid by the lessee.

At the present time, energy costs particularly are becoming items of concern. There is some thought to be given to utility stop clauses. This would mean that if the basic utility bill is paid by the lessor, any increase in the cost of utilities over the base period would be paid for by the lessee. This applies, of course, in cases where the lessor is providing some of the utilities. Such clauses would be especially applicable in multi-tenanted buildings, such as office buildings, where there are common utilities and the lessor pays the utility costs.

Entry and Inspection

"Entry and Inspection" gives the lessor the right to enter the premises at reasonable times to inspect the property in order to ensure that the terms and conditions of the lease are being carried out. It also allows the lessor (under certain circumstances) to make repairs that are deemed necessary for the proper maintenance of the property. During the last 60 days, the lease usually permits the lessor to put suitable "For Lease" or "To Let" signs on the premises in a manner which does not disturb the basic business of the lessee.

If the lessor did not have the right to enter and inspect the premises, the building could be allowed to deteriorate to a point where the economics of putting the building back into its original shape, notwithstanding the fact that this may be the lessee's responsibility, would become prohibitive. The lessor wants the right to protect his property during the term of the lease. He cannot afford to wait until the end of the lease to become aware of the fact that the property has been run down, misused or abused. This is especially true when the lessee is not a high credit tenant or one who would be financially unable to meet the responsibility of putting the property in its proper condition at the end of the lease term.

Assignment and Subletting

Assignment means that all rights, title and interest in the lease or the lessee's position are assigned to another party and that the primary lessee has no further responsibility. Subletting means that the tenant subleases the premises but still has the primary responsibility to see that the terms and conditions of the lease are carried out in accordance with the original lease.

In both instances, it is acceptable practice to have the lessor agree to any assignment or subletting; any assignment or subletting cannot take place without his permission. This is especially important when it comes to the actual use of the premises. A landlord generally would not allow any assignment or subletting which would materially change the nature of business carried on within the demised premises. In the case of assignment, the credit of the assignee would also be very important.

Hold Harmless Clause

The "hold harmless clause," in effect, says that the lessor is not responsible for damages and/or losses which occur on or near the leased property.

196

This is a financial responsibility. However, the lessor may have an ordinary tenant who has practically no net worth or very limited net worth. The lessee may cause some rather extensive damage, and, although he has agreed to hold the lessor harmless, he may not be financially able to do so. Consequently, a hold harmless clause is no better than the financial responsibility of the one who is holding one harmless. (See insurance clause below.)

Insurance Clause (Fire and Liability)

This clause determines the responsibility for carrying liability insurance. Because of the nature of recent awards, it is quite necessary to have adequate liability insurance with very high limits. It should be pointed out that, as the limits go up, the cost per $1,000 of insurance drops. Therefore, the last limits above minimum limits are generally inexpensive. As indicated, the lessee shall hold the lessor harmless, and will, in addition, carry adequate liability insurance.

Uninsurable Losses

In California there are earthquake problems; other areas are particularly susceptible to mud slides, floods, etc. In some places, insurance for these losses is either prohibitive or unavailable. This is a special consideration in a net lease. It may be stated in a net lease that the tenant will carry insurance, pay all taxes, and all other expenses incidental to the proper care and maintenance of the demised premises. The question concerning whose responsibility it is for replacing the structure in the event of an *uninsurable* loss demonstrates the economic impact of this clause.

Waiver of Subrogation

Subrogation means "to stand in place of." It is common practice to have a mutual waiver of subrogation. This, in effect, says that each party agrees that the insurance will cover the losses as described, and each agrees not to sign an agreement with their respective insurance companies permitting the insurance company to seek redress from the other party.

There should be no additional charge for a "waiver of subrogation" clause. Most insurance policies state that, if there is an agreement waiving subrogation, they will respect that agreement. The theory behind this is that insurance premiums are developed on the basis of expected losses. If the insurance company received a premium for the exposure of the possible loss, then they should not be able to go back after the party causing the loss and collect again. This, in effect, is receiving the premium twice.

From the lessor's point of view, he may have a very good, strong, local tenant who accidentally causes a loss (for instance, a fire). If the insurance **197** company had the right to go back and collect the loss from the tenant even after the insurance was paid, this could obviously bankrupt an otherwise good tenant. This would serve no useful purpose for either the lessor or the lessee.

Abatement of Rent During Repair Period

From the lessor's point of view, this is generally covered by income rental insurance. Such insurance pays the rent that the lessor would have received during that period in which the building is being reconstructed or the damage repaired from an insurable loss. This type of insurance may be purchased by either the lessor or lessee depending upon the terms and conditions of the lease.

The Destruction and Renewal Clause

This clause is interwoven with the insurance clause and presents the following problems: (1) the total destruction of the premises; (2) a partial loss and the determination of how much damage constitutes a partial or a total loss; (3) determination of who is responsible for reconstructing the premises. These determinations depend on the nature and type of the building involved.

Normally, any repair which can take place within a short period of time (for instance, 60 days) would obligate the repairs to be made. Anything over 60 days could become an option of the lessor as to whether or not to put the building back into its original condition. If the lessor does not wish to put the building into its original condition, this decision should be made within 30 days from the time of destruction. Time limits mentioned above are merely suggestions, depending on the nature of the building and the circumstances involved.

Another problem concerns what constitutes total destruction or partial destruction. Sometimes a building may not be completely demolished but is demolished to the point where it is economically infeasible to replace it in its original condition. Or, from the lessee's point of view, the lease has such a short term remaining that it would not be desirable to rebuild the property for this particular lessee, unless the lease is to be renewed or extended to make the improvements worthwhile and economical.

There should be a consideration in this paragraph of the possibility that the lessor may have a single purpose building or a building which does not conform to current zoning regulations. There should be some provision in the lease which indicates that, in order for the building to be reconstructed, the lessor will be allowed to obtain all the necessary permits from government authorities in order to put the building back into its

original condition.

Some buildings are prohibited by the local government agency or zoning board from being put back into their original condition because of what is termed a "misplaced improvement;" i.e., the buildings do not conform to the present zoning laws in their areas. In this case, if the building cannot be replaced, the lease should be terminated, with no liability or claims for damages upon either party.

Taxes

There are two types of taxes: real estate taxes and personal property taxes. The problem here is to determine who is going to pay which taxes.

It is customary, particularly in a gross lease, to have the lessor pay the real estate taxes and the tenant pay all personal property taxes. There are many variations on the real estate tax arrangements, however. There are such things as tax stops, wherein the lessor pays the base real estate tax (that is, the taxes for the first year of the lease), and then any increase in taxes over and above the base year are paid for by the lessee. In a multi-tenanted building, the increase portion of the taxes that are paid by the lessee are prorated, depending upon the square footage occupied by the lessee as it relates to the total building.

The other section in the lease concerning taxes has to do with how the taxes are to be paid, if they are to be paid by someone other than the lessor. As far as the tax collector is concerned, it is the responsibility of the lessor to pay the taxes or to see that they are paid.

Also included under taxes are any liens and/or assessments which are assessed upon the real property by governmental authorities after the commencement date of the lease; for example, street improvements, lighting assessments, sewer assessments, etc. There should be a provision in the lease for lessee's participation in assessments after the commencement date of the lease. If they have been assessed prior to the commencement date, they would probably be considered part of the taxes.

Default

There are essentially two types of defaults: One is a money default, the second is a violation of other terms and conditions of the lease, such as damage to the premises, subletting the premises when it is prohibited, etc.

It is customary to have money defaults remedied in a short time. Other defaults must have a time allotment sufficient to take care of the nature of the default. For example, damage to a building might take two to four weeks to cure, as opposed to a money default, which might be corrected in a matter of hours.

In order for a default provision to be activated, the following processes are necessary:

1. The party that is in default must be notified by the other party of the fact that there is a default. Such notice must be delivered as per the notice agreement in the lease.

2. After the notice of default has been given, sufficient time must elapse for the defaulting party to correct (cure) it. If the default has not been corrected during the appropriate time period as indicated in the lease, the lease is in default and the lessor or the lessee (as the case may be) should proceed with the appropriate legal action. The economic impact of this clause is extremely important. For example, if the tenant is in default for any reason and the lessor is unable to remedy the situation or remove the tenant from the premises, a considerable economic hardship on the lessor can occur.

Abandonment

The lessee generally agrees not to abandon or vacate the premises during the term of the lease. The problem here is to define abandonment. In retail commercial property, abandonment is defined in terms of the dollar amount of merchandise that must be available in the store and/or the store hours during which the store must remain open.

This is especially essential in a percentage lease. If there is not enough merchandise in the store and the store does not remain open during reasonable hours, it would be impossible for the lessee to generate enough volume of business to generate a percentage rent.

Abandonment of a building generally increases the insurance rate due to increased exposure to vandalism and malicious mischief. Also, empty stores do not bring in foot traffic to augment the adjacent stores in a multi-tenanted building. This works an economic hardship on the lessor.

In the event that abandonment does take place, there must be a provision for removing the fixtures and equipment of the lessee, re-entry and possession by the lessor, and re-renting of the premises. The default and notice provisions of the lease must be followed, and due process of the law must be observed in all cases.

Costs of Suit

Normally, the costs of any litigation that is involved in the adjudication of any clause or paragraph in the lease will be paid by the party who loses the suit. The prevailing party will have all of his costs paid for by the person losing the suit.

Holding Over

The tenant holding the premises beyond the term of the lease theoretically controls two very important factors. The first is that the rent must be determined during the holdover period. The second is that it must be made clear that, if there is a holdover, all the terms and conditions of the lease are still in full force and effect even if the holdover is on a month-to-month basis.

Should problems occur when the agreement was no longer in effect, the operation of law would prevail—possibly to the detriment of the lessor. It is very necessary to have all the terms and conditions still in effect, even though the term of the lease is on a month-to-month basis.

Sale of the Premises

Upon sale of the premises, the lessor is released from any further liability. The liability then transfers to the new lessor who is the buyer of the property.

Appointment of Receiver: Lessee Bankruptcy

If a receiver is appointed or if the lessee is bankrupt, then the receiver takes possession of the personal property of the lessee used in the conduct of his (the lessee's) business. Upon the lessor's option, the lease may be cancelled. If a bankrupt tenant or a tenant under a reorganization is unable to pay the rent, this has an obvious economic impact. There must be a method specified in the lease whereby, if a receiver is appointed, the lessor may repossess the demised premises.

Lessor's Bankruptcy

If the lessor is declared bankrupt and/or the real estate goes into foreclosure, the lessee is subject to having his lease cancelled depending upon the subordination clause in the particular lease agreement. In our particular example the subordination clause indicates the lessee agrees that the lease under the demised premises will be subordinate to any mortgage presently on the property and for any future mortgage put on the property. In this event the lease would be subject to being cancelled in the event of foreclosure and/or bankruptcy.

It is possible to have the tenant go bankrupt and the property not go into foreclosure. In this event the lease would still be valid. Therefore, it is incumbent upon the lessee to know the financial circumstances of the lessor in order to make a determination as to whether the lessor is of substantial financial capacity so that the threat of bankruptcy and/or foreclosure is not obvious. This is especially true if the lessee is planning to spend a great deal of money improving his premises. According to the lease, typically all the improvements would become part of the real estate and if the lessor were going into bankruptcy or the property was threatened with foreclosure there is the possibility that all this money might be lost by the lessee.

Condemnation

A condemnation clause has two problems: a partial taking or a total taking. Specific interpretations will vary from state to state, and thus special care must be taken to be aware of the provisions applicable in the state where the property is located. For example, under California law, if there is a total taking or a partial taking, there can only be one award. That award is the fair market value of the real estate taken. It is customary that the lessee receive no part of the award unless a separate award is made for the lessee's interest. The total award should go to the lessor. If there is no condemnation clause in the lease, then the leasehold value can be taken off the top and the lessor would receive only what was left over.

In a partial taking, the problem is whether the property is still viable from the lessee's point of view. This problem depends upon the nature of the building. For example, in a commercial property, the condemning agency takes the parking lot. Is the property still viable for the conduct of the business? On the other hand, a portion of the building, such as a backend or a storeroom, is taken and the sales area is not disturbed. How does this affect the business? There must be some formula for determining whether or not the property is viable from the lessee's standpoint.

The lessor is primarily interested in obtaining the total award. In the event that the property is still viable from the lessee's point of view, however, the rent must be reduced in order to cover the amount of property that has been taken and the reduced ability to conduct the lessee's business in the demised premises.

Senior Lease

The senior lease is the primary lease upon the demised premises (e.g., ground leases or master leases). In a building which is sublet, there must be a distinguishing characteristic between the senior lease and the junior lease (sublease). There should be a statement clarifying that the junior lease must not be in conflict with the senior or master lease. Also, upon the termination of the senior lease, it is necessary to have the senior lessee responsible for removing any sublessees or sub-tenants, at the option of the lessor, from the demised premises.

Subordination

Subordination is the ordering of priorities. In a lease contract, it is customary to have the lease subordinate to any mortgages presently on the property or any mortgages that are put on the property in the future.

This particular clause is usually required by lending institutions which desire their mortgage to be superior to any other liens on the property.

Insofar as the lease would be considered a lien, the lenders generally require a subordination of any leases. Then, in the event of foreclosure, the lender, in effect, has the option of keeping or terminating the lease. This is extremely important to a lessor who expects to refinance the property at some future time and the lease term has not expired. It may be impossible to get financing without this clause.

Signs

There are two kinds of signs: advertising signs, which are on the walls and sometimes on the roofs of the buildings and are not related to any tenancy on the property; and the signs of a lessee doing business within the demised premises.

Roof and wall signs can be revenue producers. The lessor should reserve the sign rights or be compensated by the lessee. In a multi-tenanted building, there is the problem of multiple signs. For example, signs should not block another tenant's sign nor obstruct the windows above. Signs in windows should be controlled.

Surrender and Termination of the Lease

With respect to the manner in which the lease is surrendered to the lessor, there must be notice of the surrender of the lease by the lessee to the lessor. In addition, the lessor should inspect the property and legally accept the premises, and this procedure should be in writing. It is not sufficient to have the lessee simply drop off the keys. As mentioned previously, it is necessary for the property to be returned to the lessor in its original condition less normal wear and tear.

Notices

The two elements involved in notices are how the notice is delivered and what constitutes receipt of notice. Notices may be delivered personally; by mail, return receipt requested; and/or tacked on the door of the premises. The second major element is the time involved in each type of delivery. For example, if communication is by mail, the notice is not officially communicated until 48 hours after postmarking. Personal delivery might be within 24 hours of personal service.

Unless the notices are properly received, none of the default provisions or any of the other provisions which require notice can come into effect. This could cause a great economic hardship, especially in unlawful detainer actions. The court would require proof that the party or defendant had been properly notified.

Cumulative Remedies Nonwaiver

If there has been a breach of the lease and the lessor has let it go by once, this does not establish the precedent for changing the original intent of the parties or modifying the lease. If, for example, the rent was due on the first of the month, and the landlord accepted the rent on the fifteenth of the month for several months running, this does not mean that the landlord must continue to accept the rent on the fifteenth. He still has the right to collect it on the first of the month as stated in the lease, even though there was a period where the lessor did permit this to happen once or twice.

Signature of the Lease

As indicated in the beginning of this section, the signatures of the lessee and the lessor must be shown to be valid. If the lessee is a corporation, there should be a corporation resolution authorizing the party signing the lease to do so. If the lease or a short form of the lease is to be recorded, it would be necessary to have the signatures notarized. Notarization of the signatures does not necessarily mean that the parties signing the lease have the authority to do so, however; consequently, it is very important to have a corporate resolution or other proof of validity, as the case may be.

Finally, the lessor sometimes requires guarantees under signatures. If this is the case, the guarantor's signature, his financial statement, etc., should be handled in approximately the same way as that of the original lessee. The guarantor should have a financial statement sufficient to guarantee the lease and also to guarantee that the party signing the lease is, in fact, authorized to do so.

Additional Lease Clauses

Renewal Options

A renewal option is a right given to the lessee by the lessor to extend the period of time that the lease covers, for one or more additional periods as agreed. This right has considerable economic effect on both parties. It gives the lessee the right to continue the use of the premises under the existing terms. This could be extremely favorable under the conditions that might exist when the original lease term expires. By the same token, it restricts the lessor from planning any use of the property until such time as the lessee has determined whether or not he will exercise the option. Since this right is strictly to the lessee's benefit, many lessors refuse to grant such privilege, and it is normally not included in a standard form contract.

Merchants Association

Where a merchants association is formed for the purposes of jointly paying common expenses and/or providing for common advertising and promotional efforts, it is customary to include a provision in the lease which requires that each lessee be and remain a member of the merchants association in good standing. This is important because the lease often is the only enforcement vehicle ensuring that merchants association fees and charges are paid. The extent to which the merchants association pays normal operating expenses of the property can have a significant effect upon the net income of the property.

Recording the Lease

It is becoming a more common practice to record the entire lease, or a short form of the lease. A lease is a transfer of property rights, and the lessee may want to have his rights in the property made a part of the public record. If this is the case and is provided for in the lease, there also should be an accompanying responsibility on the part of the lessee to execute a reconveyance of some type at the termination of the lease.

A recorded lease is considered to be an encumbrance upon the property and, if not released or reconveyed, could have considerable detrimental effects on the lessor, particularly in the case of presenting it free and clear of all encumbrances to a new lender.

Commissions on Leasing

A lease conveys rights to property and spells out each party's responsibilities in the relationship of lessor and lessee. It stands to reason that, if commissions are to be paid for the broker's efforts in the leasing process, the recitation in the lease of the responsibility to pay the broker and how much will be paid should be specified as clearly as are the responsibilities for any of the other costs which have been outlined in the balance of the lease. This responsibility to the broker for his commission is therefore formalized if the rights of either the lessee or the lessor are transferred or assigned. This provision should also cover the matters of voluntary termination or the sale of the property by the lessor to the lessee.

Security Deposits

In some leases security deposits are required by the lessor for the faithful performance of the contract. This is usually the case when there is a small local tenant of no great financial strength. In this situation the security deposit can be handled in such a manner that it is held until such time as the lease has been performed and therefore the security deposit is returned to the lessee. In this case the security deposit would not be taxable.

If the security deposit is paid to the lessor and is applied to the last month's rent or is under the full control of the lessor, then the security deposit would be taxable upon receipt. Sometimes security deposits can be rather substantial sums; therefore the advice of a tax counsel would be necessary so that it could be handled presumably in a non-taxable manner. **205**

Guarantee

In some leases, especially with weaker tenants, a guarantee is required by the lessor. This guarantee means that if the primary lessee goes into default the guarantor would take over and would agree to guarantee the rent. This sometimes happens in major corporations where the corporation guarantees the lease for some smaller corporation which is controlled by the main corporation. These can become very important when one is trying to finance a property by getting the proper guarantees. An ordinary lease can be turned into a triple A tenant lease with the proper guarantees.

There should be insurance available to pay the rent in the event of default by a lessee. This insurance permits a weak tenant to become a financially strong tenant from a lessor's point of view. Such an arrangement can appreciably enhance the value of the real estate.

Section IV

Case Studies

This section contains four case studies:

1. A downtown specialty market study

2. A broad based market study which includes both housing and retail components

3. An office space study.

4. A study of development potential for a convenience food store.

These studies are included to serve as illustrations of the overall methodology as well as the tools and technology described in this text. In each case, it is the process of analysis and not the final conclusions that are important.

Chapter 11

Downtown Specialty Shopping Center

11

Introduction

In the following case, a family corporation had made a decision to sell all of its real estate investment holdings. One of the holdings consisted of three commercial buildings which included a J. C. Penney's store as a tenant. A commercial broker was employed by the corporation to find a buyer for the property. Two other (marginal) tenants were located in the three commercial buildings. All three tenants (including the Penney's store) were on leases which had two to four years remaining or an average of three years per unit.

The general condition of the neighborhood in which the commercial properties were located was run down. Those buildings in closest proximity to the subject properties were very old and occupied by marginal tenants. Across the street, however, there was some indication of revitalization of the general area with some construction of new institutional, commercial and office space. New development that had already taken place included a bank building with office space and a chain drug retail outlet. In front of this new construction was a park-like mall which served as a major transfer point for commercial transportation. In addition to being very accessible to commercial transportation, the subject site was strategically located between two major highways.

The problem posed to the broker was what kind or type of buyer would be interested in acquiring the commercial properties in light of the fact that they were on relatively short-term leases and also in a declining neighborhood. The Penney's store, for example, had approximately 18,000 square feet of commercial space on two floors, plus a mezzanine. Along with the obvious lack of appropriate space, sales volume was declining substantially for Penney's as well as the more marginal tenants. Generally, there was a rather bleak future for these properties in their current conditions, particularly in light of the fact that the majority of commercial tenants were leaving the area at the expiration of their respective leases due to lack of space and also due to a lack of convenient parking. There was some parking provided by the city for institutional buildings, but these parking facilities were of generally no benefit to the subject property.

It was the decision of the commercial broker that the property, in its present condition, was not a true investment property because cash flows were of an extremely short-term nature and there was little possibility of re-renting the buildings to similar tenants. The basic problem then for the commercial broker was to determine what type of use or uses these properties could be put to at the end of the lease term.

In his consideration of possible use or uses, the broker noticed that signs in the area indicated that it was a revitalization area; he contacted the Community Development Office. He found that the Community Development Office had been acquiring property in the area for redevelopment into a downtown commercial project with the idea of reselling sites to those who might be interested in them for retail development. The broker then concerned himself with the ultimate desirable type of project that could "successfully" be undertaken within the area without the constraints of the existing buildings and lots. Total space available in the downtown area was approximately 90,000 square feet. Upon investigation it was found that the Community Development Office was very favorable towards some type of shopping center development.

The commercial broker conducted a preliminary economic analysis of the area which indicated a rather substantial demand for stores. A cursory study using the *Survey of Buying Power* indicated that for every $3 in purchasing power for sales of the kinds of goods and services contemplated, there was only $1 currently being spent in the area. It was therefore indicated that there was substantial opportunity for successful development of a shopping center within this particular location.

The next question was to determine who would be the most likely buyer. It was determined that it would be a developer, and the development would be done in conjunction with the renewal effort currently being carried out by the city and also in conjunction with other property owners within the area who were interested in the possibility of a joint venture. It was also determined that because of the preliminary demand/supply analysis that had been carried out, that the development should be multi-storied. The basis for the sale was on the present income and expense even though of short-term duration. This was in recognition of the fact that the value of the property based upon the proposed project was significantly greater than the value based upon the remaining short-term leases.

The terms of the sale were $100,000 down with the seller to carry back an interest-only note at 8 percent due in five years. There was a clause in the note that indicated that if the property was transferred to any partnership or other entity in which the original buyer had an interest, that the note was not due or payable within the five-year period. If the property were sold without the original buyer having any continuing interest then the entire note became due and payable. This was done to ensure that the original developer develop the property or have the property developed by some responsible party. The developer anticipated the need for a joint venture with a financial partner as well as other partners. Therefore, the note allowed for transfers of this type but not for the original developer to sell out his interests completely.

Site and Access

The site of the proposed special retail shopping center is the two-block square area in the redevelopment area of a midwestern Central Business District (CBD). The area is bounded on the east by State Street, on the north by Randolph Street, on the south by Lincoln Avenue and on the west by Warren Avenue. The proposed retail development would encompass all of the property within these boundaries with the exception of the post office building and the adjacent parking lot located at the southeast corner of the intersection of State Street and Randolph Street. The total ground area involved is approximately 4.4 acres.

The site is on the northern perimeter of the downtown retail shopping area. The three blocks north of the site and south of Sampson Boulevard are primarily church and school areas. The retail and commercial areas of the downtown extend for one block to the east. Beyond, there is a park and residential area. On the north to Dillon Street are parking and commercial facilities and beyond lie residential areas. To the west the retail section continues for another block to Ross Avenue. Fourteenth Street is primarily a commercial shopping strip. Two blocks west of the site between 14th Street and Lincoln Avenue is a small specialty shopping center known as Harrison Center.

Regional freeway and local access to the site area is excellent, although 14th Street, the major east-west thoroughfare which runs tangent to the site, is sometimes congested in the site vicinity. The Kennedy Freeway (I-78) runs east and west approximately one mile south of the site and there is excellent access from this freeway via Milford Avenue, which has been widened west of I-78 to Harnett Avenue. Center Street which is the extension of State Street south of 14th Street is planned for widening shortly after the proposed shopping center opening. This would facilitate access from I-78 to the project area.

Access from Route 27 is approximately one and one-half miles to the north of the site via the State Street interchange.

Transit buses run both east and west along Route 27 and also have feeder lines from the residential areas east and southwest of downtown.

Trade Area Population Income and Employment Characteristics

In view of the specialized nature of the proposed downtown retail redevelopment project, a detailed examination of middle-to higher income

211

residential patterns, population demographics, growth patterns, and competitive facilities was undertaken in order to analyze the trade area which would be tributary to the project. The retail competitive situation will be discussed in later sections of this analysis.

The derivation of the trade area boundaries are based principally on income and proximity considerations.

Trade Area Population

The primary trade area encompasses all of the city and extends west as far as state Route 83. The southern boundary of the trade area is defined by a line running east and west approximately along the crest of Lamont Boulevard carried west to the intersection of Route 83 and I-78. The eastern border is an irregular line extending as far east as the western end of the Lawrence Freeway, then cutting west and then north to include the areas west of 98th Street. The northern border is defined by the lake shore extending from the airport to the boundary line of the trade area. Secondary Zone "A" to the east is a narrow strip as far east as Route 24, south to Lamont Boulevard and on the north Kennedy Boulevard. Secondary Zone "B" circumscribes the cities of Westmont and Carlton and that portion of the city of Richmond west to Wilson Avenue. All portions of the secondary trade area zones are within 20 minutes driving time of the site. Though relatively close to the site, areas east of 98th Street and north of Kennedy Boulevard were not included within the site trade area because of their more modest income character.

Population statistics for the trade area are displayed in Table 1. Information used in estimating current population and projecting future population within the trade area zones was provided by the agencies listed at the bottom of the table. Population growth has been slow (less than 1 percent per year) during the first half of this decade, because of the limited amount of developable land, zoning regulation and general economic conditions. It is expected that the rate of population growth will increase slightly from this level during the remainder of this decade and into the 1980s.

The only major housing development currently planned for the trade area is an 1,800 unit single, and multi-family development to be built on the ridge between Knollwood Hospital and Hazelton College. This development would be in four phases starting in 1976 for completion around 1983.

The total trade area included 293,231 people in 1970, approximately one-third of whom were living within the primary trade area. The current population estimate for the total trade area is 307,000. It is estimated that a total of 315,700 people will live in the trade area by 1978, the anticipated first full year of operation of the proposed downtown shopping center. By 1983, the total trade area will encompass 333,700 people, 30 percent of whom are anticipated to reside in the primary trade area. The longer range projections for 1988 and 1998 for the total trade area population are 356,800 and 394,600, respectively.

Table 1 Downtown Shopping Center Trade Area Historical and Projected Total Population (1970–1998)

	1970	1975	1978	1983	Long Range 1988	Long Range 1998
Primary Trade Area	95,247	98,100	99,900	101,700	104,200	109,400
Secondary Zone "A"	92,484	97,100	100,000	107,500	115,000	127,200
Secondary Zone "B"	105,500	111,800	115,800	124,500	137,000	158,000
Total Trade Area	293,231	307,000	315,700	333,700	356,800	394,600

Sources: "Population Estimates for State Cities," May 31, 1974, Population Research Unit, State Department of Finance, County Planning Commission, City Planning Department. "Projections of the Region's Future," September 1974, Association of Area Governments.

Trade Area Higher Income Population

Since higher income persons are expected to provide the great bulk of customer support for the proposed center, it is necessary to focus on and quantify this segment of the trade area's total population. This question cannot be approached without first offering a comprehensive and workable definition of higher income population.

Because of the rapid year-to-year rise of incomes over the past decade or so, including the effects of inflation as well as gains of real purchasing power, any income level establishing a floor for inclusion in this category must be understood to be a parameter for defining real purchasing power at a given point in time. Based on experience in examining areas similar to this area, the parameter for determination of "higher income population." which best defines this segment, is members of families who in 1969 had family incomes of $10,000 or more, as indicated in the 1970 U.S. Census of Population.[1] Based upon inflationary trends, this income level equates to a current level approximating $15,000 annually. There is no reason to believe that most of these families, who because of inflation have passed a specific income level, will extensively change their buying habits and

---

1 Because of significantly better income population growth occurring east of I-78. Since 1970, census income levels for this area are not wholly representative of the actual higher income levels now characterizing this area, and an adjustment has been made to compensate for this condition.

store preferences. Therefore, the $15,000 current annual family income level has been retained as a floor in projecting higher income trade area families.

The historical and projected higher income population, by trade area segment, is exhibited in Table 2. The current estimated level of better income population in the total trade area is 189,400 people, or 61.7 percent of the total trade area population. It is projected that the higher income segment of the population will increase to 199,500 people by 1978, the first full operational year of the proposed project. By 1983, the higher income segment of the total trade area will represent almost 66 percent of the total population. This increase in higher income population as a proportion of total population is primarily due to increases in attained educational levels, the increasingly more skilled level of the work force in reaction to increasing demand for more highly skilled workers, and the continuing growth in demand for professional and government service workers in the work force.

Table 2   Downtown Shopping Center Trade Area Income Population*

					Long Range	
	1970	1975	1978	1983	1988	1998
Primary Trade Area	57,604	61,800	64,440	68,100	72,400	79,900
Secondary Zone "A"	52,190	57,200	60,400	67,600	75,600	87,800
Secondary Zone "B"	63,860	70,400	74,700	83,400	95,200	115,300
Total Trade Area	173,654	189,400	199,500	219,100	243,200	283,000

* Defined as members of families with a current mean family income approximating $15,000 or more.

Trade Area Incomes

Table 3 below shows a comparison of the estimated 1975 mean per capita incomes for the various trade zones, as defined above, for all families and for the higher income families residing in the trade area.[2] It can be seen that the Secondary Zone "A" higher income residents have a substantially higher level of income than similar residents of the primary trade area or Secondary Zone "B." This is a reflection of the inclusion of the exclusive areas as well as the area surrounding Simpson College within

---

214

2 Higher income unrelated individuals comprise a statistically insignificant proportion of trade area population and therefore are not included in the population estimates.

the Secondary Zone "A." Geographically, this area contains little modest income housing. The area is predominantly single family homes on sites of a minimum quarter acre with the general range of housing prices from $60,000 to over $100,000. In the eastern-most sections of Secondary Zone "A" housing values tend to be in the upper levels of this range.

Table 3 Trade Area Population 1975 Mean Per Capita Incomes

	Total Family Members	Higher Income Family Members
Primary Trade Area	$6,873	$ 8,167
Secondary Zone "A"	6,886	10,449
Secondary Zone "B"	5,297	7,249
Total Trade Area	6,522	8,520

Source: 1970 U.S. Census, *Survey of Current Business*, April, 1974 and April, 1975.

The primary trade area, which is principally the city, has a level of per capita income more than 10 percent greater than that found in Secondary Zone "B."

While the areas immediately surrounding the downtown shopping center project are lower to moderate income areas, the area north of Route 27 and the Milford area immediately west of I-78 as well as the area east of I-78 are included within this trade area and contain medium-to high income housing mostly of the single-family type. Secondary Zone "B," which is the eastern and central portions of Richmond and Westmont, has the full income spectrum of housing represented, with house values and incomes tending to get higher moving from the lake southward.

Housing values in the area surrounding the downtown site and between the two freeways are predominately in the $25,000 to $35,000 range both east and west of the site. To the south of Route 27, new homes are in the $40,000+ range and just west of this area tend to be slightly less expensive. West and south of the Milford intersection with Interstate 78, the homes range from $50,000 to $80,000. East of Milford homes are in a similarly high price range, up to over $100,000. In the area of Milford Avenue, homes are in the $50,000 to $60,000 range. There is very little developable land left in the area south of Route 27. Cluster housing in residential areas interspersed with industrial areas is prevalent.

Trade Area Employment

The decade of the 1960s was one of major expansion and change in employment in the trade area. The expansion of the airport in 1962 simulated a substantial increase in transportation sector employment for the western county area. The development of three regional shopping centers added substantially to retail employment. Manufacturing, the historical employment base of the area, also grew substantially during this period. Tied to the growth of population and incomes in the area was a concurrent growth in demand for services and a need for additional government employment. Government employment also climbed rapidly in the latter part of the decade.

Table 4   Trade Area Historical and Projected Employment

	1970	1980
Primary Trade Area	29,688	33,500
Secondary Zone "A"	18,853	21,000
Secondary Zone "B"	32,406	37,300
Total Trade Area	80,947	91,800

Sources: *Projections of the Regions Future*, Association of Area Governments, September, 1974.

Employment figures for the trade area are shown in Table 4. Employment in 1970 in the trade area was at a level of 80,947 people in jobs. Growth in employment is projected at approximately 1 percent per year for the decade of the 1970s. There are no reliable estimates of current employment due to current economic distortions and the fluidity of the job market. However, except for isolated cases, such as International Harvester, which is closing its local plant this July, the employment base in the trade area is growing slowly in the long run. The larger employers in the trade area have experienced some employment fluctuations but have no announced plans for permanent employment cutbacks.

Projected Per Capita and Total Available AFO Expenditures

Table 5 summarizes the per capita better income AFO expenditures for households with $15,000-plus of current annual income in both the primary and secondary zones of the total trade area.

"AFO" refers to Apparel-Accessories, Home Furnishings and Decorative Home items and "Other" specialty goods anticipated to predominate at the proposed specialty center. Experience would indicate that other types of stores expected to be included to provide balance and additional appeal to the center are basically merchandising rather than market oriented. These include restaurant and service establishments. Therefore, analysis has been confined to projecting per capita and total available expenditures for the AFO categories described above.

The projected per capita and total AFO expenditures for better income customers residing in the trade area are based upon current year dollar values, which reflect both real income and inflationary dollar gains. Based upon historical trends in the area and discounting today's very high rate of inflation as being an anomaly with respect to the long term for AFO merchandise, these per capita and total estimates reflect a 1.5 percent average annual real income gain plus an inflationary gain of 4 percent per year with respect to AFO type merchandise.

Table 5 Downtown Shopping Center Trade Area Higher Income Population Per Capita AFO Expenditures*

	1975	1978	1983	Long Range 1988	1998
Primary Trade Area					
A**	$212	$247	$315	$402	$ 623
F	37	43	55	70	108
O	147	172	218	279	432
Sub-Total	$396	$462	$588	$751	$1,163
Secondary Zone "A"					
A	$275	$320	$407	$519	$ 804
F	48	56	71	91	141
O	191	222	283	360	558
Sub-Total	$514	$598	$761	$970	$1,503
Secondary Zone "B"					
A	$187	$218	$278	$354	$ 549
F	33	38	49	62	96
O	130	151	193	246	381
Sub-Total	$350	$407	$520	$662	$1,026
Total Trade Area					
A	$221	$258	$330	$420	$ 651
F	39	46	58	74	115
O	154	179	229	292	453
Sub-Total	$414	$483	$617	$786	$1,219

Note: Projections assume 5.5 percent growth per year including both real and inflationary growth relative to AFO.

* In current (inflated) dollar values.
** A = Apparel, F = Home Furnishings/Decorative Home Items, O = Other DSTM (Department Store Type Merchandise).
Sources: 1970 *Census of Population.*
1972 *Census of Business—Retail Trade*
Survey of Current Business, April and May, 1974.

Projected per capita expenditures, when multiplied by projected population levels, yield total trade area AFO potential as shown in Table 6. These total expenditure potentials reflect the potential expenditure base from which the downtown shopping center would draw the majority of its sales. However, it is known that a portion of this expenditure base is exported to retail facilities in other parts of the area. Because of the numerous studies performed in this area, the magnitude of this expenditure export from the downtown trade area to AFO retail facilities is known. In Table 7, this estimated export has been deducted from the total trade area AFO potential. The residual trade area share of AFO expenditures represents the potential for which the downtown shopping center project would actually compete for sales.

Table 6 Downtown Shopping Center Trade Area Better Income Population Total AFO Expenditure Population*

	1975	1978	1983	Long Range 1988	Long Range 1998
Primary Trade Area					
A**	$13,102	$15,907	$21,452	$29,105	$ 49,778
F	2,286	2,769	3,746	5,068	8,629
O	9,085	11,077	14,846	20,200	34,517
Sub-Total	$24,473	$29,753	$40,044	$54,373	$ 92,924
Secondary Zone "A"					
A	$15,730	$19,328	$27,513	$39,236	$ 70,591
F	2,746	3,382	4,800	6,880	12,380
O	10,925	13,409	19,131	27,216	48,992
Sub-Total	$29,401	$36,119	$51,444	$73,332	$131,963
Secondary Zone "B"					
A	$13,165	$16,285	$23,185	$33,701	$ 63,300
F	2,323	2,839	4,087	5,902	11,069
O	9,152	11,280	16,096	23,419	43,929
Sub-Total	$24,640	$30,404	$43,368	$63,022	$118,298
Total Trade Area					
A	$41,997	$51,520	$72,150	$102,042	$183,669
F	7,355	8,990	12,633	17,850	32,078
O	29,162	35,766	50,073	70,835	106,901
Total	$78,514	$96,276	$134,856	$190,727	$343,185

* In current (inflated) dollar values.
** A =Apparel, F = Home Furnishings/Decorative Home, O = Other DSTM.

Table 7 Downtown Shopping Center Trade Area Better Income Population Trade Area Share of Trade Area AFO Expenditures* (000's)

	1975	1978	1983	Long Range 1988	1998
Primary Trade Area					
A**	$11,399	$13,839	$ 18,663	$ 25,321	$ 43,307
F	1,989	2,409	3,259	4,409	7,507
O	7,904	9,637	12,916	17,574	30,030
Sub-Total	$21,292	$25,885	$ 34,838	$ 47,304	$ 80,844
Secondary Zone "A"					
A	$12,269	$15,076	$ 21,460	$ 30,604	$ 55,061
F	2,142	2,638	3,744	5,366	9,656
O	8,522	10,459	14,922	21,228	38,213
Sub-Total	$22,933	$28,173	$ 40,126	$ 57,198	$102,930
Secondary Zone "B"					
A	$11,585	$14,331	$ 20,403	$ 29,657	$ 55,704
F	2,044	2,498	3,597	5,194	9,741
O	8,054	9,926	14,164	20,609	38,658
Sub-Total	$21,683	$26,755	$ 38,164	$ 55,460	$104,103
Total Trade Area					
A	$35,253	$43,246	$ 60,526	$ 85,582	$154,072
F	6,175	7,545	10,600	14,969	26,904
O	24,480	30,022	42,002	59,411	106,901
Total	$65,908	$80,813	$113,128	$159,962	$287,877

* In current (inflated) dollar values.
** A = Apparel, F = Home Furnishings/Decorative Home, O = Other DSTM.

Competition

There are currently no major theme specialty centers serving the higher income segment of the population. What would have been the first such center, a 268,000 square-foot complex in a larger community to the south, was recently rejected by that community because of traffic problems.

While no facilities of the type being proposed serve the trade area, there are numerous retail complexes merchandising apparel, decorative home items and the other types of goods expected to be presented at this planned center. The difference lies in physical and architectural surroundings and method of merchandise presentation, rather than in different kinds of merchandise. Recognizing that only a certain trade area expenditure base is available for the purchase of AFO merchandise, the proposed center would therefore be in competition with other AFO merchandisers.

There currently exists almost 1.1 million square feet of AFO specialty retail space in major retail centers which draw from the expenditure base of residents of the downtown shopping center trade area. Table 8 indicates competitive locations and the size of these facilities. The three largest concentrations of this space are situated peripherally to the trade area. Therefore, these facilities draw only a small portion of their sales from the total trade area which would be tributary to the downtown project.

Approximately 50 percent of the existing major specialty retail competitive space is located in smaller regional shopping centers, community shopping centers and community shopping districts. The Eastbrook Mall and Fairmont Shopping Center are both regional sized facilities that contain less than 100,000 square feet of AFO type space. Because of their regional nature, both of these facilities draw from a broader market area than the remainder of the small facilities conveniently reached from the down-town trade area.

There are only two minor specialty facilities currently serving the trade area. These are the 14th Street Center and Cambridge Center. The 14th

Table 8　Downtown Trade Area Major Competitive Specialty Retail Space (Estimated Per Sq. Ft.)

Map Key	Name/Location	Apparel & Accessory	Decorative Home/ Furnishings	Other Specialty DSTM	Total
1	Branford CBD	39,290	14,410	59,610	113,310
2	Eastgate Area	44,390	5,400	32,750	82,540
3	Kennedy Broadway S. C.	20,500	3,900	12,885	37,285
4	Winchester CBD	151,130	41,990	48,515	241,635
5	Vernon Center	40,000	—	5,000	45,000
6	Brush Shopping Area	16,550	2,730	9,160	28,440
7	University Shopping Center	19,400	2,110	15,285	36,795
8	Lakeshore S. C.	24,370	—	20,910	45,280
9	Eastbrook Mall	53,850	1,600	34,910	90,360
10	Rossmoor Square	6,025	510	8,000	14,535
11	City CBD*	9,100	4,800	7,900	21,800
12	14th Street	10,960	1,525	4,530	17,015
13	Fairmont S. C.	43,840	3,875	25,390	73,105
14	Cambridge Center	7,420	1,300	11,350	20,070
15	Richmond CBD	21.015	16,700	29,095	66,810
16	West and S. C.	106,970	3,960	50,210	161,140
	Total Special DSTM	614,810	104,810	375,500	1,095,120

* Not including specialty retail space in project area to be demolished.

Street Center, a small "town and country" type shopping center located one block south of the project site, is similar in concept to the proposed downtown shopping center. It includes approximately 17,000 square feet of competing AFO space. This center has been in operation since 1948. Cambridge Center contains approximately 20,000 square feet of AFO space.

Currently, there are no viable proposals for significant new competitive space in the trade areas to be served by the downtown shopping center project. Because of the scarcity of developable land and the existing convenient access to regional shopping facilities for residents of the trade area, it is unlikely that any major new competitive specialty retail space will be developed within the trade area prior to the maturity of the proposed downtown facility.

Sales Volume Estimates

This section contains a discussion of the methodology and estimated sales resulting from a market share analysis of the proposed downtown shopping center. The market share methodology utilizes the existing competitive situation and the population, income and expenditure levels developed earlier. Based upon the revised concept outlined in the introduction to this report, it is assumed that the 200,000 square feet of GLA proposed to be contained in the downtown project would include the following components:

Specialty Apparel-Accessories	100,000 Sq. Ft.
Home Furnishings/Decorative Home	27,000 Sq. Ft.
Other Specialty Retail	35,100 Sq. Ft.
Specialty Restaurants & Services	37,900 Sq. Ft.
Total	200,000 Sq. Ft.

The basic market shares shown for each trade area zone in the following tables have been based upon these factors:

1. The extent, location and character of AFO competition serving the proposed project's trade area.

2. The historical performance of stores, such as those proposed under the revised development concept, in serving the various income strata of the $15,000 + family market.

3. The past performance of AFO stores in similar specialty retail centers in other portions of the area. Of particular note is the appeal of these centers to the higher income population of the tributary trade areas.

4. The assumed merchandise character of the stores to be included in the downtown shopping center. It is assumed that the merchandise categories

of these stores would be similar to that found in other specialty retail centers, although the price points and taste level of the merchandise are expected to be slightly lower.

5. The expected attraction and strength of the proposed retail development concept in attracting principally the higher income residents of the trade area.

6. The strategic location with reference to access routes and public transportation of the downtown shopping center project.

The resultant market shares by AFO retail category have been applied to the trade area share of area expenditures in the following three tables. In addition to the sales from within the trade area zones derived by market share, an additional 20 percent has been added to allow for sales from beyond the trade area and from more modest income groups to arrive at a total sales estimate. All sales and productivity figures are expressed in current (inflated) dollar values.

The 20 percent figure indicated above is somewhat more than would be normally added to account for sales volume originating from beyond the trade area. This occurs because of the anticipated sales contribution generated by superior public transit and the fact that no other such specialty retail center exists in the area.

The sales volume estimates for the apparel and accessory stores in the downtown shopping center are shown in Table 9. The market shares by trade area zone are applied to the share of trade area expenditures for the year 1978, the anticipated first full year of shopping center operation, to arrive at a sales volume estimate of $8.3 million. This volume is then divided by 100,000 square feet of apparel and accessory space to arrive at a productivity in 1978 of $83 per square foot. By 1983, this sales volume is estimated to increase to approximately $11.5 million, or a productivity of $115 per square foot.

A similar approach was used to estimate sales volume for the home furnishings/decorative home stores and other specialty retail stores. The 27,000 square feet of home furnishings/decorative home space is estimated to generate sales of $2.0 million in 1978 for a productivity of $74 per square foot. It is estimated that this sales volume will increase to $2.8 million in 1983, or a productivity of $103 per square foot. In the other specialty retail category, it is estimated that the proposed 35,000 square feet of space will develop $3.7 million of sales in 1978, or a productivity of $106 per square foot, and by 1983 will develop $5.1 million, or a productivity of $146 per square foot. These results are displayed in Tables 10 and 11.

Table 9 Downtown Shopping Center Sales Volume Estimates—Apparel and Accessories

			Long Range Sales	
	1978	1983	1988	1998
Apparel and Accessories (100,000 Sq. Ft. GLA)				
Trade Area Share of Better Income Expenditures (000's)				
Primary Trade Area	$13,839	$18,663	$25,321	$ 43,307
Secondary Zone "A"	15,076	21,460	30,604	55,061
Secondary Zone "B"	14,331	20,403	29,657	55,704
Total Trade Area	$43,246	$60,526	$85,582	$154,072
Trade Area Sales Potential (000's)				
Primary Trade Area @26.9% Market Share	$ 3,723	$ 5,020	$ 6,811	$ 11,650
Secondary Zone "A" @11.4% Market Share	1,719	2,446	3,489	6,277
Secondary Zone "B" @8.4% Market Share	1,204	1,714	2,491	4,679
Total Trade Area	$ 6,646	$ 9,180	$12,791	$ 22,606
Including 20% from Beyond Trade Area and More Modest Income Groups (000's)	$ 8,308	$11,475	$15,989	$ 28,258
Productivity at 100,000 Sq. Ft.	$ 83	$ 115	$ 160	$ 283

Table 10 Downtown Shopping Center Sales Volume Estimates—Home Furnishings/Decorative Home

			Long Range Sales	
	1978	1983	1988	1998
Home Furnishings/Decorative Home (27,000 Sq. Ft. GLA)				
Trade Area Share of Better Income Expenditures (000's)				
Primary Trade Area	$ 2,409	$ 3,259	$ 4,409	$ 7,507
Secondary Zone "A"	2,638	3,744	5,366	9,656
Secondary Zone "B"	2,498	3,597	5,194	9,741
Total Trade Area	$ 7,545	$10,600	$14,969	$26,904

Table 10 *Continued*

			Long Range Sales	
	1978	1983	1988	1998
Trade Area Sales Potential (000's)				
Primary Trade Area @36.4% Market Share	$ 877	$ 1,186	$ 1,605	$ 2,733
Secondary Zone "A" @16.9% Market Share	446	633	907	1,632
Secondary Zone "B" @11.4% Market Share	285	410	592	1,110
Total Trade Area	$ 1,608	$ 2,229	$ 3,104	$ 5,475
Including 20% from Beyond Trade Area and More Modest Income Groups (000's)	$ 2,010	$ 2,786	$ 3,880	$ 6,844
Productivity at 27,000 Sq. Ft.	$ 74	$ 103	$ 144	$ 253

Table 11 Downtown Shopping Center Sales Volume Estimates—Other Specialty Retail

			Long Range Sales	
	1978	1983	1988	1998
Other Specialty Retail (35,100 Sq. Ft. GLA)				
Trade Area Share of Better Income Expenditures (000's)				
Primary Trade Area	$ 9,637	$12,916	$17,574	$ 30,030
Secondary Zone "A"	10,459	14,922	21,228	38,213
Secondary Zone "B"	9,926	14,164	20,609	38,658
Total Trade Area	$30,022	$42,002	$59,411	$106,901
Trade Area Sales Potential (000's)				
Primary Trade Area @17.6% Market Share	$ 1,696	$ 2,273	$ 3,093	$ 5,285
Secondary Zone "A" @8.2% Market Share	858	1,224	1,741	3,133
Secondary Zone "B" @4.3% Market Share	427	609	886	1,662
Total Trade Area	$ 2,981	$ 4,106	$ 5,720	$ 10,080
Including 20% from Beyond Trade Area and More Modest Income Groups (000's)	$ 3,726	$ 5,133	$ 7,150	$ 12,600
Productivity at 35,100 Sq. Ft.	$ 106	$ 146	$ 204	$ 359

Table 12 Downtown Shopping Center Summary of Sales Volume Estimates*

Store Category	1978		1983		Long Range Sales	
	Sales (000's)	Productivity $/Per Sq. Ft.	Sales (000's)	Productivity $/Per Sq. Ft.	1988 (000's)	1998 (000's)
Apparel & Accessories (100,000 Sq. Ft.)	$ 8,308	$ 83 (74)	$11,475	$115 (87)	$16,000	$28,300
Home Furnishings/Decorative Home (27,000 Sq. Ft.)	2,010	74 (66)	2,786	103 (78)	3,900	6,800
Other Specialty Retail (35,100 Sq. Ft.)	3,726	106 (95)	5,133	146 (111)	7,200	12,600
Total Specialty Retail (162,100 Sq. Ft.)	$14,044	$ 87 (78)	$19,394	$120 (91)	$27,100	$47,700
**Total Shopping Center (200,000 Sq. Ft.)	$17,400	$ 87 (78)	$24,000	$120 (91)	$33,400	$58,800
(Sales Contribution Attributable to Public Transit)						
@ 5%	$ 870		$ 1,200		$ 1,700	$ 2,900
@ 10%	1,740		2,400		3,300	5,900

* Sales shown in current year (inflated) dollar values. Constant 1975 productivity values in parentheses.
** Includes 37,900 sq. ft. of restaurants and service establishments. Sales of such establishments are based principally upon merchandising rather than marketing considerations. Sales productivity (and total sales) of such establishments assumed to be similar to that of center as a whole. Proposed 12,000 sq. ft. drug store deleted as being inappropriate to concept.

Development Recommendations

Summary of Sales Potential

The sales volume estimates developed in the preceding section for the revised shopping center concept in the downtown area have been consolidated and summarized in Table 12. The total shopping center figures include 27,900 square feet of restaurants and service establishment space. Sales estimates for this non-retail space are based on our experience, which indicates that sales in these establishments will be similar to the overall AFO productivity of the center.

As noted previously, all dollar figures in sales estimates are shown in terms of current (inflated) dollar values so as to more accurately reflect costs as they will be incurred and revenues as they will be received. Furthermore, financial analysis will require the use of inflated dollars to realistically assess shopping center performance and development costs. In Table 12, however, constant 1975 dollar values for the productivity estimates have been provided in order to measure estimated performance in terms comparable with today's dollars and to delete the effects of future inflation. As shown in the table, it is anticipated that approximately 5 to 10 percent of center sales would be attributable to public transit.

Sales Tax Revenues

Table 13 shows the gross sales tax revenues which would accrue to the city from the retail shops located in the downtown shopping center.

Table 13   Downtown Shopping Center Estimated Annual City Sales Tax Revenues

		Long Range	
1978	1983	1988	1998
$174,000	$240,000	$334,000	$588,000

These estimates are based on a sales tax rate of 1 percent applied to gross sales figures. Sales taxes from merchants currently operating within the site area are not considered in the above figures. In order to figure the net new sales tax increment attributable to the new development, the above figures should be reduced by current sales taxes realized from merchants in the site area.

Comparisons with Other Area Specialty Retail Centers

It is useful at this point to test and compare the center's anticipated sales performance with those currently being achieved by major existing area specialty centers, relative to the character of the trade areas they serve.

The productivity level estimated in 1978 for the overall downtown specialty center is slightly below those that are currently realized at comparable projects elsewhere in the area, as shown in Table 14. In constant 1975 dollar terms, the project's overall productivity level is $78 per square foot. Comparable specialty retail centers are currently achieving productivity levels ranging from $90 to over $135 in constant 1975 dollar terms. When comparing projected performance of the downtown project in 1978 with productivities now being realized in currently existing projects, it should be noted that comparable projects have been open a number of years and productivities are based on a stabilized sales rate, whereas the 1978 sales for the project is reflected in constant 1975 dollars and represents first year sales. The sales volume estimated for 1983, by which time sales will have stabilized, shows an estimated productivity of $91 per square foot in constant 1975 dollar terms.

The sales volume estimates for the downtown shopping center in the apparel and accessories category shows a sales productivity of $74 per square foot in 1978, as expressed in 1975 constant dollars. While this productivity is somewhat lower than those currently being achieved by comparable specialty centers, by 1983, trade area growth and maturity of the shopping center will increase sales volume to a stabilized constant dollar productivity level of $91 per square foot. This figure compares favorably with those of comparable shopping centers.

In the home furnishings/decorative home category, the productivity estimate for the year 1978 is $66 per square foot. The diversity of stores included in this category precludes direct comparison from shopping center to shopping center in terms of individual productivity levels. However, it can be stated that the $66 per square foot average productivity level in this category for the downtown shopping center would be sufficiently attractive to a small, aggressive merchandiser whose lines would fit into the price point categories envisioned in this shopping center concept. In the other specialty retail category, the 35,100 square feet of proposed space in the downtown project is estimated to achieve a 1978 productivity level of $95 per square foot in constant 1975 dollars. This level approximates the mean productivity level currently being achieved at existing stabilized comparable centers. By 1983, the fifth full year of the shopping center operation, this constant dollar productivity level is projected to increase to an estimated $111 per square foot which exceeds the productivity level being achieved in this category in any of the comparable centers.

Selected relevant data pertaining to comparable existing specialty retail shopping center trade areas (plus trade area data for the Capital Town and Country Shopping Center) are shown in the accompanying Table 15. The figures in each category for the comparable shopping centers have been indexed to the data relative to the downtown shopping center, which is shown as an index of 100.

Table 14   Representative Specialty Retail Shopping Centers Comparative Sales and Productivities (1975 Dollar Values)

	Apparel & Accessories		Home Furnishings/ Decorative Home		Other Special DSTM		Total Specialty DSTM	
	Sales ($ Mil)	Productivity ($/Sq. Ft.)	Sales ($ Mil)	Productivity ($/Sq. Ft.)	Sales ($ Mil)	Productivity ($/Sq. Ft.)	Sales ($ Mil)	Productivity ($/Sq. Ft.)
*Downtown Shopping Center**	$ 7.4	$ 74	$1.8	$ 66	$ 3.3	$ 95	$12.5	$ 78
Cherry Hill Shopping Center	2.2	135	1.7	195	1.5	103	5.4	136
Town and Country Village/ Plainfield	2.8	90	0.6	57	6.0	92	9.4	133
Town and Country Village/ Simsbury	1.3	88	NA	NA	1.6	85	2.9	86
Town and Country Village/ Ledyard	6.6	115	1.4	112	4.5	99	12.5	109
T and C Village Additional/ Ledyard	5.1	131	NA	NA	4.7	100	9.8	114
Town and Country Shopping Center/Capital	3.2	111	0.3	47	2.5	89	6.0	95
Total**	$28.6	$ 99	$5.8	$ 94	$24.1	$ 95	$58.5	$103

* Estimated 1978 Sales Volumes in 1975 Constant Dollar Values.

** Note: Square footage space of NA (Not Available) not included in calculating total productivity.

Source: State Board of Equalization.

Table 15 Representative Specialty Retail Shopping Centers 1969 Comparative Trade Area Data (Index)*

Name (Year Opened)	Total Families	Percent Better Income Families	Mean Family Income (All Families)	Mean Family Income (Better-Income Families)	Better Income Families by Income Group (%)			Trade Area Sq. Ft. of AFO Space Per Family	Employment	
					$10–15,000	$15–25,000	$25,000+		% Professional & Managerial	% Other Employment
Downtown Shopping Center (Proposed 1978)	80,862 (100.0)	66.0% (100.0)	$14,351 (100.0)	$19,514 (100.0)	47.0% (100.0)	40.3% (100.0)	12.7% (100.0)	8.5 (100.0)	20.3% (100.0)	79.7% (100.0)
Cherry Hill S. C. (1965)	18,083 (22.4)	77.4 (101.2)	18,224 (126.9)	23,577 (120.8)	30.5 (64.9)	43.7 (108.4)	25.8 (203.1)	8.5 (100.0)	42.2 (207.9)	57.8 (72.5)
Town and Country Village/Plainfield (1949)	36,349 (44.9)	67.7 (101.0)	15,102 (105.2)	20,827 (106.7)	38.7 (82.3)	44.6 (110.7)	16.7 (131.5)	22.5 (264.7)	37.6 (185.2)	62.4 (78.3)
Town and Country Village/Simsbury (1968)	42,144 (52.1)	73.7 (101.1)	13,414 (93.5)	18,642 (95.5)	44.3 (94.3)	45.9 (113.8)	9.8 (77.2)	18.0 (211.7)	35.6 (175.4)	64.4 (80.8)
Town and Country Village/Ledyard (1960) and (1970)	101,488 (101.3)	68.3 (101.0)	13,726 (95.6)	18.067 (92.6)	47.1 (100.2)	42.5 (105.4)	10.4 (81.9)	20.4 (240.0)	32.1 (158.1)	67.9 (85.2)
Town and Country S. C./Capital (1947)	50,565 (62.5)	63.7 (96.5)	13,391 (93.3)	17,839 (91.4)	49.2 (104.7)	39.9 (99.0)	10.9 (85.8)	16.6 (195.3)	37.8 (186.2)	62.2 (78.0)

* Index shown in parentheses—Downtown S. C. = 100.0.
Source: *1970 Census, Population.*

The downtown shopping center trade area contains a slightly lower percentage of better income families as a share of all families than do most of the others, with the exception of the Capital Town and Country Shopping Center. However, in terms of mean family income for all families and for only higher income families, the subject trade area falls into place behind only the high income Cherry Hill Shopping Center and Plainfield Town and Country Village trade areas.

In terms of trade area AFO space per family, the downtown shopping center trade area shows a very low 8.5 square feet per family. This is approximately one-half the level of competitive AFO space in all the other specialty shopping center trade areas (with the exception of the Cherry Hill trade area which maintains its high level population to AFO space ratio primarily because of the difficulty of obtaining building permits for commercial facilities in that area). The breakdown by income group shows results which are consistent with the mean incomes.

The most salient point to be made in the comparison of this data is made in the breakdown of employment statistics into professional and managerial, and all other employment. The downtown shopping center trade area shows a far lower index in the professional and managerial category while showing a considerably higher index in the other, essentially blue-collar employment categories, in comparison with all the other specialty shopping center trade areas. These employment categories are known to be a general index of taste levels among the residents of individual trade areas. A more quality-oriented taste level is generally attributed to individuals and their families in the professional and managerial employment category, while the other employment category essentially reflects a lower taste level and price point orientation. This comparison offers a reasonable explanation of the seemingly inconsistent results of this analysis.

While the market data indicate a strong base of support for the originally conceived project and a competitive gap in the area for the original project concept, the employment make-up of residents of the trade area indicates a lower taste level and price point appeal prevailing than that envisioned in the original project concept. It is for this reason that this analysis has assumed a merchandising plan based on lower price points than were envisioned in the original project proposal.

Had the original project concept been implemented, a marginal sales performance would have been projected. Specifically, analysis of the original concept yielded a sales potential of approximately 19 percent below that estimated for the revised concept. Approximately $14.0 million in first year total center sales resulted from an analysis of the original concept, compared to $17.4 million for the revised concept. Fifth full year sales under the original concept resulted in a sales potential of $19.4 million, as compared to $24.0 million under the revised approach.

230   Shown in Table 16 is a suggested tenant list for the revised specialty

Table 16 Downtown Shopping Center Suggested Tenant Types

Apparel and Accessories — 100,000 Sq. Ft.		*Other Specialty Retail —* 35,100 Sq. Ft.	
Boy's Wear	1,500	Books	1,600
Children's Wear	2,000	Florist	1,000
Family Shoes	3,000	Gifts	2,000
Family Shoes	2,000	Gifts	2,000
Girl's Wear	4,000	Gifts	1,000
Men's Wear	6,000	Paperback Books	1,000
Men's Wear	4,000	Hobby	1,500
Men's Wear	3,000	Imports	2,000
Men's Wear	2,000	Jewelry	2,500
Men's Shoes	2,000	Jewelry	1,000
Men's and Boy's Shoes	2,500	Jewelry	500
Teen Wear	4,000	Music & Records	2,000
Teen Wear	3,000	Plants	1,000
Teen Wear	2,000	Sporting Goods	2,500
Women's Wear	10,000	Sporting Goods	1,500
Women's Wear	4,500	Sewing Center	1,500
Women's Wear	4,500	Stationery	2,000
Women's Wear	4,000	Toys	2,000
Women's Accessories	3,000	Silver & Jewelry	1,000
Women's Accessories	2,000	Cards & Party Center	1,500
Women's Wear	2,500	Needlepoint & Yarn	500
Women's Wear	3,000	Bead Store	500
Women's Wear Boutique	2,500	Camera Store	1,000
Women's Wear Boutique	2,500	Crafts	1,000
Women's Wear Boutique	1,500	Art Supplies	1,000
Women's Shoes	3,000	*Restaurants and Services —* 37,900 Sq. Ft.	
Women's Shoes	2,500		
Women's Shoes	2,500	Bank	2,000
Women's Shoes	1,500	Barber Shop	500
Children's Shoes	1,500	Beauty Shop	2,500
Tennis/Ski Shop	2,500	Cleaners	1,500
Hosiery Store	500	Cocktail Lounge	1,000
Men's Shoes	1,000	Restaurant	1,500
Lingerie Shop	1,000	Finance Company	1,500
Pants Shop	3,500	Insurance Office	500
Leather Shop	2,000	Restaurant	2,500
Home Furnishings/Decorative Home — 27,000 Sq. Ft.		Photography Studio	1,000
		Real Estate	1,000
Picture Frame Shop	2,000	Restaurant	5,000
Art Gallery	2,000	Restaurant	4,500
Art Gallery	2,000	Restaurant	4,000
Bath Shop	1,500	Wine and Cheese Store	1,400
Draperies	2,000	Travel Agency	500
Rugs-Wall Hangings	2,000	Bakery	1,000
Furnishings/Decorative	3,500	Ice Cream Store	1,000
Gourmet Cooking	2,500	Deli	2,500
TV & Stereo	3,500	Health Foods	1,000
Waterbeds	3,000	Candy Store	500
Modern lamps, wall systems	3,000	Copy Service	500
		Total	200,000 Sq. Ft.

shopping center concept. It provides the balance necessary to enhance the project's attraction and appeal.

Parking Requirements

In general, parking ratios in specialty retail centers of the type being analyzed in this report are lower than those required in a more conventional regional shopping center. In specialty centers appealing to better-income high taste level shoppers, the average parking ratio is 4.0 parking spaces per 1,000 square feet of gross leaseable area, while the ratio for conventional centers is approximately 5.5 parking spaces per 1,000 square feet of gross leaseable area.

The primary factors involved in determining parking ratios, in addition to local zoning regulations, are better-income customer behavior and merchandising of the stores. In terms of local zoning regulations, the city zoning department has no requirement for providing parking for retail establishments. In terms of better-income customer behavior, studies have shown that such customers generally visit specialty centers less often than they visit conventional centers and tend to visit fewer stores but have high average purchases. Also, they tend to stay a shorter time than at a conventional regional center. This results in higher parking space turn-over and resultant lower required parking ratios.

After careful consideration of the above-mentioned factors, and recognizing the proximity of public transit, we have determined that a parking ratio of 4.5 to 5.0 spaces per 1,000 square feet of gross leaseable area would be appropriate to provide adequate parking for customers of the proposed shopping center development. This ratio translates into 900 to 1,000 parking spaces which would require 360,000 to 400,000 square feet of parking area. The architect's preliminary design for the shopping center includes provisions for 200 parking spaces one-half level below grade, and 700 parking spaces each at the minus 14-foot and 23-foot levels. The 4.5 to 5.0 per 1,000 square feet GLA ratio for parking would most likely eliminate the necessity to construct the proposed 23-foot level parking floor and the attendant cost of such development.

DOWNTOWN SPECIALTY SHOPPING CENTER PROFORMA

Total Site Area — 191,500 sq. ft.
Approx. Gross Leaseable Area: 200,108 sq. ft.

Estimated Development Cost:

Land		$1,600,000
Buildings (200,108 s.f. @$22.00)	$4,402,000	
Common Areas (63,000 s.f. @$6.00)	378,000	
Garage Improvements	350,000	
Architectural & Engr. @7%	360,000	5,490,000
Developer Expenses @10%		550,000
Loan Fee & Expenses		237,000
Leasing Commissions (assuming 10 yrs.)		463,000
Real Estate Taxes		25,000
Interest—$8,365,000 @9%)		565,000
*Tenant Construction Allow. (200,108 s.f. @$5.00)		1,000,000
Total Development Cost		$9,930,500

*Paid 30 days after tenant opens

Income Projections (not including percentage rents)

Level	GLA	@	Total
Park Level	43,365	6.42	310,469
Plaza Level	134,318	7.51	1,009,166
Lower Level	17,425	6.64	115,764
Kiosks	–0–	6,000.00	18,000
	200,108	7.26	$1,453,399

Expense Projections

Gross Rents		1,453,399
Debt Service (80%=$7,944,400— 10.48 constant=9%—25 yrs.)	$ 832,600	
Landlord's Taxes @.25 sq. ft.	50,000	
Insurance @.04 sq. ft.	10,000	
Maintenance Reserve @.10 sq. ft.	20,000	
Merchants' Assoc. @.075 sq. ft.	15,000	
Vacancy Factor @2½%	36,300	
Management Fee @4%	58,100	$1,022,000
NET CASH FLOW		$ 431,399

Cash on Cash Return on $1,986,100=21.7%
   (Free & Clear Return on $9,930,500=12.73%)
   (Net Cash Flow on 100% financing=$223,299)

Chapter 12

Development of Storrs Center

12

Introduction

The property under consideration for development is a 42-acre parcel located in Mansfield, Connecticut and owned by the University of Connecticut. It is situated to the east of Route 195 and to the south of Dog Lane at the intersection of these roads. The property includes an already existing "commercial block" of approximately 27,000 square feet situated at the northwest corner of the property.

The "commercial block" contains a post office, restaurant, drug store and other smaller operations. An older building with generally below-average rents charged to the tenants, the property has always had a problem of accessibility for automobile traffic. The theatre (parking and building), University Plaza, Willimantic Bank and Trust, Phil's Variety and the Universal Food store are privately owned properties located sporadically around the subject property (see map).

Storrs Center Study

This study was conducted in 1966 by the Center for Real Estate and Urban Economic Studies at the University of Connecticut. While an effort was made to carry out the recommendations of this report, ensuing legal difficulties between the university and the developer precluded that possibility. Even though the study is ten years old, certain of its findings and recommendations are quite relevant even in today's market. A summary of the findings of that study follows.

The university-owned, 42-acre parcel of land near the southeast corner of Dog Lane and Route 195 in Storrs has truly unique locational advantages for the development of multi-family rental housing and shopping center facilities. Thus, it should not be diverted to other university uses which could be performed as efficiently on other sites.

The university "community" (students, faculty, staff, and classified employees) will continue to grow during the next five years at the same pace that it has over the past six years. Demand for members of the university community to live in or near Storrs will outstrip the capacity of the private

234

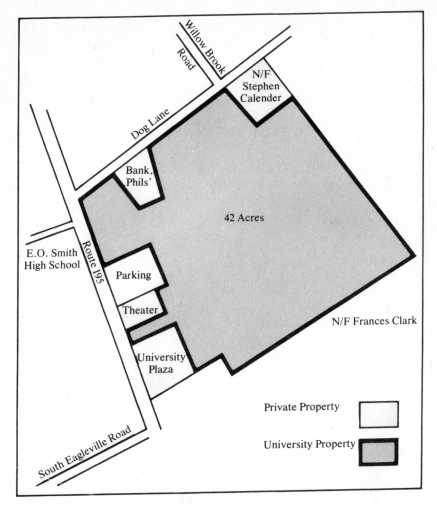

Willow Brook

Road

N/F
Stephen
Calender

Dog Lane

Bank,
Phils'

42 Acres

E.O. Smith
High School

Route 195

Parking

Theater

N/F Frances Clark

University
Plaza

Private Property

University Property

South Eagleville Road

housing market, particularly for rental units. The stability of employment and income in Storrs, as a result of the university, makes large-scale rental housing development financially feasible, even with a heavy turnover in occupancy which is a part of university life.

By 1970, even if the trend of private residential construction is maintained in Mansfield, there will be a "gap" of over 300 rental units for faculty, professional staff and classified employees alone. There is a special need for both one-bedroom or efficiency apartments for single faculty and staff members or student couples, and three-bedroom (preferably with one and one-half baths) apartments for larger faculty and staff families until they may purchase housing.

The university-owned site under consideration has the added advantage of public (university) water and sewer service; this means that much higher

235

densities can be utilized in developing the site for residential purposes. The immediately surrounding population, both university and non-university, has sufficient income and need to support some 100,000 square feet of commercial (rental and service) floor area in Storrs Center. Although the mix of uses that was found to be supportable is essentially the same as that currently found in the Storrs Center vicinity, the sizes and character of the uses must be changed in order to be profitable.

Access and parking represent critical problems for the Storrs Center commercial development; the current road network around the site is inadequate and used for too many purposes simultaneously.

The following represents the specific recommendations of the Storrs Center study.

Rental Housing

On the eastern 30 to 32 acres of the subject parcel, 296 rental housing units should be constructed, as follows:

1. 81 one-bedroom or efficiency units at $85 per month in an eight-story building;

2. 96 three-bedroom, one and one-half bath units at $140 per month in 12 eight-unit buildings;

3. 120 two-bedroom units at $110 per month in 5 three-story, 24-unit buildings.

The rental units should be owned and operated by the university and should include all utilities. Revenue bonds could be authorized and subsequently issued to meet the initial investment costs.

Commercial Development

Parking and access should be integrated in terms of design and physical flow with the commercial facilities to be built on the western 10 to 12 acres of the parcel. The university should acquire all frontage on Route 195 and Dog Lane in the vicinity of the Storrs Center parcel, including the land now owned by University Commercials, Inc.

Parking and access areas should total at least 400,000 square feet of land area. The commercial center should be developed by a private developer-sponsor, selected by negotiation with the university. The private developer should own all buildings, including that currently owned by University Commercials, Inc.; the university should lease the land to the private developer on a long-term basis at a recommended 7 percent of appraised value. The commercial development should be integrated with the current university commercial building; however, the Universal Food Store, Gulf Oil Station, University Pharmacy building, and radio and record shop buildings should be razed. There is a possibility that the Universal Food Store building can be converted to another university use.

Bonding authorization should be obtained to finance the acquisition and ownership of the commercial land. Design and use control should rest with the university. Legal authority should be obtained so that construction could begin by September, 1967.

Update of Storrs Center Study

While the projections made in the 1966 study are still considered to be relatively sound, there have been substantial adjustments in rental rates, costs of construction and financing costs as well as the size of the individual residential rental units and total commercial development. For example, total space for residential rental units was estimated in the earlier report at 142,900 square feet. It is estimated that in the current market that space would have to be approximately doubled to meet the demand in the market. In addition, rental rates projected above would also have to be approximately doubled for the new size units indicated.

Further, construction costs were estimated at $16 per square foot in the earlier study when, in fact, those costs are closer to $30 per square foot in today's market. Land at the time of the earlier study was also estimated at a value of $500,000, which has also doubled over the ensuing years and would require in the current market a lease income of approximately 10 percent of that value as opposed to the 7 percent reported earlier.

For the housing portion, in particular, the financing could very well be accomplished through other than conventional terms. Conventional terms normally would be 75 percent of value over a 20 to 25-year period with an interest rate of 9.5 percent. Either revenue bonds or state funding could very likely be obtained for approximately 100 percent of building costs for a term of 35 years and at a cost of 7.5 percent.

Rental Housing Study

The demand for residential rental space in the magnitude indicated in the earlier study has been corroborated by a study of rental housing which included the towns of Mansfield, Willimantic, Willington, Ashford, Chaplin and Tolland (partial). The study, conducted in the summer of 1975, consisted of an inventory of all one- to three-bedroom rental units in these towns. The sizes of these units ranged from a low of approximately 500 square feet to a high of 1,200 square feet. The rental range was from $145 per month to $260 per month.

Typically, heat and hot water were included in the rent except for units that were electrically heated. For the latter, electric charges are billed directly to the tenant. The vacancy rate for these units was found to be the lowest in the one-bedroom apartments and highest in the three-bedroom apartments. Aggregate vacancy was less than 4 percent for the entire market. A summary of the occupancy levels and vacancy rates for each type of unit surveyed follows:

Type Unit	Percent Occupancy	Percent Vacancy
One-Bedroom	99.4%	.6%
Two-Bedroom	95.3	4.7
Three-Bedroom	87.6	12.4

Total vacancy in the three-bedroom category consisted of 15 newly constructed units in Willimantic. Therefore, the vacancy count for this type unit is not really accurate—that is, the vacancy rate is overstated because of newly constructed units incorporated within the survey.

Because of the nature of new development that has taken place over the past ten years, it is felt that the initial projection in the 1966 study of 100,000 square feet of commercial space is excessive. Further, in order to maintain the objectives of the university regarding such a development, it would be necessary to integrate any commercial activity with the convenience needs of the immediate university market (faculty, staff, and students). In addition, there has been virtually no improvement in the traffic flow since the earlier study and commercial development in excess of the size needed to serve the immediate convenience market would only further intensify a poor and very undesirable traffic situation. Subsequent discussion of statistical data pertinent to commercial development will provide a better indication of a more appropriate size development for this market.

Population and Income Projections—Mansfield, Connecticut

Table 1 provides population figures for 1970 and projections through 1980. The average annual rate of growth for the period between 1970 and 1980 was 1.59 percent (constant growth). Census data indicated that over the prior ten-year period the number of households approximated 56 percent of the town's population. This percentage was applied to the 1970–80 projected population data to obtain an estimated number of households for the subsequent decade. It was further assumed that the number of persons per household would remain relatively stable over the period so that a figure of 2.95 persons per household was used to convert population in households to number of households over the ten-year projection period.

Median household income (see Table 2) was projected from 1970 data using a 6 percent compound annual growth rate. The 6 percent growth rate used is reflected in national trends experienced in the late 1960s. Effective buying income per household was assumed to be 85 percent of the median household income. The 85 percent level is the average rate of EBI to total personal income in the State of Connecticut over a three-year period in the early 1970s as noted in *Sales Management* magazine.

Table 1 Projected Population for the Town of Mansfield

Year	Population	Population in Households	Households
1970	19,994	10,976	3,688
1971	20,271	11,352	3,848
1972	20,560	11,514	3,903
1973	20,860	11,682	3,960
1974	21,179	11,860	4,020
1975	21,534	12,059	4,088
1976	21,860	12,242	4,150
1977	22,206	12,435	4,215
1978	22,588	12,649	4,288
1979	22,976	12,867	4,362
1980	23,424	13,117	4,446

Source: *1980 Projections of Population*, Thomas E. Steahr, Department of Agricultural Economics and Rural Sociology. *1970 U.S. Census of Population.*

Notes: 1. Population projected using 1.59 percent annual rate of growth.

2. Population in households represents 56 percent of population.

3. Households computed assuming 2.95 persons per household.

Table 2 Town of Mansfield Income Projections

Year	Median Household Income $	EBI Per Household $	EBI Sales Management (Tolland County)
1970	12,603	10,712	12,461
1971	13,359	11,355	9,925
1972	14,160	12,036	10,072
1973	15,009	12,757	11,489
1974	15,909	13,522	14,783
1975	16,864	14,334	
1976	17,875	15,193	
1977	18,948	16,105	
1978	20,085	17,072	
1979	21,290	18,096	
1980	22,567	19,181	

Source: *Sales Management, Survey of Buying Power; 1970 U.S. Census of Population.*

Median Household Income is projected using 6 percent compound annual growth rate.

EBI Per household is shown as 85 percent of Median Household Income.

Commercial Market, Projections and Rents

All projections made in this section are strictly for the University of Connecticut market. This market contains students in dormitories, commuters, faculty and all other university staff. It is felt that concern for only this market will provide a conservative estimate and any non-university affiliated individuals that may be drawn to this development will add to potential dollar sales.

Table 3   Student Projections

On Campus Retail Spending[a]

	Range	
1976	*$500*	*$700*
9,618 students in dorms	$4,800,000	$6,700,000
1980[b]	*$670*	*$940*
10,307	$6,900,000	$9,700,000
Commuting Students EBI[c]		
1976	*$1,850*	*$2,050*
6,105 students	$11,300,000	$12,500,000
1980	*$2,480*	*$2,740*
10,734	$26,600,000	$29,400,000

[a] $500 to $700 range used was from university estimates of student expenditures.

[b] Growth rates projected to be 6 percent per year.

[c] University fees for room and board from 1975/76 catalogue were added to student expenditures.

The number of students in dormitories as shown in Table 3 was derived by subtracting the population in households of the Town of Mansfield from total population. The range for student spending from $500 to $700 per year was obtained from university estimates. The number of commuting students was determined by subtracting the students in dorms from the total university enrollment of 15,732. The effective buying income of commuting students was estimated on the basis of university fees for room and board taken from the 1975/76 catalogue and added to in-dorm student expenditures.

The faculty and staff population is indicated in Table 4. As noted in that table, 402 part-time employees are excluded. Faculty and staff effective

Table 4   Distribution of Annual Salaries for 4,331 Full-Time Employees at the University of Connecticut, as of 17 February 1976
(Excludes 402 Part-Time Employees)

Annual Salary	No. of Employees
Below– 7,500	1,326[a]
7,500– 9,999	1,038
10,000–12,999	438[b]
13,000–15,999	425
16,000–18,999	383[c]
19,000–24,999	422
25,000–29,999	194
30,000–above	105
Total	4,331

[a] Includes 404 graduate assistants, all of whom receive less than $5,000 for nine months of service. Everyone else in this income class is paid between $5,000 and $7,499.

[b] Includes 80 employees with salaries specified as "$10,000 and above."

[c] Includes 2 employees with salaries specified as "$16,000 and above."

Table 5   Calculation of Retail Sales Available to Proposed Development

		(Millions)		
		1976		1980[a]
University Employee Gross Income		53.035		70.973
Employees EBI (84% of GI)		44.549		59.617
Commuting Student EBI	11.3	12.5	26.6	29.4
Total EBI	55.849	57.049	86.217	89.017
Retail Sales				
University Employees & Commuting Students (50% of EBI)	27.925	28.525	43.109	44.509
Dorm Residents	4.8	6.7	6.9	9.7
Total Retail $ Available	32.7	35.2	50.0	54.2

[a] Growth rate of 6 percent a year assumed to obtain 1980 projections.

Table 6   1972 Connecticut Statistics

State Total EBI	13,864,496,000
State Population	3,090,000
Persons per Household	2.95
No. of Households	1,047,458
EBI Per Household	13,995
Connecticut Retail Sales	7,274,000,000
Selected Services	1,163,000,000
Personal Services	70,537,000 (Part of Selected Service)

$$\frac{7,274,000,000}{1,047,458} = \$6,944 \text{ Retail Sales/H.H.}$$

$$\frac{6,944}{13,995} = 50\% \text{ (Retail Sales as } \% \text{ of EBI)}$$

$$\frac{1,163,000,000}{1,047,458} = 1,110 \text{ Services/H.H.}$$

$$\frac{1,110}{13,995} = 7.9\% \text{ (Services as } \% \text{ of EBI)}$$

$$\begin{array}{r} 70,537,000 \\ 7,272,000,000 \\ \hline 7,344,537,000 \end{array}$$

$$\frac{70,537,000}{7,344,537,000} = .0096 \text{ (} \% \text{ of Pers. Serv. to Total)}$$

Source: Connecticut Market Data 1974/75, p. 40; *1972 Census of Selected Service Industry*, p. 7-4; *1972 Census of Business: Retail Trade*, p. 7-2, 7-4.

Table 7

	1972 Retail Spending (millions)	% of Total
SIC Classification[b]		
Retail Spending[a]		
A. General Merchandise Group Stores	989	13.7
B. Food Stores	1,640	22.7
C. Apparels and Accessories	436	6.1
D. Furniture, Home Furnishings and Equipment	365	5.1
E. Eating and Drinking	533	7.4
F. Drug Store and Proprietary	236	3.3
G. Miscellaneous Retail	958	13.3
Selected Services[c]		
H. Personal Services	215	14.6

[a] Total state retail spending in 1972 was 7,217 million.
[b] Only those classifications needed are shown.
[c] Total state spending on selected services in 1972 was 1,469 million.
Sources: *Bureau of Census 1972 Retail Trade*: p. 7-3; *Bureau of Census 1972 Selected Services*: p. 7-4.

buying income was calculated at 84 percent of gross income (see Table 5). The 84 percent figure was derived from data found in the publication *Connecticut Market Data 1974/75* and simply represents per capita effective buying income divided by per capita personal income. A total gross income figure for faculty and staff was determined by taking average salary in each category shown in Table 4 times the number of employees in that categoty.

In 1972, retail sales constituted 50 percent of effective buying income in the State of Connecticut (see Table 6). Total potential retail sales was determined simply by adding retail sales for each category. Personal services were added to total Connecticut retail sales and then this figure was divided into personal services to obtain a percentage of personal services to the total in order to delineate an estimate for spending for this type of activity by students in dormitories.

A process involving several steps and using secondary data was established to determine the type and size of outlet for the commercial development. The first step was to list the SIC classifications for Connecticut retail spending in 1972 and relate each of these categories to total state retail spending (see Table 7).

The second step in the process consisted of establishing store-type sales as a percentage of total spending by subjectively identifying the type of activity within the major SIC classifications that would be considered appropriate for the Storrs Center development. The store-type sales as a percentage of total retail spending is simply a function of the percentage of total retail spending for each general SIC classification times the percentage of store-type sales to group total. For example, in Table 8, the 1.7 percent variety store sales as a percentage of total spending is simply the product of the 13.7 percent general merchandise classification as a

Table 8

SIC Classification	$ Value of Spending	% of Store-Type Sales To Group Total	Store-Type Sales As % of Total Spending
A. General Merchandise Group Stores	989		
1. Variety Store	123	12.4	1.7
B. Food Stores	1,640		
1. Retail Bakery (Baking and Selling)	34	2.1	.47
2. Candy, Nut, and Confectionary	7	.4	.091
C. Apparels and Accessories	436		
1. Women's Ready-to-Wear	148	33.9	2.07
2. Men's and Boys' Clothing and Furnishings	98	22.5	1.37
3. Family Shoe Store	40	9.2	.56
D. Furniture, Home Furnishings and Equipment	364		
1. Music Stores	16	4.4	.22
E. Eating and Drinking Places	533		
1. Restaurants and Lunchrooms	261	50.0	3.7
2. Refreshment Places	119	22.3	1.65
3. Drinking Places (alcoholic)	77	14.4	1.07
F. Drug Store and Proprietary	236	9	
1. Drug Store	226	95.8	3.16
2. Proprietary	8	4.2	.14
G. Miscellaneous Retail	958		
1. Liquor Store	197	20.6	2.74
2. Florists	25	2.6	.35
3. Sporting Goods and Bicycle Shops	41	4.3	.57
4. Jewelry	42	4.4	.59
5. Gift, Novelty, and Souvenir	22	2.3	.31
6. Camera and Photographic Supply	16	1.7	.23
H. Personal Services	215		
1. Coin operated laundries and dry cleaning	10	4.7	.69
2. Beauty Shops	47	21.9	3.2
3. Barber Shops	13	6.0	.88

Sources: *Bureau of Census 1972 Retail Trade*: p. 7-4, 7-5; *Bureau of Census 1972 Selected Services*, p. 7-4.

Table 9

SIC Classification	1976 Potential Market Area Retail Sales Millions		60% Capture Rates	
	32.7	35.2	Low	High
A. General Merchandise Group Stores				
1. Variety Store	.556	.598	.334	.359
B. Food Stores				
1. Retail Bakery (Baking and Selling)	.154	.165	.092	.099
2. Candy, Nut and Confectionary	.030	.032	.018	.019
C. Apparels and Accessories				
1. Women's Ready-to-Wear	.677	.729	.406	.437
2. Men's and Boys' Clothing and Furnishings	.448	.482	.269	.289
3. Family Shoe Store	.183	.197	.110	.118
D. Furniture, Home Furnishings and Equipment				
1. Music Stores	.072	.077	.043	.046
E. Eating and Drinking Places				
1. Restaurants and Lunchrooms	1.21	1.30	.726	.780
2. Refreshment Places	.54	.58	.324	.348
3. Drinking Places (alcoholic)	.35	.377	.210	.226
F. Drug Store and Proprietary				
1. Drug Store	1.033	1.112	.620	.667
2. Proprietary	.046	.049	.028	.029
G. Miscellaneous Retail				
1. Liquor Store	.896	.964	.538	.578
2. Florists	.114	.123	.068	.074
3. Sporting Goods and Bicycle Shops	.186	.201	.112	.121
4. Jewelry	.193	.208	.116	.125
5. Gift, Novelty, and Souvenir	.101	.109	.061	.065
6. Camera and Photographic Supply	.075	.081	.045	.049

	1976 Service Sales			
	4.46	4.57		
H. Personal Services				
1. Coin operated laundries and dry cleaning	.031	.032	.019	.019
2. Beauty Shops	.143	.146	.086	.088
3. Barber Shops	.039	.040	.023	.024

Source: *Bureau of Census, 1972 Retail Trade.*

percentage of total retail spending times the 12.4 percent of variety store sales to the total general merchandise group stores.

The third step in the process was to determine the potential market area retail sales and was determined by applying the percentages established above (store-type sales as a percentage of total spending) to the previously determined total retail sales. This was further reduced by applying a 60 percent capture rate (see Table 9). Due to the confinement of students in dormitories and the large number of commuters, it is most reasonable to assume that the proposed development will capture a larger percentage of the total retail sales available. This should also be true to some degree for university faculty and staff.

The sales per square foot for each store-type outlet was obtained from *Dollars and Cents of Shopping Centers, 1975*. For those outlets which were not clearly identified in this source material, an average of similar outlets was taken. For example, restaurants and lunchrooms and refreshment places sales per square foot are averages (see Table 10). Also in Table 10, the square footage required was derived by dividing potential market area retail sales by sales per square foot for each store-type outlet (as determined by *Dollars and Cents of Shopping Centers*). These figures were then compared to median gross leaseable area for neighborhood centers for each outlet type. The number and sizes of outlets is shown in Table 11 and reflects the calculations made in Table 10 as well as personal judgment regarding the unique characteristics of the market in which the project is to be located.

Market rents for the Storrs area as compiled in *Commercial Leasing Practice in Storrs Connecticut, 1975* suggests that an appropriate range for the types of facilities contemplated for the proposed commercial development would be between $6 and $7 per square foot. On the basis of this estimate and the projections made in Table 10 (including a University Bookstore of 10,000 square feet) this development would provide for a gross income of approximately $400,000. Expenses for this type of development, according to *Dollars and Cents of Shopping Centers*, would approximate 30 percent of gross receipts, producing a net operating income of $280,000. Construction costs are estimated to be $1,900,000.

Table 10

SIC Classification	Sales/ Sq. Ft.	Square Footage Needed		Neighborhood ULI's *Dollars and Cents of Shopping Centers* Median GLA
		Low	High	
A. General Merchandise Group Stores				
1. Variety Store	41.22	8,103	8,709	7,500
B. Food Stores				
1. Retail Bakery (Baking and Selling)	49.00	1,877	2,020	1,800
2. Candy, Nut and Confectionary	52.00	346	365	2,400
C. Apparels and Accessories				
1. Women's Ready-to-Wear	63.05	6,439	6,931	2,000
2. Men's and Boys' Clothing and Furnishings	60.00	4,483	4,817	2,000
3. Family Shoe Store	35.63	3,087	3,312	2,854
D. Furniture, Home Furnishings and Equipment				
1. Music Stores	31.00	1,387	1,484	1,440
E. Eating and Drinking Places				
1. Restaurants and Lunchrooms	52.50	13,828	14,857	2,305
2. Refreshment Places	50.06	6,472	6,952	1,600
3. Drinking Places (alcoholic)	41.82	5,022	5,404	1,658
F. Drug Store and Proprietary				
1. Drug Store	64.82	9,565	10,290	7,305
G. Miscellaneous Retail				
1. Liquor Store	79.50	6,767	7,270	2,400
2. Florists	49.97	1,361	1,481	1,207
3. Sporting Goods and Bicycle Shops	45.39	2,468	2,666	2,287
4. Jewelry	76.91	1,508	1,625	1,160
5. Gift, Novelty, and Souvenir	37.29	1,636	1,743	1,800
6. Camera and Photographic Supply	155.93	288	314	1,020
H. Personal Services				
1. Coin operated laundries and dry cleaning	15.03	1,264	1,264	1,470
2. Beauty Shops	49.85	1,725	1,765	1,200
3. Barber Shops	38.88	592	617	620
Total		78,218	83,886	

Source: Urban Land Institute, *Dollars and Cents of Shopping Centers* 1975, Neighborhood Centers.

Table 11 *Dollars and Cents of Shopping Centers* Summary of Tenant Characteristics in Neighborhood Shopping Centers

Tenant	Number of Units	Size (Sq. Ft.)
Variety Store	1	8,000
Deli/Bakery (Independent)	1	1,900
Candy, Nut, Confectionary[d]	1	300
Women's Ready-to-Wear	1	3,000
Men's/Boys' Clothing	1	2,500
Family Shoe	1	3,000
Music Store	1	1,400
Restaurant and Lunchroom	2[a]	5,000 (2)
Refreshment	2[b]	2,000 (2)
Drinking (Alcoholic)	1[c]	1,800
Drug Store	1	3,000
Liquor	1	2,500
Florist	1	1,200
Sporting Goods/Bicycle	1	2,400
Jewelry	1	1,500
Gift/Novelty, Souvenir	1	1,700
Camera/Photo Supply[d]	1	300
Coin-Operated Laundry	1	1,400
Beauty Shop	1	1,200
Barber Shop	1	600
Bookstore	1	10,000
Total		61,700

[a] *Dollars and Cents* category of restaurants with liquor averaged with restaurants without liquor.

[b] Refreshment places consist of fast foods.

[c] Cocktail lounges.

[d] Marginal contribution to commercial development as conceived.

Chapter 13

Analysis of Office Market Potential

13

Introduction

In this case study, a broker was retained by an office building developer to look for a market where development potential would continue over time. The developer was looking for an opportunity for development in an area where his expertise (and staff) could be utilized on a continuing and the most efficient basis. Initially, several markets were studied with the intention of identifying the market which had the greatest potential for continued development.

The market selected was studied in considerable detail in two phases. Phase I of the study centered on the general characteristics of the office market. Phase I was intended to describe the demand for office space based upon the growth of gross user groups in order to compare the long-term supportable demand level with the level of demand experienced during the past few years. Further, it was intended to show the current supply of office space along with the potential future supply of space.

Phase I of the report is not an economic base study projecting growth from the base industries and characteristics of Capitol County. However, these factors have been relevant to historical growth rates. It is also not intended to project over-building or excess demand since such predictions must be based upon knowledge about who will build, what they will build, and in what time frame. At this point, only some builders' intentions are known. This phase of the study only measures the point of time in which the market was studied. It does, however, provide a basis of knowledge on which to measure the effect of changes in intentions and new actions, whether initiated by a builder, land owner, user or government in the future.

Phase I of this report does not describe the product that would do well in the market. It does describe the share of the market that a suitable product should expect. To prepare a suitable product, the following kinds of knowledge from various sources will be necessary:

- Tenant types
- Number of employees
- Space required

- Internal division of spaces
- Amenities required, including courts, patios, kitchens, baths, parking, landscaping, bars, materials
- Source of tenants, local or others
- Tenants being supplied by other builders
- Tenants not being supplied by other builders
- Growth of tenants
- Lease term of potential tenants
- Tenants represented in Capitol City and those not represented
- Marketing agents and their commitments, points of view, contracts and presentations
- Other marketing aids

Much of this information comes from a survey of existing buildings and tenants both in the subject area and in "source" areas. Potential marketing agents also supplied information regarding tenants, building requirements and marketing tools.

Phase II of the study shows that marketing to insurance, business, law firms and certain other types of business activities through a marketing approach based on the existing positive features of the selected community and location will maximize the rate of office absorption on the subject site. This is in contrast to marketing approaches relying on extensive cold calling and selling.

Phase II also maintains that the marketing approach, type of marketing target and type of competition indicates that an integrated site plan involving small buildings or a "small office park" would have the best results. This portion of the study is based on samples. Samples may be biased, but the sample size in this study was large enough in all but certain areas, which will be discussed, to give a fair picture of the market. However, whenever views of tenants or the proportion of a single type of user are cited in this report, the views and proportion are of the sample and not of the total population.

This phase of the study was done from information gathered in February and March, 1977. As tenants move and new buildings are built, the facts will change from those shown.

It should be emphasized that the studies that follow typically are not done by the commercial broker. However, the commercial broker is often the catalyst in having the study conducted and is in a position to interpret the information from the studies which are invaluable to the developer, the lender and the leasing program.

General Market

Capitol County had a population of 686,300 in 1975. It is a community that grows steadily but not rapidly (about 1.5 percent per year). The basic industry is government, which lends to the area a growth rate that cycles with growth of the state (but more smoothly) plus a heavily centered income distribution and sometimes erratic or noncooperative policies.

The typical historical condition of the real estate market in Capitol City has been that of over-building. With substantial buildable and zonable land, developers consistently, though not drastically, have been ahead of the market. Many builders preferred the lower margins to the boom or bust cycle of other areas.

Most recently, Capitol City has reached the size where the business of serving the population is almost as big as the business of government. As a result of government and the city's new dimension, Capitol City did not suffer the real estate depression as severely as did other places, and is now building at a record rate.

Capitol City's growth rate is expected to continue at about the same level as it has in the past and certainly through the term of the subject project. A burgeoning basic industry, a lower cost of living and a still rural aspect and life style in a growing state are all factors which indicate continued growth.

Government Influence

All three levels of government have been growing during the past year, although state and local government have been expanding much more rapidly than federal government. Most government operations are housed downtown, but there has always been leasing of suburban space. In 1971, after a long program to provide state buildings for state workers, for instance, only 50,000 square feet were being leased. At the present time, there are 2,119,663 square feet. This program is being tried once more through state support of the Capitol Area plan.

The state GSA has been mandated to lease only in the downtown area and to build two new office buildings to house suburban employees. These are budgeted currently, but will probably not start construction until 1979. These two buildings will hardly hold the expected growth in government employment between now and the time they are completed.

Of greater early impact is the state's willingness to lease older renovated structures. These will absorb a percentage of government growth. While there is little space remaining downtown, there are no new private build-ings planned because of the disparity between the high cost of high-rise construction and the low rental rates paid by government on which builders must depend in large part.

Rural space is being rented in the Lake Avenue area, largely because of rent levels. Few buildings will be affected either way by the Capitol Area plan.

Assumptions

Capitol County is expected to grow by 10,000 persons per year as projected by the Department of Finance. The major growth of the county will continue to be in the northeast and southeast sectors, served by two interstate highways. With 75 percent of the growth occurring in these areas, comparable growth should occur in the office centers serving them. In future years, some growth will be lost to competing areas, thus shifting some office emphasis to downtown.

The number of jobs required to service and support the same population is increasing from the existing average of 365 to 387 jobs per thousand of population. In relation to new population, the number of jobs must be approximately 480 per thousand in order to gradually continue this trend. By 1980, there would be 288,600 jobs for 736,000 people or 392 jobs per thousand. A slightly larger proportion of the new jobs will be office-oriented.

In 1970 and 1975, transportation, communications and utilities, government, finance, insurance and real estate and business services accounted for slightly less than 49 percent of total employment. The boost in government growth will increase this figure to just over 49 percent by 1980, requiring about 2,650 office jobs per year until then. With the assumption of 200 net square feet per employee, demand is expected to be about 530,000 square feet per year.

Over the next five years, transportation, communications and utilities will retain the same relationship with population at five employees per thousand population. In addition, federal government will increase employment to 44 employees per thousand of population and state government will retain a relationship of 52 employees per thousand of population. Local government will increase the number of employees to 53 per thousand of population due to new programs. Finance, insurance and real estate will increase the number of employees to 18 per thousand of population, and business services will increase the number of employees to eight per thousand of population. On the basis of the foregoing assumptions, annual growth by office worker category would be as follows:

Annual Employment Growth

Transportation, communications and utilities	50
Federal government	729
State government	520
Local government	801
Finance, insurance and real estate	329
Business services	217
Total Annual Employment	2,646

The Lake Avenue corridor is expected to capture various percentages of this growth. Capture or penetration for transportation, communications and utilities should be in the neighborhood of 50 percent in the market area. The capture or penetration rate for federal government is anticipated to be 30 percent in the subject area, with 60 percent downtown and 10 percent scattered. The reason for the high percentage in the market area is the proximity of the federal building. State government will not locate in the subject area due to the Capitol Area plan. Local government is expected to locate 10 percent in this area with 50 percent downtown and 40 percent scattered.

About 80 percent of finance, insurance and real estate will locate in the eastern portion of Capitol City due to the population growth in this area. Of this, 15 percent will locate at East Range, leaving the remainder, or 65 percent, for the Lake Avenue Corridor. About 80 percent of the business services employees are also expected to locate in the eastern portion of Capitol City, 65 percent along Lake Avenue and 15 percent along East Range.

Capture Rates

	PCU	Federal	State	Local	FIRE	Business Services	Total
Downtown	25	437	520	401	33	22	1,438
Lake	25	318	—	80	213	141	677
East Range	—	—	—	—	50	32	82
Other	—	74	—	320	33	22	499
Total	50	729	520	801	329	217	2,646

Construction costs and the low rents paid by government will prevent much new construction in the downtown area, other than by government itself or through rehabilitation. Since downtown is basically full, it can be assumed that three-quarters of federal, state and local employees will fill space left by firms wishing to upgrade. The state is trying to build two new buildings, one to consolidate the justice department and one general purpose building containing 350,000 square feet. Although the funds were budgeted this year, construction (as previously indicated) will probably not begin until 1979.

With the three to five-year construction lag, government projects will hardly be able to accommodate even one-quarter of the expected growth in demand for office space over the short term. If the remainder of replaced firms wish to upgrade, and 60 percent of these go to Lake Avenue, 10 percent go to East Range and 30 percent go to others, the distribution of space would be as follows:

Distribution of Space by Location

	Employees	Space	Percent
Downtown	359	71,800	14
Lake	1,325	265,000	50
East Range	190	38,000	7
Other	772	154,400	29
Total	2,646	529,200	100

New private employees equal 596 persons per year, or 113,240 square feet of space. One rule of thumb generally quoted is that for every square foot of space demanded by new tenants, 1.6 square feet is demanded by upgrading tenants. While the ratio may vary widely, this factor results in 181,000 square feet of upgraded space. The downtown redistribution method used here results in 215,800 square feet in upgraded space.

There are about 2,200 doctors and dentists in Capitol County or one for every 311 persons. The growth rate expected for the subject area is only 600 persons per year and would indicate at most two new practitioners. However, the Lake Avenue Corridor is considered the choice location for many specialists who do not need to be as close to their patients. Therefore, the growth in the northeastern area, for purposes of estimating, is 6,000 persons per year or 20 new practitioners. If each employs two persons and each worker requires 275 square feet of space, another 16,500 square feet is added to the demand of the Lake Avenue Corridor. In addition, the demand from medical practitioners desiring to upgrade their space has more than equalled the demand from growth. On the same basis the absorption of new space by medical offices in Capitol County is probably about 60,000 square feet a year.

Office Centers

The Lake Avenue Corridor, including University Circle (where the subject site is located) and Westhaven, has become an office center for Capitol City. The reasons for this development include: (1) the predominance of government downtown; (2) the growth of the city to the east; and (3) the completion of both interstate highways to the east.

River Road is something of an office center, but it is inhibited by slower growth in South Capitol City and lower incomes. A single developer has been the main developer in the area, and government has provided many of his leases due to lower rents.

The East Range area is an emerging center with a huge amount of planned new offices. It is expected that this will provide space for professionals serving a more local clientele because of the distance to freeways. If this is true, the area could be vastly overbuilt. Rentals in the one well-planned project now under construction are going well.

Sampson Avenue probably would have been the office center corridor since it connects both interstate highways and is the most used traffic artery in the country. While development is proceeding, Sampson Avenue has been upended by the existence of University Circle and Westhaven on Lake Avenue. These projects are assumed to be filled out of the demand for "other" locations rather than those from the Lake Avenue Corridor since they do not form a center. The project approved for Sampson and Attica is large, but is not very relevant since its success is doubtful at any time during the next several years.

Office Demand

The demand for office space is based on growth of population and size of the population. Both growth and size are instrumental in determining the types and level of office services. Office users include transportation, communications and utility groups (growth in this category is generally in office personnel) government, finance, insurance and real estate groups and business services (which are also largely real estate oriented). As growth in population occurs, these groups generally grow. When the population reaches a certain size, the service level of these groups may change (from a local insurance agent to an area office, for instance). Both growth and size of population encourage new firms and expansion and upgrading of existing firms.

These users typically want to locate in a prestige area and in an area where others are located. The Lake Avenue Corridor has established itself as such an area through the early emergence of University Circle.

Such users also want to locate generally close to the residence of the administrative executive, to "where the action is" and in a location accessible to through-city and through-state traffic routes. Lake Avenue is closest to the major residential areas in Capitol City. The greatest amount of new development is occurring in that eastern quadrant with the two interstate highways providing the accessibility.

The foregoing are the principles on which much of the assumptions listed earlier are based. It results in the Lake Avenue Corridor capturing 45 to 50 percent of the total office demand in the Capitol City area or 250,000 square feet per year over the long term. Medical demand constitutes another 30,000 square feet. Medical space is, however, more related to location and the number of customers in a service area.

Historical Absorption

During 1976, Capitol City absorbed about 750,000 square feet of space. This absorption level was above normal, forming the peak of the cycle and the new trend to office upgrading at higher level services. It also reflects the revolving door phenomenon in that many of the industries absorbing the office space are also the ones dependent upon its construction. By 1978, the wave should slow down to its longer term rate of about 600,000 square feet per year.

Correspondingly, the Lake Avenue Corridor absorbed about 436,000 square feet of space, or about 55 percent of the total for the area. This percentage should taper off, but only slightly as East Range and Sampson Avenue move into the market.

Among the three parts of Lake Avenue Corridor, University Circle has always been dominant. It is the most prestigious, the most attractive and the most developed. It is also located closest to some of the finest residential areas in Capitol City.

On the other hand, a circulation problem has developed at the corner of College and Lake that is a very great concern to potential tenants. A leading leasing agent is leaning very heavily on this as a selling point in a promotion of Westhaven, and it is effective. The publicity, marketing and talk on the street is that Westhaven is the new thing. Office tenants, as cited before, tend to prefer the "in" place, which is expected to be Westhaven in 1977. This fad is reflected in the number of projects planned for Westhaven during the next year or so. In three to five years an overpass is planned for Lake Avenue and College which will return University Circle to a dominant position. University Circle can accept this decision only temporarily due to the availability of land.

Two projections of the division of market between the areas in the Lake Avenue Corridor are shown below. They are only slightly different from each other, depending upon the degree of success at Westhaven.

Division of Market within Lake Corridor Projection

Percent Share	1976	Alternate I 1977	1978	1979	1980
University Circle	40	35	35	50	55
Lake Avenue	32	30	25	15	10
Westhaven	28	35	40	35	35
Percent Share	1976	Alternate II 1977	1978	1979	1980
University Circle	40	30	35	50	50
Lake Avenue	32	35	25	15	15
Westhaven	28	40	40	35	35

Certainly if all planned projects are built in early 1977 in Westhaven, there will be considerable overhang in 1978. Lake Avenue also will have some space in 1978. University Circle will come out with only a small amount.

Conclusions, Phase I

Based on either Alternates I or II, University Circle land is shown in the next tables to be absorbed during 1981. The tables combine the recent rate of absorption with the estimated long-term or supportable rate of absorption and the ability of the Lake Avenue Corridor to capture its share. A table is shown for both Alternates I and II.

A drastic change in the marketplace will be necessary to extend the absorption period beyond 1982. Government, of course, has the capacity to make drastic changes.

Capitol County Absorption of Office Space
(000 square feet)

| | Alternate I | | | | |
	1976	1977	1978	1979	1980
Capitol City Absorption	750	675	600	600	600
Lake Avenue Corridor	436	337	300	270	270
(Percent of Capitol City)	55	50	50	45	45
University Circle	172	118	105	135	145
(Remaining Space)*	639	521	416	281	136
Lake Avenue	141	101	75	40	27
(Remaining Space)*	409	308	233	193	166
Westhaven	123	118	120	95	95
(Remaining Space)*	653	535	415	320	225
	Alternate II				
Capitol City Absorption	750	675	600	600	600
Lake Avenue Corridor	436	337	300	270	270
(Percent of Capitol City)	55	50	50	45	45
University Circle	172	101	105	135	135
(Remaining Space)*	639	538	433	298	163
Lake Avenue	141	118	75	40	40
(Remaining Space)*	409	291	216	176	136
Westhaven	123	135	120	105	105
(Remaining Space)*	653	518	398	293	188

* Using midpoint of potential future space; adding back what has been absorbed so far in 1977. There are differences between the various parts of remaining University Circle land. The subject property is at the end of office development, has the most difficult access and is the furthest from the shops. On the other hand, it is adjacent to the river, is quiet and has the University Circle ambience.

Phase II

The purpose of this phase of the study is to determine the most likely user of office space in the subject property of the University Circle complex and Capitol City during 1977 and 1978, in terms of their business activity and former location. From this information, a marketing plan and building design is to be developed that will best satisfy this tenant.

Methodology

A field survey was made of the tenants of 15 office buildings in the Lake Avenue Corridor which includes University Circle, Lake Avenue and Westhaven. One other complex at Sampson Avenue and River Drive was also surveyed. Each tenant was asked about the nature of the business being conducted, the number of employees, the square footage occupied, the former location and the prospects for moving. The question about the lease term was answered some of the time, but one on rent was hardly ever answered.

Where firm figures were not available on square footage, estimates were used. Where tenants could not be interviewed, the name, the type of business and square footage were included, but the number of employees in the former location was left blank. In a recently completed building, only those tenants occupying space were surveyed.

A second part of the survey consisted of 15 buildings which were chosen from "former locations" identified by current tenants in the market area. These buildings were taken evenly from downtown and east. One-half of the tenants were telephoned and asked the following questions:

1. What is the nature of the business?

2. How many people work in the office?

3. How long has the business occupied the space?

4. If and when the office is next moved, what location in Capitol City will be chosen and why?

If no answer was forthcoming to Question 4, another question was asked: "Are there any reasons for being in any particular location in Capitol City?" Answers were not used from short-term, temporary or uninformed personnel. In most cases, a long-term employee was reached.

In the mid-town section, many companies did not answer the telephone, indicating a one-person office. Many of these buildings have been largely taken over by public service firms or agencies, and the portion occupied by others is small. As a result, the sample is small.

The telephone survey seemed to indicate that the cast area has the greatest mobility and failure rate.

Results of the Survey

Of a total of 139 tenants surveyed in the 15 buildings, there was 496,000 square feet of leasable office space accounted for, or 3,572 square feet per tenant. The breakdown of offices by size is skewed on the average to the large size, as shown by the following table.

Firms/Tenants by Office Size

Square Feet	Lake Avenue Corridor	Percent	University Circle Only	Percent
Less than 1,000	45	32	9	27
1,000–1,999	45	32	8	24
2,000–3,999	23	17	6	18
4,000–5,999	8	6	4	12
6,000–9,999	8	6	2	6
10,000 or more	10	7	4	12
Total	139	100%	33	99%

While 28 percent of the space surveyed was in University Circle, only 19 percent of the under-4,000 square foot spaces was located there. Much of this is accounted for by the predominance of insurance companies and other very large users of space. University Circle has 95,506 square feet and 12 offices averaging 7,959 square feet each. Furthermore three of the insurance "firms" are related through the same parent and might be considered one firm.

Of the currently renting buildings in the Lake Avenue Corridor, space sizes are broken down in the following way:

Firms/Tenants in Currently Renting Buildings by Office Space

Square Feet	1445 Foster	1485 Foster	2020 Carey	425 College	Total	Percent
Less than 1,000	3	—	—	1	4	23
1,000–1,999	3	—	2	3	8	47
2,000–3,999	—	—	1	1	2	12
4,000–5,999	—	—	—	—	—	—
6,000–9,999	—	—	—	—	—	—
10,000 or more	1	2	—	—	3	18
					17	100%

While the local telephone company and one insurance company have filled a very large amount of this currently-renting space, the predominant firm size is between 1,000 and 2,000 square feet. Judging from the spaces being prepared in these new buildings, this space size will continue to satisfy the bulk of tenants.

A clear difference between University Circle and the rest of Lake Avenue is shown in the distribution by business activity. Insurance is the predominant activity in both areas, but far more so in University Circle. It is followed in University Circle by very distant seconds in legal and other business activities. In the corridor generally, government and transportation, communications, and utilities are more important.

Sources of New Firms

This phase of the study was also intended to determine the source of firms locating in the Lake Avenue Corridor. It was clear that University Circle attracts more firms from downtown than the rest of the Lake Avenue Corridor, but fewer from mid-town and east areas. It is also important to note that University Circle keeps its own firms when they move to larger spaces. The area as a whole is greatly influenced by the formation of new firms. Twenty-two percent of the tenants derived from this source—largely among attornies in University Circle. Insurance companies are from a wide range of locations. While the out-of-town group is not large in terms of the numbers of firms, it constitutes some of the largest space users.

Among the new buildings, most users are from the east area (7 of 15) while five are new, one from mid-town and one from downtown. Telephone interviews were conducted with 127 firms to determine the number of employees by tenant/firm. An additional purpose of this interview was to verify and refine the space requirements per employee.

In the downtown area, where occupancy periods are much longer, approximately four calls were made for every three responses. In mid-town, five calls were made for every two responses and in the east, three calls were made for every two responses. In addition, many of the offices in mid-town were occupied by service agencies, both public and private. It was judged that calling these groups was not beneficial.

"Potential" Movers

Through the survey, one group of firms was identified as "potential" movers. These are the firms that had no business ties downtown and those that voiced an interest in moving east in general or to the Lake Avenue Corridor. In the downtown area, the greatest number of "potential" movers were those in the other category of business activity. A larger number were also in the insurance business. Far fewer lawyers (a very small portion of the total number) were interested in moving. Downtown is the preferred location of litigating attorneys, certified public accountants (because of the proximity of head office banks) and associations that lobby.

As noted before, back-up data shows the strong inclination for public service groups to locate in mid-town. The reason is the low rent and proximity to clients. Another group interested in mid-town are the professions in the arts or quasi-arts—architecture, engineering, graphics and printing. These firms need large spaces, do not wish to pay high rents in general and enjoy the older buildings.

Very few of the lawyers, small accounting firms and insurance firms still remaining in this area have any tie to it. There is an exception to this, but that exception is located directly across the street from the

County Courthouse. The 60-man legal firm occupying that building is a further exception in that it owns the building.

Over one-third of the tenants in University Circle came from the east area and University Circle itself. These firms moved because they are new and growing. They move within the area because their clients are there, their homes are there and their employees are there.

The largest portion of the "potential" movers in the east are insurance firms. Many are from the Sampson Avenue Corridor, which, while it has a number of office buildings, is basically a retail corridor with half again to twice the traffic as Lake Avenue.

Tenant Market for University Circle

Much of the foregoing has been combined into three graphs to illustrate the type of tenant most likely to be attracted to University Circle. Graph 1 (page 261) shows the amount of space occupied by each type of business activity in University Circle, along with the "potential" movers by business activity. The first scale is space and the second is employees, but the interesting parts are the peaks. University Circle has successfully attracted insurance firms first, other types second, and legal firms third. Of "potential" movers, insurance firms form the greatest number, other firms are second and legal firms are third.

Graph 2 (page 262) shows that University Circle has most successfully drawn firms from the east, secondarily drawn from downtown and has also been successful with new firms. Of the "potential" movers,, the largest percentage of those are in the east. The largest number of "potential" movers are downtown, of course, but they are a smaller percentage of the total firms and much harder to find.

Graph 3 (page 263) combines this information for the three main groups: insurance, legal and other business activities. The following interpretations are given to the graphs:

1. Insurance is especially attracted to University Circle and is a "potential" mover from all three Capitol City areas.

2. Legal firms will be mostly new (inmigrating) firms moving from established downtown locations. The "potential" movers from either midtown and the east are from too small a sample to be relevant.

3. Other business activities show a high "potential" mobility, particularly in downtown.

The most common reason for moving from downtown was a lack of parking. Secondary reasons were the distance to the decision-makers' homes and traffic congestion. The reasons for moving from mid-town were the dilapidated surroundings and the unsavory character of the clients of some nearby firms. The most common reason for moving from one location to the other in the east was for more space.

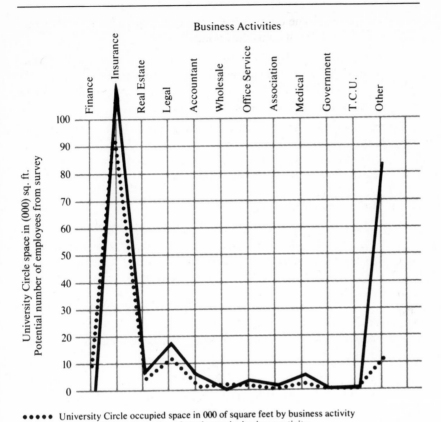

Business Activities

●●●●● University Circle occupied space in 000 of square feet by business activity
━━━ "Potential" movers number of employees by business activity

GRAPH 1

Marketing Program

In addition to advertising, marketing consists of a number of factors, some of which include the leasing agent, leasing terms, product design and marketing approach. It should be the intent of the marketing program to build upon the qualities of University Circle to attract the tenant most likely to move and to prefer the location.

We have concluded that these would include insurance companies from downtown, mid-town and east; law firms, particularly new law firms, from downtown; and other business activities, particularly from downtown.

The reactions most often listed concerning University Circle are as follows:

Prestige—Positive
Integrity of design—Positive
Proximity to the river—Positive
Good neighborhood—Positive

261

Market Areas

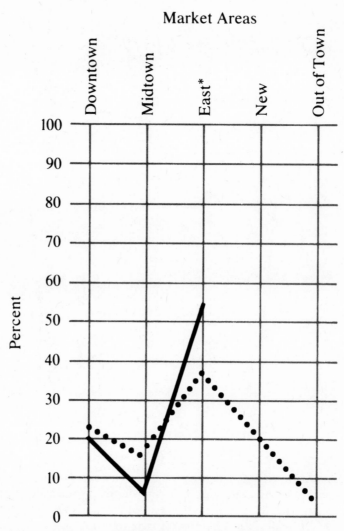

● ● ● Former Location of University Circle firms as a
        percentage of total firms

━━━ Locations of "potential" movers by percent of total
       employees

 ＊ East includes University Circle

GRAPH 2

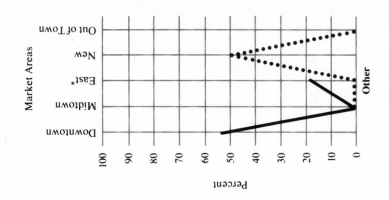

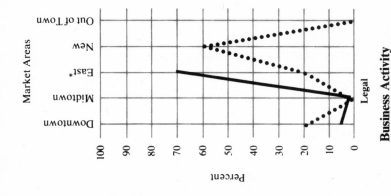

Business Activity

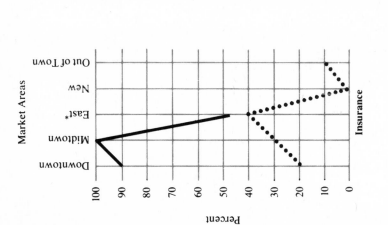

●●●● Former location of firms in University Circle as a percentage of total by business activity

──── Location of "potential" firms as a percentage of total by business activity

* Includes University Circle

GRAPH 3

263

State university—Positive/Negative
Congestion at College and Lake Avenue—Negative
Lack of restaurants—Negative.

The positive factors are extremely important to all three likely business categories and should be maintained as marketing factors. The negative factors should be ameliorated as far as possible.

Approach

The approach to the market should be based upon the quality and prestige of the University Circle community and the residential area surrounding it. It is not as accessible to all freeways as Westhaven and for the time being the congestion at College and Lake is a detriment. Again, the point is to emphasize the positive while reducing the negative.

Structuring the marketing program around the community should be advantageous in reaching the targets of the market program. The insurance companies are interested in a prestige location where other insurance companies are located. They are, however, scattered in all three major tenant source areas. A direct sales pitch over the telephone will probably not be appropriately timed so as to sell to the one of many that might be ready to move and will also not convince such a firm of the quality of University Circle.

In addition, the new lawyer groups that are also targets are downtown, but scattered in existing offices. A direct pitch to any individual in this group could be downright embarrassing.

Third, 10 of 32 responses as to why the east area was chosen was the relationship to the decision-makers' homes. The community approach should reinforce the ties between decision-makers living in University Circle and the surrounding residential areas and the University Circle office area.

Last, this approach implied cooperation among all University Circle builders. The forms that this approach may take are varied:

1. Community reception or community events through the association or generally in cooperation with others in the community.

2. Greater attention to newspaper releases. One builder's release on his new building in University Circle was one column, several lines long. It is not difficult to get pictures and better headlines if the release is structured around the community. Follow-up releases as the building progresses will get traffic.

3. Direct communication with the community as to the progress of a building.

264   4. Association with or other work on community problems, such as the overpass at Lake and College. This is good press because the promise of a resolution is as salable as the resolution itself.

5. The community of insurance firms should have much the same treatment. Events and existing firms in the community should be a subject for a press release, emphasizing the community and the decision-maker as well as the event and the firm. Insurance firms located outside the community should be made aware of the progress of construction of an office building as well as other community events.

6. One of the negative factors affecting the site is its position at the end of the College Avenue office community. Another is the state university student enclave at the footbridge. An alternative use would provide a destination point, thereby increasing traffic flow, buffering the enclave, and increasing the need to restrict student parking on College Avenue, all of which would be desirable. A restaurant has been mentioned. This alternative would also help sell the office space by providing a luncheon place within walking distance. Westhaven and Lake Avenue both have good restaurants nearby, but the subject property does not. Such a restaurant could not be the conventional chain type or similar type which require heavy traffic. It would have to be an individual and unique endeavor which in itself would complement and add to the community feeling. It may be difficult to find such a user. It has also not been determined if this use would be allowed by the city, but it is a reasonable use for the site adjacent to the footbridge across from the commercial area. Such a location would also attract some professional staff from the university.

Leasing Agent

Only two out of 139 surveyed firms were first approached by a leasing agent and thereby motivated to move. Of the others, the vast majority drove around looking at buildings and then called up the broker listed on the sign. A large percentage of the signs on buildings in the area belonged to the leading leasing agent in the area.

Builders of a number of the buildings in the general area have an arrangement with the leading leasing agent whereby they can both lease space. In one of those buildings, all tenants said they had gone directly to the builder.

One builder (who is reputed to have provided the inspiration for University Circle) does most of his own leasing—his reputation of providing the most beautiful buildings being sufficient advertisement. Another builder/developer of a planned structure in the area will probably do the majority of his own leasing.

The advantages of going with the leading leasing agent are its well-known name to both Capitol City residents and outside companies coming in and

265

the fact that the buildings will not advertise themselves given their location at the end of College Avenue.

The disadvantages of going with the leading leasing agent are the agent's heavy commitment to the Westhaven community and the fact that it has too much business to have the time or inclination to market any one building. It is believed that the leasing agent would not direct anyone to the subject site unless the client specifically and firmly asked for it.

University Circle as an area is already sufficiently well-known to market to Capitol City firms without the leasing agent. The firms that are entering from outside Capitol City, which are few but often quite large, will very likely approach the leasing agent first. If these are insurance firms, they will inquire as to the location of existing insurance offices and at least will become aware of University Circle. Other types of business categories may not find out about University Circle at all.

The best system would seem to be a cooperative one where the leasing agent could lease and receive commissions, but leasing would also be done in-house. In-house leasing, however, would be successful only with a good working relationship between the on-site employee and other office builders. Under this program, the location, community and product would "sell" the property rather than the leasing agent doing so.

Leasing Terms

The majority of the new leases are written for three to five years. The insurance companies and established lawyers want longer terms, while new law firms and other types of business activity want shorter terms to accommodate growth.

All new leases are being written as full service contracts where the owner pays the cost of utilities, taxes, maintenance, landscaping and usually twice-a-week janitorial service. The lessee pays only for the telephone.

New leases are being written with escalation clauses tied to a local area cost of living index, usually with one-half of percent per month maximum increase. A few, however, were as high as one and one-half percent per month.

New leases are being written from a low of 65 cents to a high of 75 cents in most buildings. No individual leases higher than 72 cents were noted except at one new building which was developed by the area's leading office building developer.

Tenant improvements are standard in that carpet, paper or paneling on 50 percent of the exterior dimensions of the space, signs, full wall dividers and counter space are provided.

There is, however, an obvious difference in quality in carpets, paneling, paper and dividers. The River Commons Office Park and another location on College Avenue both use excellent low shag nylon carpet. One other location on a street perpendicular to College has a very good multi-colored industrial weave. Some paneling offered is rough cut or finished hardwood rather than the more common ready-made walnut veneer. Some walls show exterior block. Dividers are usually smooth or textured removable wall board type, but a few are rearrangeable panels.

All ceilings are acoustical tile with flush fluorescent lighting. No one offered special ceiling effects in reception areas such as blown ceilings and drop light fixtures. All entrance doors to reception areas were flush to the hallways regardless of whether the hallway was exterior or interior. No one offered recessed entrances.

Design Factors

Office buildings in Capitol City include modern high-rises in downtown such as the 14-story Capitol Mall building, a number of old high-rise buildings, 1950 style two-story buildings in mid-town with colored panels or latticed facades over windows, and modern low-rise buildings in the east.

The east area buildings break down into five types:

1. Two-story, multiple structures around courts

2. One-story ranch style

3. Two-story architecturally unique buildings

4. Small building office parks

5. Basic buildings

The majority of new buildings are two-story multiple structures around courts. These buildings combine structures and parallel pairs with one exterior court between them. The main entrances are at the ends of the buildings with stairs to the second floor. In most typical situations, the second floor has an exterior covered walkway that connects the two buildings at each end over the entrance. The courtyard is landscaped and trellised at the second floor eve. Landscaping, walks and creeks are arranged between the pairs of buildings. Restrooms are at one end of the building reached by the exterior hall or courtyard. Building lengths range from 104 to 205 feet.

Types of Designs

There are a variety of other types of design in the general market area, but, as indicated previously, the courtyard building predominates. The disadvantages to a courtyard building are the exterior hallways (when employees must go outside to reach even the rest rooms), the greater cost of construction (many exterior walls), the greater utility costs (with more exterior window and wall per square foot plus more exterior door), and the plain exterior (flat roofs, little exterior detail—all the show is inside).

The leading developer in the area excels at architecturally unique buildings. His buildings on River Drive are two-stories with massive roofs, intricate shapes and soaring lobbies. Both an existing building and a planned building on College Avenue are lower cost take-offs of this design type. These University Center buildings have no courtyards. All offices are off six-foot wide interior corridors. Office depth is about 30 feet which provides a large two-room system. The advantages of such a style are the reduced construction costs, the ability to put more emphasis on the exterior, minimum utility costs and weatherproof corridors. The disadvantages are the dark corridors, dark reception areas and no tenant identity.

A fourth type of building is the small office park type. A good example consists of seven small two-story structures on a heavily wooded site. Most of the buildings are about 4,000 square feet, but they vary to accommodate the trees. If the site is on a hill, the second story is level entry. Tenants have a great deal of identity (public exposure) since clients and employees alike may park in front of their own building with their own sign in front.

The most recently approved building plans in Capitol City are in Westhaven and are for four separate one-story buildings ranging in size from 7,000 to 8,000 square feet. Firm identity is the special feature here. Parking convenience is also a factor. At least one of the four buildings is being built for a single attorney's office.

Another type of building is the basic straightforward structure—either a one-story store-front type or a two-story interior corridor type. The eye is not drawn to these buildings; without an appreciable difference in rent, they may suffer during less active times.

Considering the large size required by some insurance firms, other business activities and the smaller size of some law firms, it is apparent that a two-tiered system of spaces is necessary to maximize rentals at the subject site.

Because of the marketing decision to maintain the character of University Circle, exterior architectural features will be necessary. This will also be helpful in keeping the attention on the river side of College Avenue since several of the buildings on the interior side are the basic building type.

Small Office Park

Since University Circle does not have the small building office park type of design to offer at present, and since prestige and identity is important to the marketing target, it is felt that this type will be most marketable. The small office park has the additional advantage that individual buildings may be sold to tenants. The ability to divide the sites should be one of the factors dictating the design of the complex. This style is in keeping with the overall ambience of smaller structures coordinated within each other.

This style is also easily adaptable to the two-tier system of space sizes. One tier of the system would allow about 7,000 square feet of space with firm identity from the outside. The second tier would accommodate the two office system of smaller spaces with less identity from the outside. The principle to be maintained is the smaller building with parking attached to each. The two tiers could be in separate buildings or the large tier on the first floor and the small office tier on the second floor of a two-story building. The two tiers would not be mixed since the small office firms have more flexibility to grow if they adjoin other small offices.

Of other design features, these are the most important:

1. Parking is generally fixed at one space per 250 square feet of rentable office. Since most offices have one employee per 200 square feet and a requirement for visitors, this level is a minimum.

2. All two-story structures have elevators.

3. Landscaping is grass and trees and heavy berming. Landscaping sometimes divides parking areas. The subject site is treeless and totally flat.

4. Materials concentrate on horizontal, vertical and diagonal wood siding, medium cut and in lighter to natural tones. Brick and stone veneers are used heavily.

5. Windows are large but an effort is being made to reduce air-conditioning needs with deep overhangs, blinds, sideshades, recessed windows, and tinted and reflective glass.

Chapter 14

Convenience Food Store Development Potential

14

Convenience goods shopping centers include food, drug and liquor stores. Because of the nature of the market, these facilities serve primarily the needs of those residents in close proximity to the convenience goods location. Since more than one convenience "center" can serve a single residential area, the market penetration of a particular center is dependent upon the size and quality of food stores, which are almost always the major tenants of a center.

For the facility under consideration in this case study, delineation of the trade area was determined by examining such factors as existing competition and the accessibility of residential areas to the site. The boundaries of the trade area (approximately one mile radius from the site) reflect an assumption that the new facility would be of high quality and range in size from 20,000 to 25,000 square feet.

The National Picture

Business Week's March 21, 1977 issue examined in depth the $7.4 billion "mushroom" called convenience stores. Today's 27,500 stores double the 1970 total and represent the fastest growing segment of the retail food industry.

These small stores specialize in a different sales mix than do supermarkets. Most sell no fresh meat, little or no produce and a limited line of dry groceries. They stock an average of 3,000 fast-moving impulse items, compared to the 12 to 15,000 carried in today's supermarkets. Thus they in no way compete for the family's weekly grocery shopping. Instead, located close to bedroom communities, they are handy for the buyer who has forgotten something during routine shopping. Merchandise like snack foods, baked goods, soft drinks, beer and cigarettes account for 60 percent of all sales. The modest average individual sales tape of $1.38 supports what convenience store operators know—that the average customer is in the store less than five minutes, that the goods bought are usually consumed in half an hour and that more than half their customers are men.

Traditionally stocking only top-selling brands, often at premium prices, their inventory stays fairly constant. Recent consumer resentment over rising prices has resulted in many of the smaller companies (those with fewer than ten units) swallowing price increases in crucial products like candy, coffee and tobacco. This has forced down gross margins—on a national average—a full percent, to 26.6 percent in 1976. Medium-size chains, who set prices between those of supermarkets and the largest of the convenience chains that operate in 39 states, are doing what they can to persuade customers to buy "more than just what they have to have." And the largest operations are moving more to private labels in items like coffee and salad dressings.

But even as they take steps to keep merchandise costs at a workable level, they worry over how to cope with soaring costs of land and construction. It is becoming increasingly difficult to find good locations with ample parking space at prices practical for this kind of business. One chain employs a computer study of more than 100 site characteristics to narrow its list of possible locations.

The threat of slowing suburban expansion and abandonment of the once respected practice of staying three-quarters of a mile away from an existing convenience store are negatives of the changing picture. Supermarkets met the early threat of convenience stores by expanding their business hours, which has proven to be another retarding factor in growth of this small type operation.

Laggard operations are given a limited time to turn around to profitable operations. Daily sales and inventory reports are processed overnight so changes are spotted almost before they can be sensed on the scene. This fine-tuned examination of the day's operations allows management to make better use of space occupied by unprofitable items, suggests to them the addition of new "hot-to-go" goods processed through microwave ovens or perhaps using that same space for a stronger assortment of print and audio merchandise.

Energy-conscious customers may welcome the addition of gasoline pumps. Some stores are focusing their location choices so gasoline service stations are combined with convenience merchandise. One chain has even established a credit card arrangement with a major oil company, allowing both gasoline and store merchandise to be charged.

Whatever new concepts are developed, convenience stores have earned their place on the retail merchandising scene.

The Facility Under Consideration

The study proposed a convenience food store as indicated above. The trade area delineated for the proposed development was one mile radius from the site. On the basis of time-distance studies and the type of facility being considered for development, the following demand potential has been projected.

The total demand potential available to any food store within a designated trade area of a projected convenience center is a product of the total population within the trade area and the population's anticipated annual per capita expenditure. The table below presents the current and projected population within the trade area, the estimated per capita expenditures and the total demand potential.

Convenience Food Facility Market Share Analysis

	1977	1980	1985	1990
Population	16,800	16,900	17,900	17,900
Per Capita Food Expenditure	$ 655	$ 660	$ 680	$ 695
Total Demand Potential (000's)	$11,000	$11,150	$11,830	$12,440
Required Sales Volume @ Sales Productivity Level of $140.00 per Square Ft.				
20,000 sq. ft. (000's)	$ 2,800	$ 2,800	$ 2,800	$ 2,800
25,000 sq. ft. (000's)	$ 3,500	$ 3,500	$ 3,500	$ 3,500
Market Share of Total Demand Potential				
20,000 sq. ft.	25%	25%	24%	23%
25,000 sq. ft.	32%	31%	30%	28%

The population figures indicate that the 1977 population of the trade area being considered was 16,800 and is expected to increase to about 17,900 by 1990. This growth is anticipated to occur largely within the market area and to the south of the market area. The projected per capita expenditures were derived by examining the income level of the population within the trade area and from the *U.S. Census of Business-Retail Trade.* The result of these two projections is that the total demand potential available in the trade area is anticipated to be approximately $11.2 million in 1980, increasing to $12.4 million by 1990.

This analysis assumes that a new food facility would range in size from 20,000 square feet to 25,000 square feet. The required sales volumes in 1977 dollars for such a facility would be between $2.8 million to $3.5 million. In order for a new facility to achieve this level of sales, it would have to receive a market share of the total trade area demand potential of between 25 percent and 31 percent in 1980. This market share, although at the high end of an achieveable range, can be realized. The market share requirement is expected to decrease slightly in future years as the total market potential increases. The table above presents the format for market shares for selected years through 1990.

Convenience Goods Summary

The conclusion that is derived from the market shares presented in the table above is that there is sufficient demand potential for the construction of a new 20,000 to 25,000 square foot food facility. However, it can be expected that a new facility of this size will have an adverse impact upon the sales of existing facilities which now serve trade area residents since the new facility would be attempting to realize approximately 25 percent to 30 percent share of the total market potential.

Food store facilities are usually the major tenants in convenience centers. If there is sufficient demand to support a major food facility, then development experience has demonstrated that a developer can secure and successfully develop a full neighborhood shopping center. Therefore, in addition to the food center, it is anticipated that a convenience center would have a drug/discount store and numerous smaller shops as well.

Section V

Annotated Bibliography

Annotated Bibliography

Books

Applebaum, William. *Shopping Center Strategy*. New York: International Council of Shopping Centers, 1970, 202 pp.

This is a case study of the planning, locating, and developing of the Del Monte Center, Monterey, California. It traces the history of a regional shopping center and its development and assesses the outcome of various decisions on the entire venture.

Atlas, Martin. *Tax Aspects of Real Estate Transactions*. Washington, D.C.: BNA, Inc., 1966, 361 pp.

The author presents concepts of what can and cannot be done in advance tax planning. He explains the tax implications of raising mortgages; making exchanges; organizing sales; drafting leases; and figuring income, expenses, and deductions.

Boyce, Byrl N. (Ed.). *Real Estate Appraisal Terminology*. Cambridge: Ballinger Publishing Company, 1975, 306 pp.

The development of this handbook was sponsored jointly by the Society of Real Estate Appraisers and the American Institute of Real Estate Appraisers. A compilation of appraisal terminology (including the areas of investment analysis, statistics, mathematics, and computers) and detailed appendices are included in the volume.

Clark, John. *Coastal Ecosystems*. Washington, D.C.: The Conservation Foundation, 1974, 178 pp.

The purpose of this guidebook is to present the main principles needed to implement improvement in the use of coastal lands and water. The book stresses the importance of an environmental management program embracing the entire ecosystem.

Davies, Pearl Janet. *Real Estate in American History*. Washington, D. C.: Public Affairs Press, 1958, 228 pp.

This book traces the history of land ownership and development in America. The main focus is on the rise of the professional real estate person.

Davis, Jerry C. and Tatum, Charles A. (Ed.). *Appraisal Classics*. Chicago: Society of Residential Appraisers, Inc., 1961, 639 pp.

This anthology of articles on appraisal was compiled by the Society of Residential Appraisers. It covers the period of 1935–1960.

Dorfman, Robert (Ed.). *Measuring Benefits of Government Investments*. Washington, D.C.: The Brookings Institute, 1965, 414 pp.

A series of papers presented at a conference sponsored by the Brookings Institution, November 6–7, 1963 is the main part of this book. The purpose of the conference was to develop new techniques for measuring the benefits and costs of public investments.

Downs, James C., Jr. *Principles of Real Estate Management*. Chicago: Institute of Real Estate Management, 1964, 441 pp.

The purpose of this book is to provide an academic background for property management and provide the property manager with a working knowledge of important fundamentals.

Frieden, Bernard J. *The Future of Old Neighborhoods*. Cambridge: MIT Press, 1964, 205 pp.

This book proposes a policy of gradual and continuous rebuilding of old areas, keeping up with the abandonment of housing, and replacing surplus housing.

Friedman, Edith J. (Ed.). *Encyclopedia of Real Estate Appraising*. Englewood Cliffs: Prentice-Hall, Inc., 1968, 1160 pp.

The volume is a revised and enlarged edition of the 1958 Encyclopedia. The purpose of the volume is to give practical, up-to-date information on how to estimate the value of real estate.

Graaskamp, James A. *A Guide to Feasibility Analysis*. Chicago: Society of Real Estate Appraisers, 1970, 134 pp.

This "sketchbook" defines feasibility, explores the concept of feasibility analysis, and provides the appraiser with the methodology needed to pursue his assignments.

Hanford, Lloyd D. *Feasibility Study Guidelines*. Chicago: Institute of Real Estate Management, 1972, 131 pp.

The text gives step-by-step directions and explanations of how a feasibility study is put together, starting with the developer contract and working through the economic, geographic, and financial analyses to the final report.

Heilbrun, James. *Real Estate Taxes and Urban Housing*. New York: Columbia University Press, 1966, 195 pp.

The book examines the effect of taxes on urban housing. It deals mainly with the effect of taxes on urban renewal concerning the maintenance of improvement of existing housing and not the part under new construction.

Jacobs, Jane. *The Death and Life of Great American Cities*. New York: Random House, 1961, 448 pp.

The author states that the purpose of this book is to introduce new principles of city planning and rebuilding that are different and sometimes opposite to those principles being taught.

Jacobs, Jane. *The Economy of Cities*. New York: Vintage Books, 1969, 202 pp.

In this book, the author explains why some cities grow and other cities stagnate and decay. She develops a theory of city economic growth.

Kotler, Milton. *Neighborhood Government*. New York: Bobbs-Merrill Co., 1969, 105 pp.

This book examines the current movement of local areas demanding control of local planning bodies. The author explores the meaning of this neighborhood movement.

McKeever, J. Ross (Ed.). *The Community Builders Handbook*. Washington, D.C.: Urban Land Institute, 1968, 526 pp.

In this handbook, a practical manual for residential and commercial land development is presented. It is directed to the builder's procedures, so he may become a community developer instead of just a home builder.

Messner, Stephen D., Schreiber, Irving and Lyon, Victor L. *Marketing Investment Real Estate—Finance, Taxation, Techniques*. Chicago: REALTORS NATIONAL MARKETING INSTITUTE®, 1975. 353 pp.

The major purpose of this book is to fit real estate into the total investment program. The volume is of interest to commercial-investment real estate brokers, accountants and attorneys as well as to the investor and the members of his team.

Nelson, Richard L. *The Selection of Retail Locations*. New York: F. W. Dodge Corporation, 1958, 422 pp.

Major expositions of the comprehensive scientific procedures of locating retail facilities are presented. Included are compilation of exacting techniques and new techniques for research, market analysis, and statistical consideration of locational problems.

Neutze, Max. *The Suburban Apartment Boom.* Washington, D.C.: Resources for the Future, Inc., 1968, 170 pp.

The author examines the reasons for the suburban apartment boom in suburban apartment construction. He also attempts to answer what is encouraging this boom—market imperfections or public policy.

Randall, William J., *Appraisal Guide for Mobile Home Parks.* Chicago: Finance Division of Mobile Homes Manufacturers Association, 1966, 55 pp.

This volume presents a brief summary of the methods and procedures of appraising a mobile home park. A concise procedural guide is outlined.

Seldin, Maury and Swesnik, Richard H. *Real Estate Investment Strategy.* New York: John Wiley and Sons, Inc., 1970, 238 pp.

This book serves as a guide to the real estate investor in developing investment strategy and making investment decisions which are profitable. The authors stress the importance of learning, analyzing, evaluating, and planning before investment is considered.

Selected Readings In Real Estate Appraisal. Chicago: American Institute of Real Estate Appraisers, 1953, 1299 pp.

This is a compilation of articles on appraisal from 1933–1952. The book was compiled by the American Institute of Real Estate Appraisers for students in the Institute's courses, but is a good reference source for the practicing appraiser.

Silk, Leonard S. *Forecasting Business Trends.* New York: McGraw-Hill Book Company, Inc., 1963, 107 pp.

The author has described essential facts needed to provide competent and accurate business forecasting. The book is divided into three parts: (1) explanation of principles of forecasting; (2) evaluation of forecasting data; and (3) sources for establishing a library of current economic information.

Scribner, David. "How to Find the Best Location for your Business," In J. K. Lasser's *Executive Course in Profitable Business Management.* New York: McGraw-Hill Book Company, Inc., 1952, pp. 381–406.

The successful procedures of finding the best economic location for a business are discussed. Factors stressed are pattern of metropolitan district, price a business can afford, public control, and various special considerations.

Simmons, James. *The Changing Pattern of Retail Location*. Chicago: University of Chicago Press, 1964, 192 pp.

The economics and theories behind the changes in the pattern of retail sites are discussed and analyzed.

U.S. Department of Housing and Urban Development, *Developing New Communities*. Washington, D.C.: U.S. Government Printing Office, 1968, 210 pp.

This book stresses the importance of developing housing programs which provide people with decent housing while preserving and enhancing individual freedom. Such programs should guarantee that the poor will have new opportunities and options within communities.

Webber, Michael J. *Impact of Uncertainty on Location*. Cambridge: MIT Press, 1972, 299 pp.

This book is a preliminary account which compares theories of the location of economic activity under certainty and uncertainty. The author defines some of the ways in which uncertainty affects decisions and modifies location patterns.

Weintraub, Andrew, Schwartz, Eli and Aronson, J. Richard. *The Economic Growth Controversy*. White Plains: International Arts and Sciences Press, Inc., 1973, 229 pp.

This volume contains proceeding papers from a symposium held at Lehigh University on October 17–19, 1972. The symposium was devoted to a discussion of the problems of economic growth.

Wendt, Paul F. and Cerf, Alan R. *Real Estate Investment Analysis and Taxation*. New York: McGraw-Hill Book Company, Inc., 1969, 355 pp.

The objective of this book is to provide individuals and institutions with the analytical framework for real estate investment decisions. Long-run investment decisions are given primary attention.

Monographs, Reports and Studies

Allen, Muriel I. (Ed.), "New Communities: Challenge for Today." Washington, D.C.: American Institute of Planners, 1968, 34 pp.

This report was prepared by the American Institute of Planners Task Force on New Communities. Planners felt that there is a critical need

281

for national policy on settlement patterns, new communities, and urbanization.

Bailey, Austin E. and Bailey, George R. "Trends of Office Building Design and Comparative Operating Studies of New and Old Buildings." Chicago: American Institute of Real Estate Appraisers, 1963, 63 pp.

This study was sponsored jointly by the National Association of Building Owners and Managers and the American Institute of Real Estate Appraisers. Seven case studies are presented for study comparisons.

de Leeuw, Frank, "Operating Costs in Public Housing: A Financial Crisis." Washington, D.C.: The Urban Institute, 1969, 61 pp.

This report attempts, through analysis, to measure the relative importance of various influences on rising operating costs and to assess the financial outlook for public housing.

"Financing the Lodging Industry: A Survey of Lender Attitudes." Philadelphia: Laventhol and Horwath, 1975, 24 pp.

Designed to assess and convey the thoughts and concerns of lenders, this survey focuses on three main areas: (1) problem loans—extent and causes; (2) evaluation, monitoring and response to problem loans; and (3) the future.

Reilly, William J. "Methods for the Study of Retail Relationships." Austin: Bureau of Business Research, The University of Texas, 1959, 50 pp.

The methods, techniques, theories, and economics necessary in the study of retailing are explored.

Richards, Brian, "New Movement in Cities." New York: Reinhold Publishing Corporation, 1966, 93 pp.

The report discusses various methods that have been or could be applied to improve movement in cities; it covers a 100-year period.

Suelflow, James E. "Market Potential—Its Theory and Application." Madison: Bureau of Business Research and Service, The University of Wisconsin, 1967, 46 pp.

This monograph explores the theories and the application of those theories in developing market potential.

"Urban Renewal and Redevelopment." Chicago: American Institute of Real Estate Appraisers, 1963, 172 pp.

The principles and procedures involved in urban renewal and development are discussed in a series of articles that were published in *The Appraisal Journal* from 1953–1963.

Articles

Alao, Nurudeen. "An Approach to Intraurban Location Theory." *Economic Geography*, January 1974, pp. 59–69.

Discussed in this article are the ways in which land inputs, transport, and externalities interact. Several existing models are explained.

Alexanderson, K. W. "Bank Branch Location Feasibility Analysis." *The Real Estate Appraiser*, July–August 1969, pp. 43–48.

The author states that since good sites are scarce and building costs are high, some formula for predetermining the success of bank branch sites is imperative. He suggests feasibility analysis as the solution.

Anderson, Gordon J. "Financing Special Situations with Commercial Properties." *real estate today*®, January 1974, pp. 12–15.

The author stresses the importance of the broker knowing all available information about new financing techniques regarding commercial properties.

Appel, James R. "Preparation of the Feasibility Report." *The Real Estate Appraiser*, November 1964, pp. 33–38.

This article discusses the techniques that are necessary for the proper preparation of a feasibility report.

Applebaum, William. "Methods for Determining Store Trade Areas, Market Penetration, and Potential Sales." *Journal of Marketing Research*, May 1966, pp. 127–141.

Improved methods for determining trade areas and market penetration of existing stores are presented. An analog method for estimating potential sales at a given location is also discussed.

Applebaum, William. "Teaching Marketing Geography by the Case Method." *Economic Geography*, January 1961, pp. 48–60.

This is a classic article. The author stresses the importance of practical experience in operating a business—a concept anyone in the field of marketing geography should understand.

Ashton, Peter. "Multiple Regression Analysis: Uses and Abuses in Real   **283**

Estate Valuation." *The Real Estate Appraiser*, July–August, 1972, pp. 16–21.

The purpose of this paper is to: (1) review notable applications of multiple regression to real life situations; (2) discuss further applications of multiple regression analysis; and (3) analyze most of the commonly encountered criticisms of the process.

Babcock, Henry A. "Valuation Methods as Related to Property Classification and Kinds of Value." *ASA Appraisal and Valuation Manual*, Volume 9, 1966–1967, pp. 195–207.

The author makes proposals concerning the classification of properties for the purpose of valuation, the kinds of value that properties possess, and the methods of determining those values.

Bailey, John B. "Market Analysis—Fundamental to Defensible Valuations." *The Appraisal Journal*, October 1972, pp. 644–649.

This article explains why market analysis is an important and necessary part of any appraisal.

Baratta, Philip J. "The Appraiser's Role in Mobile Home Park Development and Investment." *The Real Estate Appraiser*, January–February 1972, pp. 16–26.

The author stresses the fact that the appraiser needs to be acquainted with all the special problems inherent in mobile home park zoning and development.

Beaton, J. Wallace. "Valuation of Real Estate as a Part of a Business." *The Real Estate Appraiser*, November–December 1972, pp. 40–43.

The author discusses the economics of real estate in the process of business valuation—the interrelationship of market value, value to the owner, and value in use.

Birnkrant, Michael. "Shopping Center Feasibility Study: Its Methods and Techniques." *Journal of Property Management*, November/December 1970, pp. 272–279.

This article discusses feasibility studies for regional shopping centers. Highlighted in the report are the objectives, methodology and limitations of these studies.

Bohling, John E. "Highest and Best Use: A New Definition, a New Opportunity." *The Real Estate Appraiser*, January–February 1976, pp. 33–36.

The definition of highest and best use that appears in *Real Estate Appraisal Terminology* is discussed and expanded.

Bookhout, L. T. "Indoor Tennis Clubs: A New Problem?" *The Real Estate Appraiser*, September–October 1973, pp. 29–34.

In this article, the author discusses the use of feasibility studies in regard to the development of tennis clubs.

Bourne, Larry S. "Physical Adjustment Processes and Land Use Succession: A Conceptual Review and Central City Example." *Economic Geography*, January 1971, pp. 1–15.

The objectives of this paper are to present a synthesis and expansion of existing concepts of succession and to present an empirical summary of the dynamic structure of succession.

Bourne, Larry S. "Trends in Urban Redevelopment—The Implications for Urban Form." *The Appraisal Journal*, January 1970, pp. 24–36.

This paper presents a review of the results of recent research on private redevelopment trends in Toronto, Canada. It is well documented with tables.

Bowes, W. A. "What is Market Analysis?" *The Real Estate Appraiser*, July–August 1968, pp. 11–14.

The author contends that true market analysis is *not* finding out what the market is. Market analysis is the study of reasons why certain prices are being paid.

Boyce, Byrl N. and Higgins, J. Warren. "Tax Shield Considerations in Real Estate Investment Decisions." *The Real Estate Appraiser*, November–December 1973, pp. 38–44.

The authors examine two aspects that are necessary when determining the investment value of property—the tax shield provided by depreciation and the cash flow net of taxes.

Brener, Stephen W. and Gamoran, A. Carmi, "Appraisals of Budget Motels." *The Real Estate Appraiser*, March–April 1974, pp. 18–20.

The property residual technique is used in determining the fair market value of a site for a proposed motel.

Brener, Stephen W. and Gamoran, A. Carmi. "How Much Value in the Inn?" *The Real Estate Appraiser*, March–April 1976, pp. 37–41.

The paper discusses ways to determine the fair market value of a site for a proposed Holiday Inn in downtown Montpelier, Vermont.

Brener, Stephen W. and Rushmore, Stephen. "Valuing Motels and Hotels

285

in the Current Market." *Real Estate Review*, Fall 1972, pp. 59–62.

The authors present capitalization rate guidelines for five investment positions in the hotel-motel field.

Brown, William J. "Cooperation Between Architects and Real Estate Appraisers in Planning and Developing New Projects." *The Real Estate Appraiser*, September–October 1971, pp. 30–32.

This article stresses the need for the team approach in the development of new, complex projects. An appraiser should be a member of this team. Also discussed is a new organization called SPECTRA, devoted to the concept of sharing staff, resources, and ideas.

Bruckner, Clarence A. "Appraisal of a Condominium Converted from an Apartment Building." *The Real Estate Appraiser*, March–April 1972, pp. 13–17.

The specifics of an appraisal of an apartment building being considered as a proposed condominium development are presented. Both the cost approach and market approach to value are presented.

"Building A Golf Course? What Should It Really Cost You?" *The Real Estate Appraiser*, March–April 1971, pp. 27–30.

This paper offers guidelines for building a golf course, emphasizing the assets of such a project and ways in which the developer can save money.

Buzzell, Robert D., Gale, Bradley T. and Sultan, Ralph G. M. "Market Share—A Key to Profitability." *Harvard Business Review*, January–February 1975, pp. 97–106.

An ongoing study of 57 companies is featured. This study reveals that there is a link between ROI and market share—the bigger, the better.

Camins, Bernard W. "Appraiser-Analyst: A Special Meaning." *The Real Estate Appraiser*, May–June 1974, pp. 33–34.

This article is an essay on the complexities of the real estate market that an appraiser-analyst must be capable of facing.

Carestio, Ralph M., Jr. "Land Absorption in Industrial Parks." *The Real Estate Appraiser*, November–December 1971, pp. 40–44.

Presented in this article is a case study from which a model may evolve that can be used to measure price and absorption rates. The model would be used in the cash flow process.

Gibbons, James E. "Apartment Feasibility Studies." *The Appraisal Journal*, July 1968, pp. 325–332.

A definition of valuation is presented and examined. The author also discusses feasibility studies as they apply to apartments.

Gipe, George W. "Developing a Multiple Regression Model for Multi-Family Residential Properties." *The Real Estate Appraiser*, May–June 1976, pp. 28–33.

Presented in this article is the concept of using multiple regression analysis as a tool for developing a computer-assisted apartment appraisal system that will estimate market value.

Glassman, Sidney. "Merchandising New Apartment Construction." *Journal of Property Management*, January–February 1969, pp. 38–41.

The purpose of this article is to present methods of merchandising that will give the property manager rapid rentals to a good clientele. The author stresses the importance of good planning before apartments are constructed.

Gottlieb, Jerry R. "Industrial Park Appraisal in the 1970s." *The Appraisal Journal*, October 1972, pp. 600–610.

The author presents an overview of the development of the industrial park. He comments only on those considerations affecting the market value appraisal.

Graaskamp, James A. "Dollars and Cents of Shopping Centers 1969." *The Appraisal Journal*, October 1970, pp. 612–614.

The author presents a review of the 1969 Edition of *Dollars and Cents of Shopping Centers*.

Graaskamp, James A. "A Rational Approach to Feasibility Analysis." *The Appraisal Journal*, October 1973, pp. 526–533.

A detailed definition of real estate is given in this article. The author lists decision processes that are necessary when undertaking feasibility analysis.

Graybeal, Ronald S. "Condominium Computerized Feasibility Analysis." *The Appraisal Journal*, October 1973, pp. 526–533.

This article demonstrates the use of a condominium feasibility computer program for the appraiser. Included in the programming are: property facts; rate of return for no conversion, conversion, and tenant and investor purchasers; and summary.

Griefen, R. John. "The Impact of the Industrial Park." *The Appraisal*   **291**

Journal, January 1970, pp. 83–91.

> The author discusses the impact of an industrial park on the region in which it is located and the impact of the park on the region's economy.

Gunsteens, Kenneth M. "Back to Basics—The Law of Supply and Demand." *real estate today®*, September 1973, pp. 4–13.

> The author contends that the basic law of supply and demand can be used as a listing tool. He presents methods in how to use it effectively.

Haar, Charles M. "Airport Noise and the Urban Dweller: A Proposed Solution." *The Appraisal Journal*, October 1968, pp. 551–558.

> This article is an essay on the problems of noise for those who live near urban airports. The author cites many court cases.

Hagood, Wayne D. "Feasibility Studies for Commercial Developments in Small Towns." *The Real Estate Appraiser*, August 1967, pp. 12–16.

> A formula is presented which can be applied in the preparation of feasibility studies: "research and more research plus experience and market knowledge plus application and good judgment equals a good feasibility study."

Haley, Byron K. "Outdoor Recreation Subdivisions." *The Real Estate Appraiser*, September–October 1971, pp. 14–18.

> Leisure-time activities and how they should fit into the developer's plans are discussed. Fourteen of the most popular leisure-time activities are listed.

Hall, Thomas H. "The Motor Hotel: Appraisals and Feasibility Studies." *The Appraiser Journal*, October 1971, pp. 568–575.

> The author discusses the most important factors involved in an appraisal/feasibility study of an existing motel or a potential site for a motel.

Halstead, Clark P., Jr. "Financing the Project." *real estate today®*, August 1974, pp. 28–30.

> Evaluating the financial aspects of a project is a critical function of any feasibility report, according to the author. The developer must be sure of the marketability of a project before he begins.

Harris, William W. "Feasibility Studies in Urban Renewal Projects." *The Real Estate Appraiser*, October 1967, pp. 21–29.

> This article discusses the role that the appraiser plays in urban renewal

such as acquisition appraisals, reuse appraisals, land utilization and marketability studies, etc.

Harrison, Thomas. "The Advent of the Super Regional Shopping Center." *The Appraisal Journal*, January 1968, pp. 91–97.

The appraiser and market analyst must understand and must be aware of the impact the regional shopping center has on existing markets and development patterns.

Hart, Gerald T. "Economic Background of Office Buildings." *The Appraisal Journal*, April 1961, pp. 207–212.

The author stresses the need for understanding of the economic base of the community, not only in the past and present, but in the future. This is necessary if a proper appraisal is to be conducted.

Hawk, Stephen L. and Kroncke, Charles O. "Some Refinements in the Real Estate Investment Decision Process." *The Real Estate Appraiser*, January–February 1974, pp. 13–19.

The differences that the IRR and NPV approaches can lend in real estate are discussed. The author presents ways in which to handle these differences.

Heidrick, Harold H. "Determining Utility Market Value." *The Appraisal Journal*, April 1970, pp. 253–271.

The determination of utility market value is discussed, and a procedure for determining utility market value is outlined.

Hepditch, G. D. "The Appraisal of Sand and Gravel Deposits." *ASA Appraisal and Valuation Manual*, Volume 4, 1959, pp. 149–158.

This article is concerned with the appraisal for taxation purposes of the value of sand and gravel deposits. Although the subject is treated at the local level, it has general application.

Herd, John J. "A Broker's Observation of Office Buildings." *The Appraisal Journal*, July 1961, pp. 328–332.

The author suggests that technical training and ethical standards of the AIREA need to be implemented by the practical experience of the appraiser, if real property is to be properly merchandised.

Hertz, David B. "Investment Policies that Pay Off." *Harvard Business Review*, January 1968, pp. 96–108.

The author discusses the conventional approaches to risk and then describes a more sophisticated approach—involving the use of computer-based risk analysis techniques to compare probable payoffs.

Hodges, M. B., Jr. "The Market and the Mini Computer." *The Real Estate Appraiser*, July–August 1975, pp. 31–36.

The uses of a desktop computer are demonstrated in three analyses of site value for a model garden apartment. The analyses show the changing value of the land over a nine-year period.

Jeffrey, D. "Regional Fluctuations in Unemployment within the U.S. Urban Economic System: A Study of the Spatial Impact of Short Term Economic Value." *Economic Geography*, April 1974, pp. 111–123.

This study attempts to delimit regional subsystems of cities displaying distinct regional cyclical patterns in their economic fluctuation over time.

Jeffrey, D., Casetti, E. and King, L. "Setting: A Bi-Factor Analytic Approach." *Journal of Regional Science*, December 1969, pp. 397–404.

The authors present a tentative look at some of the lines of analysis which could be developed into tools for predicting demand for office space.

Jennings, Christopher R. "Predicting Demand for Office Space." *The Appraisal Journal*, July 1965, pp. 377–382.

When valuing different spatial levels in local economic activities, different analytical models need to be used if the analysis is to be pertinent.

Johnson, Clifford R. "Appraising Successful Service Stations." *The Appraisal Journal*, July 1971, pp. 438–448.

This article concentrates on the appraisal of an existing proven station site for its whole value. The same valuation technique is then used to estimate damages due to partial takings and restriction of access.

Johnson, Philip M. "Rehabilitation Feasibility Financing." *The Real Estate Appraiser*, January–February 1970, pp. 20–26.

The author feels that coordinated programs are needed to uplift neighborhoods. Planners must gear structural and economic feasibility techniques to the existing problems.

Kahn, Sanders A. and Weintraub, Alvin M. "Real Estate and the Trucking Industry." *ASA Appraisal and Valuation Manual*, Volume 8, 1964–65, pp. 189–197.

The various types of terminals associated with the trucking industry are discussed and then methods to finance these terminals are presented.

Kaufman, Arnold. "The Sell/Hold Decision Process in Real Estate Liquidation." *The Real Estate Appraiser*, November–December 1972, pp. 21–29.

The author presents guidelines to be used in making sell/hold decisions. He suggests six potential categories and analyzes each category in detail.

Kelly, John F. "Motels and Freeways." *ASA Appraisal and Valuation Manual*, Volume 1, 1955–56, pp. 35–50.

This study pertains to the effect of the freeway or the access-controlled highway on motels. The author conducted a survey among motel owners for this study.

Kinnard, William N., Jr. "Tower Lines and Residential Property Values." *The Appraisal Journal*, April 1967, pp. 269–284.

The results of a study to see how location of residences to power lines affects the market value of these residences are presented. The author surveyed 17 subdivisions in nine central Connecticut towns to obtain the data.

Klink, James J. "Accounting for Real Estate Sales—It's A New Ball Game." *real estate today*®, February 1974, pp. 70–73.

The author discusses new rules and guidelines for regulating and reporting sales and profit from real estate sales.

Larson, William W. "Real Estate vs. Wall Street." *real estate today*®, May/June 1974, pp. 14–16.

The author presents a set of questions and answers for the real estate broker and his client concerning investment opportunities in real estate.

LaFaever, James H. "The Appraisal of Tidelands." *ASA Appraisal and Valuation Manual*, Volume 4, 1959, pp. 190–198.

According to the author, every parcel of tideland must be evaluated on its own merit and no general rule is applicable.

Level, Edward E. "Special Purpose Properties." *ASA Appraisal and Valuation Manual*, Volume 9, 1966–67, pp. 346–355.

This speech was delivered at the 1971 ASA International Conference. Just compensation is discussed.

Lewis, David M. and Bolton, David R. "Houston—A City Without Zoning." *The Real Estate Appraiser*, November–December 1970, pp. 39–43.

A discussion of Houston's growth without zoning is presented by the authors. They list the alternatives to zoning that are actually used such as traffic control, full-time city planning department, and the city building department.

Lindeman, Bruce. "Components of Land Values in Speculative Markets." *The Real Estate Appraiser*, January–February 1976, pp. 37–40.

This article examines the forces which establish market values of land in a speculative market.

Lomas, D. A. "Valuation in an Infiltrated Neighborhood." *The Appraisal Journal*, April 1971, pp. 247–253.

This paper focuses on the importance of studying trends, shows how trends affect value, and follows up the discussion with examples of case studies.

Lum, Tan Tek. "Feasibility Analysis of Condominiums." *The Appraisal Journal*, April 1972, pp. 246–252.

The author feels that the feasibility study of condominiums is unique for each project. The entire planning for a condominium project needs the cooperation of many professional individuals.

McFarland, John A. "Hidden Costs in Land Development." *The Real Estate Appraiser*, July–August 1972, pp. 46–49.

The builder or developer incurs many hidden costs such as water service, pavements, landscaping, etc. The author presents a checklist for residential land development that will help lessen these costs.

McNece, Elmer R. and Cook, Edgar D., Jr. "Evaluation of Land Development Corporations." *The Real Estate Appraiser*, November–December 1973, pp. 45–47.

The authors discuss the valuation of shares of a closely held corporation whose sole asset is unimproved land. The analyst can estimate land value free and clear of all restraints or can estimate land value in terms of stock of a closely held corporation.

McNeeley, W. S. "Money Making in Real Estate is a Numbers Game." *Real Estate Review*, Spring 1972, pp. 13–17.

The effective use of discounted cash flow and other investment techniques to assess one's standing in the real estate market is presented.

Mandel, H. Robert. "Appraisal or Feasibility Report (What Does the Client Want?)" *The Real Estate Appraiser*, September–October 1968, pp. 52–53.

The author contends that clients ask for an appraisal when in reality they want a feasibility study because they are interested in economic data of an area and want to know if a market exists for whatever project they are considering.

Miles, W. Porcher. "Applied Multiple Regression Analysis." *The Real Estate Appraiser*, September–October 1975, pp. 29–33.

This article examines the use of multiple regression analysis in determining the value of single-family residences.

Mills, Edwin S., "Transportation and Patterns of Urban Development." *American Economic Review*, Volume 57, 1976, pp. 197–210.

The purpose of this paper is to put forth a simplified, aggregative method that will help explain the sizes and structure of urban areas.

Moses, Leon and Williamson, Harold F., Jr. "The Location of Economic Activity in Cities." *American Economic Review*, Volume 57, 1967, pp. 211–222.

The purpose of this article is to provide insight into the development of large, core-related cities and insight into the factors which are affecting the economic activity in these cities.

Mullet, Gary M. "A Statistican Appraises Multiple Regression Analysis." *The Real Estate Appraiser*, May–June 1976, pp. 39–43.

This article stresses the importance of properly interpreting appraisal models using multiple regression analysis. Simple data sets are used to illustrate proper interpretation.

Opelka, T. Gregory. "Condominium Value Does Not Equal Sales Price." *The Real Estate Appraiser*, March–April 1971, pp. 43–44.

The author discusses the value base of a condominium construction loan.

Pendl, Charles R. "The Appraisal of Recreational Land on Inland Lakes and Streams." *The Appraisal Journal*, October 1971, pp. 583–591.

Factors that influence the value of recreational land are assessed. These factors include lake quality, water depth, desirable features to the owner, land grade, sanitation, quality of water, comparable sales, etc.

Piper, John B. "Condominium Economics." *The Appraisal Journal*, April 1973, pp. 260–263.

This article presents a study of a seven-year-old apartment complex which was converted into a condominium complex.

Poorvu, William J. and Stevenson, Howard H. "Making the Right Real Estate Bet." *The Real Estate Review*, Winter 1976, pp. 61–64.

According to the authors, in order to make the best decision in real estate investment, it is necessary to develop a refined investment return analysis.

Prior, Robert E. "Marketing Office Space." *Journal of Property Management*, March–April 1975, pp. 53–57.

In this paper, the author suggests methods of finding where good tenants exist before marketing office space. It is also necessary for the leasing agent to know his product from beginning to end.

Pyhrr, Stephen A. "Analytical Methods Can Reduce Income Property Loan Losses." *The Real Estate Appraiser*, March–April 1975, pp. 33–41.

The purpose of this article is to describe some of the improved methods and procedures for loan analysis and to encourage lenders and appraisers to integrate modern financial and computer techniques into the loan underwriting process.

Pyhrr, Stephen A. "A Computer Simulation Model to Measure Risk in Real Estate Investment." *The Real Estate Appraiser*, May–June 1973, pp. 13–31.

The author shows the application of a few financial theories and procedures in making risk analysis more explicit. He briefly outlines methodologies for assessing probability distribution inputs and discusses the use of risk simulation models.

Rams, Edwin M. "Markets, Risk, Feasibility, and Real Estate Ventures." *The Real Estate Appraiser*, May–June 1974, pp. 29–32.

Presented in this article is the author's idea of the legal concept of real property and how this concept has evolved.

Rams, Edwin M. "Rehabilitation In Urban Renewal Areas—A Real Estate Viewpoint." *ASA Appraisal and Valuation Manual*, Volume 8, 1964–65, pp. 169–179.

The author gives the reader practical case studies for implementing techniques in appraising urban renewal areas.

Rams, Edwin M. and Brown, Robert K. "The Role of Buyer Motivation In Neighborhood Analysis." *ASA Appraisal and Valuation Manual*, Volume 4, 1959, pp. 253–260.

The article discusses the role of certain variables which condition a buyer's weighing of alternative housing values. The analysis is directed toward an appraisal point of view.

Ratcliff, Richard U. "Appraisal: Is It Measurement or Prediction?" *The Real Estate Appraiser*, November–December 1972, pp. 4–6.

This article presents a condensed version of the central thesis of the author's book, *Valuation for Real Estate Decisions.*

Reed, Robert D. and Dunn, Paul A. "Valuation of Cedar Point Marina." *The Appraisal Journal*, April 1967, pp. 207–222.

The author presents a detailed appraisal of the fair market value of a marina. He lists criteria for the appraisal.

Rickey, Clyde W. and Clettenberg, Karel J. "Forecasting Real Estate Demand." *real estate today®*, January 1973, pp. 52–55.

A simplified explanation of the economic base analysis in forecasting real estate demand is presented in this article.

Roberts, Thomas L. "Valuation of the Special Purchase Property." *ASA Appraisal and Valuation Manual*, Volume 9, 1966–71, pp. 358–361.

This article is the text of a speech presented at the 1971 ASA International Conference. The speaker discusses the fair market value on properties on which there is a lack of sales comparison.

Robertson, Terry and Rufrano, Glenn. "Equity Yields: A Cash Flow Verification." *The Real Estate Appraiser*, March–April 1976, pp. 42–45.

This paper discusses the application of discounted cash flow analysis to abstracting the composition of the equity yields that investors are assumed to require in the traditional capitalization techniques.

Robinson, Michael J. "Urban Rehab: Are the Profits Worth the Risk?" *The Real Estate Appraiser*, January–February 1973, pp. 38–43.

The advantages and disadvantages of investing in urban rehabilitation are examined. The author stresses location, the market, construction, and financing as the important factors when making judgments on this type of investment.

Roulac, Stephen E. "The Impact of Securities Regulations and Financial Reporting Responsibilities on Real Estate Investment." *The Real Estate Appraiser*, November–December 1974, pp. 19–26.

This article focuses on the needed change in both the private sector and the regulatory agencies in the control of tax shelters.

Rountrey, J. E. and Burton, R. C. "Feasibility Study of Richmond Coliseum." *The Appraisal Journal*, April 1970, pp. 273–292.

The purpose of this study is to conduct a survey of the feasibility of constructing a coliseum-arena complex. The scope of the study includes: analysis of potential demand for facilities, scope of facilities and services, indirect benefits, and potential problem areas.

Rowlson, John F. "The Feasibility and Appraisal of Garden-type Condominiums." *The Appraisal Journal*, July 1973, pp. 338–349.

The author lists procedures that are necessary in a feasibility study of garden condominiums. He feels the procedures must be listed in outline form, which he does.

Rowlson, John F. "Land Utilization and Marketability." *The Real Estate Appraiser*, May–June 1968, pp. 52–55.

The need to determine forces that influence growth in predicting realistic land use is stressed. These forces include population, labor, capital, natural resources, transportation, and housing.

Rule, Thomas M. "The Metropolitan Analysis in the Appraisal Report." *The Appraisal Journal*, April 1972, pp. 224–230.

The author explores the steps in preparing a city analysis report. He stresses the importance of population in such a report.

Runnion, James F. "Predicting Success Analytically." *real estate today*®, August 1974, pp. 16–19.

This article stresses the fact that the feasibility report is of vital importance in predicting the outcome of a development project.

Schaaf, A. H. "Rising Vacancy Rates Aren't Always Bad." *Real Estate Review*, Winter 1973, pp. 101–104.

In this article, the following question is answered: Can a surplus of new housing units be handled by the market for ten consecutive years?

Seneker, Harold. "Big City, Small City—More People Choose Latter." *House and Home*, 1975, p. 22.

The demographic shift in population from urban areas to the small city is discussed.

Seymour, Charles F. "More and More of My Reports are Valueless." *The Appraisal Journal*, October 1967, pp. 453–463.

The author presents examples of his appraisal reports that were *not* made for the purpose of setting forth a value.

Shanahan, John E. "Statistical Applications for the SREA Market Data Center, Inc., Part II." *The Real Estate Appraiser*, November–December 1973, pp. 48–51.

This is the second article in a two-part series on the application of statistics to the SREA Market Data Center residential market data book. This article deals with multiple regression analysis.

Shenkel, William M. "The New Valuation System." *The Real Estate Appraiser*, November–December 1971, pp. 21–34.

The conventional appraisal processes in use for the last 25 years are reviewed and examples of new valuation systems are explored.

Shenkel, William M. "Refining Valuation Estimates with Census Data." *The Real Estate Appraiser*, September–October 1973, pp. 11–20.

The author discusses the common deficiencies in narrative appraisal reports. He suggests ways in which to remedy these deficiencies and suggests ways in which to properly use census data.

Shenkel, William M. "The Valuation of Multiple Family Dwellings by Statistical Inference." *The Real Estate Appraiser*, January–February 1975, pp. 25–36.

A review of the concept of income valuation is presented. Then the author discusses income multipliers and the variations in multiple regression techniques.

Shurberg, Merwin. "Economic Factors in Property Valuations." *ASA Appraisal and Valuation Manual*, Volume 8, 1964–65, pp. 55–61.

This article is concerned with the economic data used to evaluate the effect of highway improvements on property values.

Silverstein, Larry A. "There's Money in Conversions If you Know How." *Real Estate Review*, Fall 1971, pp. 10–14.

A step-by-step process of investing in an old structure in New York is presented, and converting such a venture to a profit is explained.

Simeral, William B. "A Guide to the Appraisal of Ski Areas." *ASA Appraisal and Valuation Manual*, Volume 9, 1966–71, pp. 16–33.

The author explains the pattern that has emerged in conducting appraisals of ski areas. He gives tables for costs of improving hillsides, lift capacities, and shelters.

Simon, Robert E. "The Effect of Concepts on the Value of Land." *ASA Appraisal and Valuation Manual,* Volume 8, 1964–65, pp. 107–112.

Discussed in this article are the extrinsics and intrinsics of valuing land. A case study is included.

Smith, Arnold R. "Feasibility Study of a Shopping Center." *The Real Estate Appraiser,* July 1967, pp. 9–15.

The author feels that it is a fallacy that only the specialists can prepare a feasibility study. He lists several observations to support his position.

Smith, Guy V. "Decreased Divergence in Service Station Appraisals." *The Appraisal Journal,* January 1971, pp. 82–93.

According to the author, the appraiser must understand the oil industry before he can possibly conduct an accurate appraisal of a gasoline station.

Smith, Larry. "Economic Factors and their Analysis." *ASA Appraisal and Valuation Manual.* Volume 1, 1955–56, pp. 51–68.

The author provides a checklist that will be helpful in the development of shopping centers.

Sortor, Charles H. "Evaluation of Deep Water Wells." *ASA Appraisal and Valuation Manual,* Volume 4, 1959, pp. 327–336.

A step-by-step procedure for appraising deep water wells is presented. The author uses the cost-less-depreciation method, modified by applying corrections as shown by a photographic survey and a study of utility value.

Spaeth, Robert L. "Measuring the Cost of Airport Noise: Formulas and Pitfalls." *The Appraisal Journal,* July 1972, pp. 412–419.

In this article, the weaknesses of the Hall-Beaton factor formula are discussed. Many court cases are cited concerning airport noise.

Stettinius, Joseph. "Correlating Information." *real estate today®,* August 1974, pp. 20–27.

The author states that it is necessary to arrange the structure and content of a feasibility report in such a way that the best, most comprehensive development design for the project becomes clear.

Suter, Robert C. "Tax Implications in the Ownership and Transfer of Real Estate." *The Real Estate Appraiser,* November–December 1974, pp. 15–18.

The purpose of this article is to acquaint the reader with some of the rules and regulations of certain tax implications in real estate activities.

Swango, Dan L. "A Basic Methodology for Estimating the Market Value of a Subdivision Land Development." *The Real Estate Appraiser*, November–December 1971, pp. 13–20.

This article focuses on a methodology for estimating the value of a subdivision or land development when individual land units or lots are ready for retail sale.

"They Do Repair Jobs on Small Companies." *Business Week*, February 17, 1973, pp. 50–51.

"How to" overhaul a sick company relatively quickly, without intensive months of analyzing, is explored in this article.

Thorne, Oakleigh J. "Cash-Flow Analysis and Investment Strategy for Industrial Park Development." *The Real Estate Appraiser*, November–December 1971, pp. 45–54.

The author presents two alternative methods for analyzing cash flow and investment strategy for industrial park projects.

Thorne, Oakleigh J. "The Corporate Muddle with Real Estate." *The Real Estate Appraiser*, September–October 1974, pp. 33–37.

Real estate development and real estate ownership as a product and and as a possible corporate investment are discussed.

Tischler, Paul S. "The Importance of the Highest and Best Use Analysis." *The Real Estate Appraiser*, May–June 1972, pp. 35–36.

A central business area is used as an example of the scope and importance of a proper highest and best use study.

Trippe, Robert R. "A Statistical Method for Determining When to Accept an Offer to Purchase." *The Real Estate Appraiser*, May–June 1976, pp. 13–16.

This article attempts to establish criteria for developing the optimal pricing strategy for a seller.

Troxel, Jay C. "Functional Analysis of Industrial Property." *The Real Estate Appraiser*, January–February 1974, pp. 35–38.

The objective of this paper is to assert that the functional adequacy of internal industrial plant operation relates to its ability to achieve economy or to avoid waste.

Tucker, Grady. "Site Selection for Suburban Shopping Centers." *Real Estate Review*, Summer 1974, pp. 70–76.

The author discusses how the developer plans a proposed suburban shopping center to complement its potential market. He stresses such items as site size, land use controls, liquidity, retail sales potential, etc.

Viele, G. R. "Appraising Lake and Recreational Properties." *The Real Estate Appraiser*, September–October 1971, pp. 5–13.

According to this article, there is a wide range of types of lake and recreational properties. The largest number of appraisals in these areas are made on second residences. Methods of appraising such properties are explained.

Vollman, June R. "Here's A New System for Figuring Project Feasibility." *House and Home*, October 1973, pp. 110–117.

This article discusses a new system for projecting feasibility of public housing programs. Stressed are: calculating financial impact on the community and computerizing information so the developer can simulate his options.

Wagner, Percy E. "Analysis of Land Development." *The Real Estate Appraiser*, May–June 1974, pp. 43–52.

The purpose of this article is to introduce real estate appraisers, developers, and brokers to the physical and financial problems which a developer must face when he develops raw land into a salable subdivision of improved lots.

Wagner, Percy E. "Analyzing and Appraising Condominium Projects." *The Appraisal Journal*, October 1971, pp. 576–582.

The advantages of condominiums over apartment units are presented. Also featured are the appraisal problems that are unique in condominium development.

Wall, Norbert F. "Organizing and Implementing a Real Estate Investment Program for Corporations: One Approach." *The Real Estate Appraiser*, January–February 1973, pp. 15–23.

The author emphasizes the need to incorporate the goals and objectives of the corporation before considering real estate investment. Long-range planning is needed before a decision is made.

Wall, Norbert F. "Pollution and Real Property Values." *The Real Estate Appraiser*, January–February 1972, pp. 5–11.

The effects of air pollution on a single-family residence, which is ten years old and contains 1,100 square feet of area, are examined. The author presents a detailed analysis.

Wall, Norbert F. "Strategy for Real Estate Investment." *The Real Estate Appraiser*, May–June 1975, pp. 41–43.

According to the author, the objective of the investor is the most important aspect of investment in real estate. These objectives fall into four basic categories: income, turnover, shelter, and long-term appreciation.

Wendt, Paul F. and Gilreath, Morgan B. "A Technique for Analysis of Apartment-Condominium Conversions." *The Real Estate Appraiser*, May–June 1974, pp. 35–42.

This article provides a decision rule through which investors can use conversions either as an entry into profitable situations or as an exit from undesirable ones.

White, John Robert. "Attitude of Investment Trusts Toward Office Buildings." *The Appraisal Journal*, April 1971, pp. 194–199.

Two recent periods in the history of real estate equity trusts relating to the office property market are contrasted in this article. One is a period of stability and tranquility and one a period of inflation and expansion.

Williams, Lawrence E., Jr. and McNichol, Daniel. "Valuation of Air Space." *The Appraisal Journal*, April 1973, pp. 234–253.

The authors discuss in depth the ways and procedures for valuing and appraising air space. They present actual appraisal procedures with tables and other data.

Wilson, Peter M., "Marinas: Development and Economic Factors." *The Appraisal Journal*, April 1967, pp. 199–205.

This article stresses the need to have careful planning in the development of marinas. Modular programming is needed so that facilities can be constructed in stages.

Woodard, F. O. and Epley, D. R. "Feasibility Study of Richmond Coliseum: A Comment." *The Appraisal Journal*, April 1971, pp. 285–292.

The authors reply to an article by Rountrey and Burton on the development of a proposed coliseum. They criticize the conclusion of the Rountrey-Burton article and suggest an alternative approach.

Wright, Colin. "Residential Location in a Three-Dimensional City."

Journal of Political Economy, July–December 1971, pp. 1378–1387.

A residential land use model is presented that includes the concept of a "high-rise" gradient and a third dimension concept.

Young, G. I. M. "Feasibility Studies." *The Appraisal Journal*, July 1970, pp. 376–383.

The cost and value of feasibility studies are discussed. Included in the discussion are: economic demand, investment yield, prediction of revenue, operating expenses and possible complications in the real market.

Zaloudek, Robert F. "Practical Location Analysis in New Market Areas." *The Real Estate Appraiser*, May–June 1972, pp. 47–50.

The author outlines a practical approach to location analysis in new market areas without requiring rigorous quantitative exercises. He presents a broad look at the socio-economic patterns, commercial development, residential patterns, highway networks and physical features.

Zerbst, Robert H. "Locational Attributes of Property Values." *The Real Estate Appraiser*, May–June 1976, pp. 19–22.

According to this author, students of appraisal need more exposure to concepts of location, such as accessibility, physical environment and fiscal environment.

Index

317

Utility, diminished, 7

Value, appraised
  defined, 87
Value, present
  defined, 163
  profile, net, 180, 181
Variable
  dependent, 52
  independent, 53
"Variances"
  squared differences, 49

Volume, gross sales, 189

Waiver of subrogation, 197
Wendt, Paul F., 85, 86
Wilburn, Michael D., 15
White, John R., 43, 78, 79, 80
Wording
  in questionnaires, 57

Z-table, 50
  defined, 44